PLOMLEY'S PICK
OF DESERT ISLAND DISCS

PLOMLEY'S PICK

OF DESERT ISLAND DISCS

Roy Plomley

Weidenfeld and Nicolson
London

Published in Great Britain by
Arthur Barker Ltd
91 Clapham High Street
London SW4 7TA

ISBN 0 297 78149 9

Printed in Great Britain by
Butler & Tanner Ltd, Frome and London

To Derek Drescher

producer of *Desert Island Discs*
with gratitude for his ready
help and guidance, and for his
cheerful co-operation

Contents

Acknowledgements

The pictures in this book are reproduced by kind permission of the following:

Jeffrey Archer, photograph by Billett Potter (Jeffrey Archer); Lauren Bacall (Aquarius/Pic, London); John Blashford-Snell (Thames Television); Mel Brooks (National Film Archive); James Cameron (Fergus Cameron); Arthur C. Clarke (Arthur C. Clarke); Tom Conti (Aquarius/Pic, London); Roald Dahl (Penguin Books); Les Dawson (Norman Murray and Anne Chudleigh); Lord Denning (Keystone Press); Mark Elder, photograph by Clive Barda (Mark Elder); John Fowles (Fay Godwin's Photo Files); Brian Glover (Brian Glover); Helene Hanff, photograph by Richard Butler (Helene Hanff); Russell Harty (Universal Pictorial Press); Earl Hines (Valerie Wilmer); Freddie Jones (Freddie Jones); Tristan Jones, photograph by Donal F. Holway (Tristan Jones); Ronald Lockley (Ronald Lockley); Fitzroy Maclean, photograph by Terence Spencer (Fitzroy Maclean); Paul McCartney (BBC Copyright Photograph); V.S. Naipaul, photograph by Jerry Bauer (V.S. Naipaul); David Niven (Ronald Grant Archive); Gregory Peck (Aquarius/ Pic, London); Donald Pleasence (Donald Pleasence); Robert Powell (Robert Powell); Otto Preminger (Ronald Grant Archive); Ralph Richardson (BBC Copyright Photograph); A.L. Rowse, photograph by Sydney Canverson (A.L. Rowse); Edmund Rubbra (Radio Times); Erich Segal, photograph by Edouard Boubat (Erich Segal); Peter Sellers (Ronald Grant Archive); Stephen Sondheim (Stephen Sondheim); Derek Tangye (Woman's Weekly); Margaret Thatcher (BBC Copyright Photograph); Maria von Trapp (Maria von Trapp); P.L. Travers, photograph by Jerry Bauer (P.L. Travers); Freddie Trueman (Patrick Eagar); Peter Ustinov (Aquarius/Pic, London); Natalie Wood (BBC Copyright Photograph); Barbara Woodhouse (Universal Pictorial Press).

Picture research by Cathy Ellis

Introduction

Since I devised the radio programme, *Desert Island Discs*, forty years ago, I have had the privilege of interviewing well over 1,600 brilliant and distinguished people. To pick extracts from just forty or so of these interviews can only be an arbitrary matter, because there is enough excellent material to fill about forty books of this size. (The figure forty seems to be pursuing me!) However, during the past six or seven years, the programme has been granted a longer playing-time, and whereas it used to run thirty minutes, it now runs forty. (Forty again!) This has enabled my guests to digress a little more than was formerly possible, so, seizing on a guiding principle, all but one of the chosen interviews have been broadcast since the beginning of 1976, which was when Derek Drescher took over as producer. The one exception is the interview with Peter Sellers, which dates back to 1957. It is included not only because it strikes me as exceptionally amusing, but because it marks the point when Peter decided to stop merely clowning and become the master of comedy character acting which he remained until his death.

A list of the discs my guests chose, together with their one book (apart from the Bible and the Complete Works of Shakespeare, which are on every island) and their one luxury, will be found at the back of the book.

Jeffrey Archer

Jeffrey Archer radiates buoyancy and confidence. He is convinced that if he were to be cast away on a desert island he would, somehow, be off it by lunchtime – and one believes him. After all, to be nearly half a million pounds in debt and then become solvent again, within three or four years, by writing highly entertaining books, is no mean achievement. His is an extraordinary story, and an inspiring one.

RP: You were Conservative member for Louth, in Lincolnshire, at the early age of twenty-nine.

JA: At that age, there was no hope of early office, so one sat down on the back benches and tried to learn the tricks of the trade.

RP: In your private life, you were involved in playing the money market.

JA: Yes, I enjoyed the Stock Exchange, and seeing how money could work when you'd made some.

RP: Until there came a day ...

JA: Yes, to begin with it all went very well and was very profitable, and I began to believe almost everything I touched would succeed – until I was advised by the Vice-President of the Bank of Boston to invest a large sum in a company called Aquablast, and he was able to show me papers proving that the bank themselves had invested large sums in Aquablast. Well, I thought, if they've invested, they must have done the research, and I not only invested everything I had – which was an act of arrogant stupidity – I also borrowed money to invest even more. Only to discover that the

1

Vice-President himself was stealing the money. He disappeared abroad, and all eighty-two investors lost, between us, eight million.

RP: How much were you down the drain for?

JA: The worst statement that came through my letter-box read minus £427,727.

RP: How long would it have taken to pay that back on your MP's salary?

JA: It would take 137 years, and that would be without interest.

RP: The alternative, of course, was bankruptcy.

JA: The alternative at that time was bankruptcy, because one didn't see a way out. The sum was so large that one couldn't see how one could honourably borrow it, or honourably raise it, and promise to pay that person back.

RP: So?

JA: So I sat down and wrote my first book.

RP: Just like that?

JA: Well, I couldn't get a job, Roy. Once you've trained to be an MP, unless you're a lawyer, you're not trained to be anything else. One or two people offered me directorships, but I had to say to them, 'I think, in about six weeks time, I'm going to go bankrupt for a very large sum of money,' and they, of course, couldn't have directors who were going to go bankrupt. I realized I just wasn't going to get a job anywhere, so I sat down and wrote *Not a Penny More, Not a Penny Less*.

RP: How could you reasonably expect to make the sort of money you needed out of writing a first novel?

JA: I had absolutely no knowledge about writing. I assumed that if one went away and spent six or seven weeks writing a hundred thousand words, then the result was bound to be published, and if it made a couple of thousand pounds, then I could put that couple of thousand pounds in the bank. I went into the wilderness with absolutely no knowledge, and it was probably a great advantage to have no knowledge, because people who write books know that only one in a hundred gets published, and one in a hundred of those hits the best-selling list.

RP: Had you a story in mind?

JA: I always thought that the idea of four young men losing their money, and then sitting down and planning to steal it back from Mr Big ... not a penny more, not a penny less ... would capture the public's imagination.

RP: Was this a kind of fantasy of yours, having lost all your money?

JA: Certainly the first half of the book, as I suspect is the case with many authors, is autobiographical. What I hadn't realized was that most people in the world have had some sort of financial down-crash ... and therefore were able to identify with my four heroes who were trying to get their money back.

RP: How long did the writing take you? You said six or seven weeks. Did you do it in that?

JA: The first draft took six or seven weeks – but there were eleven drafts, and it was just over a year until it was submitted to publishers.

RP: Did you have an agent to help you?

JA: Through luck, yes. Again with no knowledge, I absolutely hit gold, because the secret is to get a good agent.

RP: So the book hit the bookshops. How much of that vast sum were you able to pay back?

JA: To begin with, almost nothing – because the first cheque in was for two thousand. But then, eleven days after publication, Warner Brothers bid a quarter of a million for the film rights. That changed things overnight. I reported to all my creditors what was happening, and was able to say to them, 'I will pay you off in time,' and the bankruptcy proceedings were dropped and I never even reached the courts, which was marvellous. It took three years to pay everybody off, one by one.

RP: Had you something in mind for your second book?

JA: In the case of *Shall We Tell the President?* all I had in mind was the idea of a young man, aged twenty-seven, having the biggest secret in the world. He goes out with a fellow operator in the FBI, and discovers that the President is going to be assassinated. How boring! Here we go again! 1,572 people every year threaten the President's life, so naturally the FBI don't take every one of them seriously. He and his colleague go back and tell their chief. At nine o'clock that night, five people know about this particular threat.

By nine-thirty, four of them are dead, and the one man who knows realizes that it's no longer just another threat. The President is going to die in seven days and one hour, and he is the only person alive who knows. He doesn't know who to turn to, and he knows the people who've killed the other four are looking for him.

RP: Did you spend much time in Washington researching all this?

JA: Six months. I went and worked with the FBI. I lived with a senior agent for three weeks – in his car, in his office – watching everything he did. So that one got those little touches that people seem to like in books, such as – an FBI man never does up his middle button; he always wants to be sure he can get to his gun – and he always carries in his pocket ten dimes, because he's not allowed to pick up a phone and say, 'This is Nick Staines, FBI. Put me through to the Chief,' he has to put ten cents in the slot and dial, the same as any other human being. So, if you're ever stopped by an FBI man, Roy, say: 'Turn your pockets out.' Because if his pockets aren't full of dimes, he's not with the FBI.

RP: It's been stated that those first two books brought you in a million pounds between them.

JA: Yes, that's what the tax man keeps telling me. I get about thirty fan letters a week, and thirty little brown buff envelopes which make the same claim that you're making.

RP: You don't confirm or deny?

JA: Absolutely not.

RP: What about your third book?

JA: *Kane and Abel* was a totally different enterprise. I decided I wanted to try something a little harder, and go up from a 250-page thriller to a real saga, and that took considerably more research and much harder work. It took nearly two years to write.

RP: Where did you research that one?

JA: England, Poland and America. It's the story of two men, both born on the same day in 1906: one to a gypsy in a Polish forest, born with nothing; one to a Boston multi-millionaire, born with everything.

RP: The research must be the fascinating part.

JA: A lot of people think research is a matter of going into libraries and reading books, which of course has to be done because you must check your facts very carefully – but in the case of *Kane and Abel*, rather than just read books about people who'd made a million or been born with a million, I searched for Mr Kane and Mr Abel, to live with them. I sought out two very distinguished Americans and spent my time with them, watching them run their empires. That's real research. It's then that you notice the problems they have, the lives they lead, the things they do. Of course, they have all the same problems that you and I have. They're no different – except that during the day they probably move millions of pounds backwards and forwards.

RP: How do your family take to your frequent disappearances?

JA: I think my wife takes it very well; I mean she's realistic about what's happening in my career, and knows that my book will be published in other countries as well as Britain – but the children don't take it at all well. They don't understand, and they think I should stay at home. I remember once when I had to go over and edit *Kane and Abel* with the American publishers, my youngest son, who was then aged four, came to me and said. 'Do you really have to go abroad, Daddy? Can't you stay and play football?' So I tried to explain to him that this particular editor was a very distinguished man and that it was a privilege for me to have my book read by him and to iron it out with him. And my youngest said, 'If I wrote a best-seller, would you stay at home?' So I said, 'Yes, of course. If you wrote a best-seller, I could stay home and play football all the time.' I went to bed that night, knowing that I was going to New York the next day and that I was catching an eleven o'clock flight – and he woke me up at six. I was just about to strangle the little monster, because I could have done with two hours more sleep, when I saw he was clutching in his hands some pieces of paper, stapled together, with the letters of the alphabet in different colours on every page, and all he said was, 'Now you won't have to go abroad.' And I took him upstairs, trying desperately not to let him see what effect it had had on me, and I found my six-year-old son in the front room busily writing *Nicholas Nickleby*. Well, I tried to explain to him that what he was doing was what is called plagiarism, and that if you write a best-seller it has to be original. He just went on writing – he had got to about page fifteen – and I went on trying to explain. Finally I said, 'Look, millions of people have already read this book. It's one of the world's greatest stories. Everbody's read it.' And he looked at me and shook his head, and said, 'No, I went round my form yesterday, and nobody's read it.'

RP: So the whole family's in the best-seller business. What's your writing discipline? Do you write so many hours a day, or so many words a day?

JA: I like to start work at seven in the morning and write until ten. It works out at about 3,000 words a day, but it can be as low as 2,000 and as high as 3,500. I've never been above 3,500. Then I like an hour's break until eleven. Then I correct it through between eleven and one, take the afternoon off, and then read it once more between six and eight in the evening. The discipline is to keep that up for six weeks without a break. I'm terrified of saying, 'I think I'll take a day off today,' because I'm always fearful that I'll never go back to it.

Lauren Bacall

Many show-business autobiographies are expendable – but I recommend Miss Bacall's, which is entitled *By Myself*. It is a long book – although not nearly as long as she originally wrote it – and it is very honest, very emotional and, at times, unbearably sad. Through it all, as through my interview with her, is that laconic wit which is typical of the New York Jewish people, and, while reading or listening, one pictures that challenging, quizzical, beautiful look with which she faces the world. She has the deepest voice of any woman I know.

RP: Now, you're a Brooklyn girl, and you became stagestruck: can you trace that back to any particular event?
LB: Funnily enough, I don't consider myself a Brooklyn girl; I lived there for five years, but I was brought up in New York, on Manhattan. No, I cannot trace it back to anything, but it seems to me that for as long as I can remember I wanted to be someone that I wasn't.
RP: Did you go to the movies a lot, as a youngster?
LB: Yes, a lot.
RP: Who were your heroes and heroines on the screen?
LB: Bette Davis was my heroine, and Leslie Howard was my hero.
RP: Did you go to the theatre as well?
LB: The theatre was a little beyond me, because it was too expensive. The first play I ever saw was John Gielgud in *Hamlet*. That absolutely did me in. I mean, I was so moved by it, even though I was really very, very young, that I remember bumping into people as I was leaving the theatre. I was really dazed. You know, I first

7

wanted to be a ballerina: then I realized, with the help of a pro-
nouncement by a famous Russian teacher named Michael Mord-
kin, who had been a dancer, that I really didn't have the feet for it. I
was in constant pain when I was on points. No Margot Fonteyn I.

RP: As what kind of actress did you see yourself? – as Juliet, as
Bette Davis, as Ethel Merman? As what?

LB: I played the Potion Scene from *Romeo and Juliet* at drama
school; I would have liked to have seen myself as that, but I don't
think I really did. I don't think I saw myself as anything in
particular. Bette Davis was the great heroine; I acted all her parts
out after I saw the films, but I knew that they weren't really me.

RP: You went to the American Academy of Dramatic Art, but
money ran out after only one year. When you left, were there any
jobs going?

LB: I was hoping they'd give me a scholarship, but they needed
young men more than they needed girls. I just started to look for
work – and then I went into modelling on 7th Avenue, because I
had to make some kind of money. I was going in and out of
producers' offices, and I was determined that I was going to be
noticed, so I prevailed on the man who published *Actor's Cue*, the
magazine which gave tips as to what was being cast, to let me sell
it outside Sardi's, the theatrical restaurant, during my lunch hour.
I would rush up from the garment centre, get my papers, and
buttonhole anyone that I recognized.

RP: For a while, you were a theatre usher – what we would call a
programme seller here, but in civilized New York they don't
charge for programmes – and you were such a very good theatre
usher that you were given a notice by one of the critics.

LB: Oh yes, that was George Jean Nathan. Always at the interval,
I would say, 'No smoking, please,' and I would always deliver this
line differently, playing all kinds of I don't know what dramas.
Every year, Nathan listed the Bests and the Worsts of the Year,
and I was in the Bests column as The Prettiest Usher at The St
James Theatre.

RP: A man of great taste. When was the first time you walked a
stage professionally?

LB: It was in a play called *Johnny Two-by-Four*, in which I had what

I called an outstanding walk-on. I mean, to anyone else a walk-on is a walk-on, but to me if you walked on the stage in each of the three acts, that was outstanding.

RP: And the first time you spoke a line?

LB: That was in a play called *Franklin Street*, which was directed by George S. Kaufman and produced by Max Gordon, who was one of the men I'd buttonholed outside Sardi's.

RP: The records say that it opened in Wilmington, Delaware; where did it go from there?

LB: It went to Washington from there – and then down the drain.

RP: So it was back to modelling for a while.

LB: Yes, but then I was fortunate in that I was able to get into photographic modelling, and thereby hangs a tale. To start with, it was big money. I mean, big money for me – ten bucks an hour. That was not, as we say in America, hay. Then there was a picture which got on the cover of *Harper's Bazaar*. I was a blood donor, standing in front of a Red Cross door.

RP: This was wartime, of course.

LB: Yes. Anyway, Slim Hawks, who was then married to Howard Hawks, had seen my photograph in other *Harper's Bazaars*, and then she saw the cover, and she thought that I was worth looking at, and she told Howard.

RP: So you were off on the train to Hollywood. How old were you?

LB: I was seventeen.

RP: So there were tests, and all that sort of thing?

LB: There was a lot of waiting before the tests – much waiting, much hanging around.

RP: Was there a long process of grooming and teeth straightening, and all the rest of it?

LB: No teeth straightening, oh no! I was taken to Perce Westmore at Warner Brothers, and Perce sat me down in front of a mirror and looked at me, and he said, 'Well now, we'll tweeze your eyebrows and make a thin line, like Dietrich's, and then we'll straighten your teeth, and then we'll do something to your hair-line,' – and I was panic stricken. I rushed to the phone to call Hawks, and I said, 'Oh, they're going to change everything.

Please, please come down. Help, help.' And he came down, and he said, 'No, Perce, leave her just as she is. I want the crooked eyebrows, the crooked teeth, the crooked hair, the crooked every-thing.' And that's what he got.

RP: Were you broken-in easily by being given bits and pieces to play, to accustom you to the atmosphere of film-making?

LB: No, not at all. For my test, I played a scene from a play called *Claudia,* which Howard directed, and as a result of that test he signed me to a personal contract. Then, before I was put into *To Have and Have Not,* which was a lap dissolve of some months – in fact, nigh on a year – I had to test for that so that Jack Warner, who owned the studio, could give his approval and also buy half of my contract, in order for him to allow me to play in the film.

RP: So, straight away, a starring part, opposite Humphrey Bogart. Were you a fan of his? Was he one of your favourites?

LB: No, I knew he was a good actor, but I didn't think he was my type.

RP: He had already had terrific successes – *The Petrified Forest, Casablanca* and others. Now, during the shooting of *To Have and Have Not,* you and Bogart fell in love, and you stayed together in a number of pictures – *The Big Sleep,* for example, which was written by Raymond Chandler. There was a bit of script trouble during that, wasn't there?

LB: Oh yes, that was funny. One day during the shooting, Bogie walked in and said, 'Howard, who pushed Owen Taylor off the pier?' 'Oh now, let me see,' said Howard, thinking of this sequence in the picture, 'I don't know.' So Howard rang Raymond Chand-ler – and he didn't know either. *The Big Sleep* was quite a mystery, but it was terrific.

RP: You were launched with a tremendous publicity barrage. 'The Look' – and there you were, looking sexily from under your eyelids. Whose idea was that? Was that the studio's gimmick? – how are we going to launch this new girl?

LB: No, it wasn't the studio at all, it was Howard Hawks. It was also because I was a nervous wreck and I used to shake all the time – now, I only shake some of the time – and I discovered that if I held my chin down I was able to keep my head a bit steadier. Then I looked up at Bogart, and that became 'The Look'.

RP: The great Jack Warner took half your contract and had to give approval of everything: did you find him a very difficult man?

LB: I found him very difficult and not great.

RP: Right, that sums him up. Now, the other Hollywood films you made, without Humphrey Bogart. What about *Confidential Agent*, for example, from a book by Graham Greene.

LB: Oh! Why do you bring that film up?

RP: You played an upper-class English girl, and you've gone on record as saying that you were miscast and terrible. Mr Greene has been writing to the papers to say that you were excellent and absolutely right.

LB: Mr Greene is adorable to have done that, but Mr Greene is mistaken. I was not good and I was not upper-class English. I was just me, not knowing what I was doing – that's what I was.

RP: Graham Greene doesn't think so. We must see the film again.

LB: No, I won't see it again. Enough is enough. I've been in films that I've loved, but not many of them – and not that one.

RP: You had the extreme misfortune to lose your husband; did you stay on and live in Hollywood?

LB: I stayed on for – oh, I guess just under two years. Then I really couldn't take it any more; I mean I just didn't feel that I belonged there. So I came to England.

RP: And the days of the big studios were more or less over; nearly everything was being made on location. You've had some interesting locations; you went to India for one picture.

LB: That was *Flame Over India*. That was why I came here, in 1959, to be in that film. It was a reason for me to travel, so I loved that. Then I went back to New York, because I was offered a play, and I had my two young children with me. It takes a while, you know, to organize your life again, so that you know you have one.

RP: You said you've been in films that you've loved; which were they?

LB: I loved *How to Marry a Millionaire*, and I enjoyed *Woman's World* very much. I kind of liked *Young Man with a Horn* – or some of it. I adored *Designing Woman* – that probably is my favourite film – and I loved *Murder on the Orient Express*. I've not been in that many good ones, certainly, and I haven't been in that many altogether.

John Blashford-Snell

In one of those far-too-rare collaborations between the BBC and commercial television, Derek Drescher and I were approached by the producer of the Thames Television series, *This Is Your Life*, to ask if we would help with the 'pick-up' of the soldier and explorer Lieutenant Colonel John Blashford-Snell whom they wanted as the subject of one of their programmes.

The scheme evolved was this: when we had finished our *Desert Island Discs* recording with him, which was to take place in one of the BBC outposts known as 1 Portland Place, Derek and I would bring him out of the front door at exactly 5 pm, turning left along the pavement in the direction of Broadcasting House. We would be photographed by a camera placed above the portico of the old Langham Hotel, which is opposite. When we reached the end of the short street, we would be picked up by another concealed camera, which would follow us as we crossed the road to a traffic island, on which was a lonely figure, leaning on a bollard and reading an evening paper. As we reached the island, the figure would drop his newspaper, revealing himself as Eamonn Andrews, and he would say, 'Colonel Blashford-Snell, This Is Your Life', and we would all go by taxi to the Thames Television studios in Euston Road, where an audience would be waiting to see the rest of the programme.

An admirable scheme, and seemingly foolproof, but –

Derek and I brought the unsuspecting victim out of 1 Portland Place at exactly 5 pm, having delayed him with talk of a press photographer who wished to take pictures of us in Broadcasting House. We fell in neatly, as we had been instructed, with Derek walking on the inside by the wall, the Colonel in the middle and me on the outside by the kerb.

What we could not have anticipated was that Blashford-Snell's agent, an affable Welshman, would be waiting in the hall to talk to his client about a future engagement. As Derek and I were under instructions to carry out the television director's plan to the second, we had swept Blashford-Snell past the agent who, surprised and rather aggrieved, had followed us out, with protesting cries of, 'I say! Just a minute ...'

Then, in the street, a fifth man joined our small procession. He was a purposeful-looking young man, who carried a raincoat over his left arm.

Out of the corner of his eye, Blashford-Snell saw the new arrival. It so happened that he had recently been serving in Northern Ireland, where he had developed an aversion to being followed closely by purposeful-looking men with raincoats over their arms and, instinctively, he quickened his pace, to give himself space to manoeuvre if necessary.

Our neat formation was now broken up, and we crossed the few yards to the traffic island with the rapidly-walking Blashford-Snell in the lead, followed by Derek and myself, pursued by the Welsh agent, still crying, 'I say, just a minute', with the unknown raincoat-carrier in fifth place.

Eamonn dropped his newspaper, expecting to see an orderly trio approaching him, but before he could say his line, Blashford-Snell was past him and heading for Broadcasting House, with the rest of us strung out behind him. All Eamonn could do was chase after us in sixth place, calling out, 'I say! Just a minute ...'

When we saw the scene on the screen, it looked very untidy and very funny, and it was surely the first time that Eamonn had uttered his famous line, 'This Is Your Life', practically at the double.

Incidentally, the purposeful man with the raincoat turned out to be an innocent BBC technician.

RP: You're a Jerseyman, I believe.

JBS: By domicile. I was born in England, but my real home is Jersey; my father came from Jersey, and all my attachments are there.

RP: You decided to go into the Army. Do you come from an Army family?

JBS: My father was an Army padre and my godfather was in the Army, but the rest of my distant relatives were sailors.

RP: You formed a private army when you were about fourteen.

JBS: A little before I was fourteen. This was in Herefordshire, where my father was the local parson. I became very worried that Hitler might invade the district, and I decided that I hadn't much faith in the Home Guard and that I would form a defensive force from the girls and boys of the choir. We did, in fact, fight many successful campaigns against scrumpers, and we even had a piece of artillery, mounted on an invalid carriage, with which I eventually shot our gardener.

RP: Scrumpers were people who raided orchards?

JBS: That's right. I remember one very good battle, but unfortunately we damaged the church roof, which cost me an awful lot of pocket money.

RP: You were in charge of bell ringing occasionally.

JBS: Yes, my father considered, quite rightly, that I was a useless sort of son, and that I should be put to some sort of worthwhile work during my school holidays, and he said that I should ring the church bell to summon people to Communion on a Wednesday morning at seven o'clock. I discovered that if I opened my window I could actually see the church bell from my bed and, with the aid of a thirty-calibre rook rifle I could hit it nine times out of ten. This produced a most wonderfully solemn note, unfortunately followed by a sort of ping! This increased the congregation no end, because they all came to pray for deliverance. I also became involved when my father acquired a new device which was a sort of gramophone connected to a speaker on the church roof, and it was my job at ten minutes before Matins to put on Bow Bells. An extension of this device was that those who were hard of hearing could sit in the front pew and they could insert a thing in their right lughole and this would sort of turn them on to

Bow Bells. One day, for a wager with a rather wicked girl who sang on the decani side, I slipped on a record called 'He Played His Ukelele as the Ship Went Down'. The result was that all the old ladies coming up the road to church were jogging happily, and then I turned the switch over to full volume for the hard of hearing in the front pew, and really it was most extraordinary: Father was up in the pulpit, and he watched the entire front section of the congregation begin to bounce up and down. Father soon recognized that my vocation was not the church.

RP: In due course you went to Sandhurst; what branch of the Army did you opt for?

JBS: I wanted to be an explorer and I wanted to be involved with conquering obstacles. The people who do both are the Royal Engineers, so I tried very hard to get into the Sappers and, perhaps foolishly, they accepted me.

RP: When you left Sandhurst you had six weeks leave, and you decided to go round the world during that time, without spending much money.

JBS: That's quite true. I had a girl friend who was in the Women's Royal Army Corps – I eventually married her – and she was operating a telephone exchange in Malaya, and I thought it would be rather fun to go and visit her. I got stuck, because there was a revolution in Iraq and I had to offer my services as attendant to a consignment of monkeys going to London – but that failed, and in the end the Americans gave me a lift for the remaining 18,500 miles, taking me across the States and back to London that way.

RP: Where was your first posting?

JBS: Cyprus. I was posted to a field squadron which was on active service, and I had a glorious three and a half years, the first part of which was spent playing Cowboys and Indians chasing General Grivas. Later, I had the chance to do some exploration in the Libyan desert.

RP: It was on that trip that you nearly died of thirst – and didn't you find some relics of the war-time Libyan campaign?

JBS: Yes, we did. We were far south in the Sahara, and we came across what was probably the most southerly battlefield of the Long Range Desert Group. We found the ruins of vehicles, and graves where members of that illustrious force had fought to the end against the Italians. Everything had been exceedingly well preserved in the desert atmosphere. The cross which marked the graves had fallen down, and we re-erected it and reported the site to the War Graves Commission when we got back. We had to exercise very great care, because most of the hand grenades that were lying around were still very much alive.

RP: After your three or four years in the Mediterranean area, you were posted to a Junior Leaders Regiment. What's that?

JBS: You may well ask. The Royal Engineers have their Regiment at Dover, and it's designed to train very tough, very fit, selected young men to be future Warrant Officers and NCOs in the Corps. They are trained to be professional obstacle breakers, because the Sapper is at war the whole time, either against nature or, in less peaceful times, against men. There we teach boys to overcome swamps, mountains or deserts, before they go on to man service at the age of eighteen.

RP: Then, in 1963, you were appointed instructor at Sandhurst with responsibility for organizing adventure training. Did that involve launching expeditions all over the world?

JBS: Yes, it did.

RP: And did you continue to sort some out for yourself?

JBS: Yes – with cadets from the Military Academy, and from Dartmouth and Cranwell.

RP: If I may mention one of your failures, on your first expedition to Ethiopia, you failed to find Osgood's swamp rat.

JBS: The Natural History branch of the British Museum asked us to seek out that extraordinarily rare mammal, and I can't tell you of the agony we endured during months in the long wet grass of Ethiopian swamps, with swirling mists and hostile natives. We laid countless traps each day, but eventually we had to come back to Britain, with our heads held low, and say, 'We're sorry, we failed.' And a very delightful white-coated, bearded scientist looked at me over his horn-rimmed glasses and smiled, and said, 'Do you know, that's most interesting. After you'd gone, I looked it up, and they don't exist at all – they're a complete myth.'

RP: And in Ethiopia you made the first successful descent of the

Blue Nile, after many expeditions had broken their hearts trying. That was pretty hairy, wasn't it?

JBS: It was certainly the most frightening expedition I've ever done. We ran into bandits, crocodiles, rapids and hostile tribesmen. We had new types of inflatable boats which no one had really tried, and I think we scared the pants off everybody there.

RP: Weren't you running a private war part of the time?

JBS; Oh, we were. I sometimes think we were the cause of it. Haile Selassie was very complimentary about it, and it was all a great success, but it was something of a miracle that we got through alive - and, tragically, one man was killed.

RP: Then you led the British Trans-Americas Expedition, driving from Alaska to Cape Horn. How many miles is that?

JBS: According to the clocks on the vehicles, it was 17,018. Of course, it was done by a very large team, of which I was the leader and mainly concerned with the central portion.

RP: It meant crossing the Darien Gap. Will you tell me about that?

JBS; The Darien Gap is three hundred miles of the most unpleasant tropical jungle in the world. It's swamp, it's dense, it's 150 feet high, it's full of mosquitoes and snakes and funny little pigs called peccary which chase you. It has hostile inhabitants, and we had seven Colombians killed in an ambush.

RP: What was your rate of progress?

JBS; I suppose we made about three miles a day. Everything combined against us: we had a lot of breakdowns, the rains were late in stopping; we had just one hundred days in which to get across, and I think we made it by eight hours.

RP: Some of us may still have ideas that exploring means two or three Europeans travelling in litters, with a column of native bearers carrying stores on their heads, but it's got a lot more sophisticated than that, hasn't it?

JBS: It has indeed; exploration today is very scientific. You can't have one man with the knowledge in his head to solve all the problems, so we have servicemen and civilians who have administrative expertise together with scientists who need to get into very remote areas to solve their problems. If you can bring the two factors together, as our organization, the Scientific Exploration Society, has done, then you've got a marvellous team, but sometimes it has to be a fairly large team.

RP: You maintain a pleasant link with the past yourself; on tropical expeditions, you still wear a solar topee.

JBS Well, it's rather like the Vickers machine-gun; it went on for a great many years before somebody found something better. Even as I speak, various hatters in Bond Street are working by candlelight to produce an improved version, but I can promise you that the Wolsey Helmet, which is the one I wear, is still the best.

RP: 1974 was the centenary of Stanley's trans-Africa expedition, in which he crossed the continent from east to west following the Congo River. You decided to make the same trip, despite the fact that only a third of Stanley's expedition survived. So you knew it was going to be a rough one.

JBS: Yes, we did, and we knew we would have casualties, but there was tremendous scientific work to be done in that vast area, which is, of course, the size of Western Europe.

RP: How many casualties did you have?

JBS: The Senior Medical Officer worked out that we had about fifty per cent – a little over, actually – which worked out at about seventy men and women.

RP: Women?

JBS: Yes, we've always taken girls on expeditions. Going back to the question of casualties, a casualty is defined as someone who is seriously ill for more than twenty-four hours. I'm very happy to say that on that expedition, by a miracle, nobody was actually killed.

RP: How many boats did you lose?

JBS; Two. One was gobbled up by a hippopotamus, which was left looking rather perplexed. It was an inflatable boat and he was obviously suffering from a disastrous attack of wind. The other one was caught up under some trees and disappeared over a waterfall.

RP: It must have been quite a moment when you came out into the Atlantic after – how long?

JBS: It took us just over three and a half months. It had taken Stanley 999 days.

18

RP: How much portage did you have to do?

JBS: Only a few miles. The river is 2,700 miles long, and it is extraordinary; it really is a river that goes on flowing for ever. When we got to the Atlantic, the Army padre put on his cassock and surplice and held a service. It was a very moving ceremony, with the water underneath our hulls no longer tugging and pulling at us but absolutely placid. We only had an improvised cross, and our ten-minute thanksgiving service frightened the life out of our black helpers, who couldn't understand English and were quite convinced that we were going to sacrifice them.

RP: On an expedition to a very different climate, you found evidence which gave you some views about the Yeti – the Abominable Snowman.

JBS; I went out to Nepal on what was really a holiday-cum-expedition and, right at the end, I was walking along the bank of a river with my daughter, Emma, and we found some extraordinary footprints. I couldn't believe my eyes, because these footprints had enormous toes. I said to Nema Tenzing, who is a relation to the famous Sherpa Tenzing, who climbed Mount Everest with Hillary, 'What on earth is that? Who made that print?' He said, 'A man.' I said, 'I don't believe it. Look at the size of the toes.' Anyway, it turned out to be the footmark of the Holy Man of the village, who had deformed feet. Many people in Nepal have a mutation, a deformity, with one toe at right angles to the foot. Sir Edmund Hillary has noted exactly the same thing with Sherpas at eighteen thousand feet up in the snow, where they still go barefoot. One of my own theories is that many of the reports of the Yeti may be attributed to a man with deformed feet.

Mel Brooks

This American film director, producer, writer, actor and comedian makes very funny films and is a very funny man. He told me that the two great daydreams in his life were to be marooned alone on a desert island and see if he were able to survive, and to live with a strange woman in Finchley Road. He claimed to have achieved his second daydream, but had not yet coalesced the vapour of the first one.

RP: You're a New Yorker, aren't you, Mel?

MB: Yes, born and bred in Brooklyn.

RP Things could be pretty tough in Brooklyn: do you look back on your childhood as a deprived one?

MB: A child tends not to know whether he's rich or poor, as long as he's well fed and is having a great good time. My father died when I was only two, but I had three older brothers who adored me, and my mother loved me very much, and there were uncles and aunts, and somehow that Bohemian life was very exciting, and I loved being a little boy in Brooklyn.

RP: I believe music was your first love.

MB: Oh, yes. We had a Philco radio, and there were great squabbles and fights about who would hear what. When I was very young, I wanted to hear all the adventure programmes – The Lone Ranger and Jack Armstrong and what have you – and my brothers wanted to hear Tommy Dorsey, and finally they won out and that's why I'm such a swing aficionado. Ever since then, I've loved jazz and I've loved swing. A titbit of information: only a few blocks from where we lived was Buddy Rich, the famous swing drummer –

one of the best that ever lived. He taught me some elementary paradiddles.

RP: That's right, you began as a drummer. When did you start?

MB: When I was about thirteen and a half, or fourteen.

RP: When did you first play for money?

MB: At fifteen. I played at weddings, at bar mitzvahs, on subway platforms – any place where I could get a couple of bucks. It was through being a drummer that I got into show business, so to speak, as a comedian. I was playing in a hotel in the Catskills, in one of those Jewish mountain resorts where immigrants would go to speak their own language – Ukrainian, Jewish, Russian, Polish and so on – and that's where many comedians and musicians got their beginnings. While I was working there, I made some wonderful observations: for example, that Jews had a tendency to eat too much sour cream, and then to rock it off, so to speak. They would sit in rocking chairs on the verandahs of those hotels and rock. Sometimes, they would sing a song, and normally they would sing a song in the wrong key. Now, it is very dangerous to sing 'Dancing in the Dark' in the wrong key, because it goes very high, so many of them would suffer terrible fainting spells and strokes. I saved many Jewish lives simply by instructing them to start in a lower key. A pitch pipe and smelling salts – that's all you needed to save them.

RP: You were going to tell us how you got up from your drums and became a comedian.

MB: The comic fell ill and I, the drummer, knew all that bad material he was using, and I was asked by the owner of this hotel to replace him. So I jumped on to the stage and took over, and I did these kinds of jokes: 'Good evening, ladies and gents. I just flew in from Chicago and, boy! are my arms tired! I got a room in Chicago that was so small that the mice were hunchbacked – that's how small this room was. I met a girl there who was so skinny – I mean she was really thin – and I took her to a little restaurant, and the waiter said, "Check your umbrella, sir?" I mean, that's how skinny this girl was ...' Well, I didn't make it as a comic, because of that material. So I decided to become a writer. The television industry was growing up, and I moved in.

It was new, it was live, it was exciting and it was in black-and-white.

RP: What was your first job?

MB: The first job lasted for eight or nine years; I was a comedy writer for Sid Caesar on *The Show of Shows*. The leads in it were Sid Caesar, Imogen Coca, Carl Reiner and Howard Morris, and the writing staff consisted mostly of Mel Brooks, Woody Allen and Neil Simon.

RP: That's not a bad team.

MB: Quite a nice bunch of writers to have turning out material for you.

RP: After you left Sid Caesar, you devised and wrote a very successful send-up spy series.

MB: Yes, Buck Henry and I created a series called *Get Smart*, based on the exploits of Maxwell Smart, an American secret agent who was a blunderer and could do nothing right. He had a shoe telephone, and always spoke to his shoe and embarrassed everybody.

RP: You started your film career by writing and directing a short movie called *The Critic*.

MB: Well, there were some avant-garde colour and light cartoon shorts made by Norman McLaren, the Canadian, and I thought they were fabulous – but sitting next to me in the moviehouse was a little Jew from Minsk or Pinsk or somewhere, and he kept trying to make sense out of these surrealistic forms, and he was saying things like, 'It must be a cockroach, it looks like a bug. Somebody'll kill it. No, it's a bus – it's a boy – it's a car. What the heck! I came to see a dirty French movie, and I'm looking at this stuff.' So I said to myself, This is precious, this is a diamond of a concept. So I went to Ernie Pintoff, who was doing wonderful cartoons at the time, and I said, 'Ernie, you draw it, and I'll be the voice of the little old man, and we'll do it.' We did it as a lark. We never intended to release it, but we did and it was a big success – and I won an Academy Award for it.

RP: That Academy Award must have evened things up nicely at home, because your wife, Anne Bancroft, had got one for *The Miracle Worker*. You could have one on each end of the sideboard.

MB: Well, we don't have our Academy Awards. She gave hers to her mother and I gave mine to my mother. We're very good children.

RP: That's very nice.

MB: And our mothers, for some reason, both keep them on their television sets.

RP: Was it the success of *The Critic* which opened the way for your first full-length film?

MB: No, *The Critic* didn't mean a thing; the offers I got were to write television shows, and I wanted to go on to films. So I starved for a year or two, and I wrote this script, *Springtime for Hitler*. I wrote the title song, too – about one of the most misunderstood sweethearts in history, Hitler. I understand he was a wonderful dancer and a very good cook, but people are just upset by the political aspect of the man's career. I took the script to everybody, and everybody said, 'No, it's in shocking bad taste, and we won't do it.' So I just bummed around for a while, and I couldn't make a nickel and I was in a lot of trouble, but I wouldn't give up. Finally, I met an independent producer who said, 'It's before its time, but let's give it a whirl,' – so we went to see Joseph E. Levine, who had just formed Embassy Pictures. Joe said to me, 'Listen, kid, from the bottom of your heart and don't lie to me, do you think you can direct a real movie?' I said, 'I think I can.' So we shook hands, and he gave me the job, and ten months later we had the film in theatres everywhere, and the title had been changed to *The Producers*.

RP: And you got another Oscar – so your mother's got two of them on the television.

MB: Yes, I got an Oscar for the screenplay. You know, first-borns are a majestic miracle, and I'm still very proud of that film. It did well in large cities and died in the provinces.

RP: You put it on record that the character played by Zero Mostel was based on a man you'd worked for when you were fifteen.

MB: Yes, it was. You know, Zero Mostel was one of the world's great grotesque comics. Zero was Promethean. It wasn't enough for him to be on the screen or on the stage. If you went to a restaurant, sometimes a crazy cook would walk out of the back

23

with his white hat and apron, with filth and garbage and lettuce all over him, and he'd shout in Italian that there wasn't enough bread in the kitchen, and go back through the doors. And, of course, everybody would get up and leave. I mean, they said, 'My God! That's the cook!' And that would be Zero Mostel.

RP: Who was very welcome everywhere!

MB: Anyway, Zero liked the script, and he took a chance on this new young director. And I was lucky enough to have Gene Wilder in the film. My wife and Gene had been together in the Brecht play, *Mother Courage*, on Broadway – he'd played the chaplain – and I'd watched Gene every night and realized that his was a very special talent. I told him I was writing a movie for him, and he laughed and didn't believe me. Two years later, when I'd finished the script, I went to see him in his dressing-room – he was in a play called *Love* – and it was a very emotional moment. I threw the script on the table, and said, 'There it is. You're going to be in this movie. You've got the lead.' And he just broke down and wept, and wept, and wept. So I dried his eyes, and kissed him . . .

RP: He hadn't read it yet.

MB: No, but he had been a great big fan of Sid Caesar and myself and *The Show of Shows*, and he trusted that it would be funny. I'll never forget the moment. Then he wept again when I told him what I was going to pay him.

RP: You followed *The Producers* with a Russian story.

MB: *The Twelve Chairs* – but not being allowed into Russia to film it, because it was rather anti-Communistic, I got into Yugoslavia, where they were a little softer about it. I had a dreadful time in Yugoslavia, because Tito had the car. There was only one of them. There was a green Dodge, and Tito used it most of the time. So on Saturday nights I just walked about in Belgrade Square, which was lit by one ten-watt bulb – rather bleak – and they didn't even have spaghetti. I don't know what we were doing there. Anyway, we had a good time; we made the film. The Yugoslav people are wonderful; they're brave, they're courageous, they're strong and willing workers, and they helped to make the experience palatable. I shot for 106 days, six days a week, and I lived there for nine months of my life and gave birth to *The Twelve Chairs*, which I am very proud of.

James Cameron

❧❧❧❧❧❧❧❧

James has reported wars and disasters in every corner of the globe. It is, perhaps, because of the vast amount of suffering and tragedy he has seen that he is such a gentle and compassionate person.

RP: Were you born in Scotland?

JC: It's a very well-kept secret, but I have to say that I was not. When my parents realized that I was on the way, they decided that they would never be able to have another holiday after I was born, so they went down to the South of France, intending to return to have me born where every one of my family has been born for generations – in Scotland. But, unfortunately, I hopped untimely from the womb as we were passing through London. But then I was brought up in France until I was fifteen.

RP: How did that happen?

JC: There's a sort of tradition in Scottish families, of having their children sent to France – it's derived from the Auld Alliance. But chiefly it was because my father was a very impoverished writer, and, by a strange paradox, in those days the pound was worth infinitely more abroad than it was here, so my father thought his £6 a week would go further if we went to live in France.

RP: So you began in a French elementary school?

JC: In a black alpaca smock and wooden shoes.

RP: Very useful to get a bi-lingual education.

JC: Probably would have been more useful if it had been Japanese.

RP: What did you want to be?

JC: Well, here I was in this extraordinary position of having been to thirteen or fourteen elementary schools in France, and finishing

25

up at fifteen with having to get a job of some kind because my family finances had collapsed, and there was I with no qualifications, and virtually illiterate in two languages – quite something. What other trade could possibly accept such a person as I except journalism – which is used to illiterates.

RP: Where did you start?

JC: Dundee.

RP: Working for whom?

JC: Gulpingly I say, D. C. Thomson and Co. If you work in Dundee, who else can you work for?

RP: In those days, I believe the Thomson Press was rather an eccentric firm.

JC: Still is. Very eccentric, very powerful, very idiosyncratic.

RP: The best form of grounding, because you had to do everything, didn't you?

JC: Everything. Setting myself stories, subbing the stories, writing the headlines, doing the drawings – everything except selling the papers on the streets. It was very useful in later years, when I moved into more civilized surroundings, because no sub-editor could blind me with science.

RP: What papers did you work on in Dundee? Did you work on the famous Thomson comics?

JC: No, I worked on the *Dundee Courier*, the *Dundee Evening Telegraph* and a thing called the *Red Star Weekly*. I don't know whether it still exists or not.

RP: What was your job on it?

JC: My job was to read, endlessly, new versions of *The Tragedy of Maria Marten*: every year we published it in a new form, with an author being paid about one pound per thousand words.

RP: There's a story you once told me about choosing the covers. I believe you were the nearest the *Red Star Weekly* had to an art editor.

JC: Yes, I had to choose some particularly dramatic incident from that week's instalment of whatever we were running, and get an artist to draw a cover. I had one cover which I thought was a masterpiece; it showed a young woman who had just had her throat cut, and she was in a lamplit back alley with moist pavements, blood all over the place, her throat cut from ear to ear and revealing every single blood vessel there was ... it was a really terrible thing. I thought our readers would love it. So I took it into the office of our chief man, who recoiled from it in horror, and said, 'Laddie, you can never get away with this. Look, the lassie's skirts are way above her knees.'

RP: Did you write any of the fiction yourself?

JC: No, I wrote very little in those days. It was enormously pure, you know. We published stories of the most gruesome murders, but sex was never allowed to intrude in any way at all.

RP: James, you married very young, and had the misfortune to lose your wife in childbirth. You undertook to bring up your baby daughter on your own, from a few weeks old.

JC: From ten days old actually. I did it for about four years.

RP: How could you organize it?

JC: I was fortunate, if you can call it so, in that I was working on a newspaper at night. So I could put the child to bed at five o'clock in the evening, go to work, and come back at three o'clock in the morning. Very kindly, the landlady with whom I was staying looked after her during the sleeping hours. But it did mean that I was getting only about two hours sleep a night. It really did get me down a bit in the end.

RP: I should think so. How long did you stay with the D.C. Thomson group?

JC: About fifteen years. I finished up in Glasgow, which I thought was promotion. Eventually, I got myself sent down to London to the *Daily Express*.

RP: Was that about the beginning of the war?

JC: That's right.

RP: So the *Express*, as was the case with all newspapers at that time, was in the process of becoming a four-page paper.

JC: Indeed, it was very, very constrained ... and the staffing problems were ridiculous.

RP: Working with such a very small staff, I suppose it was really back to doing several jobs.

JC: Except that you could hardly be expected to do as you had done in Glasgow, being told to carry the type about.

RP: I believe at one point you took over Osbert Lancaster's Pocket Cartoon for a while.

JC: Yes, while Osbert was in Athens for the War Office. I drew them for about a year but, not having his enormous inventiveness, I could only do about three a week.

RP: Then after the war you became an *Express* Foreign Correspondent. That must be a very unsettled life, being woken at three o'clock in the morning and told to catch the five o'clock plane to Nicaragua.

JC: A deeply, profoundly unsettling life that went on for twenty-five years or more. It gave me opportunities for seeing the world that I would never have had otherwise. It's a kind of life that's all over now. I mean, I was the last of the dinosaurs, because there aren't any of us left. No newspaper could afford us nowadays.

RP: You became, in fact, the *Express* roving reporter. You could go more or less where you liked.

JC: More or less.

RP: Even to Tibet.

JC: I got about twenty miles into Tibet. When the Dalai Lama was being expelled, I went to a place called Kalampong, in North Bengal. The only way to get to Tibet was to walk, and I walked for about 250 miles, and I got to Yatung, which is the very first village you come to in Tibet. The police stopped me, and I said, 'I want to go to Lhasa, please,' and they said, 'It's just up the road there ... another 480 miles.' I turned round and walked all the way back again.

RP: Why did you leave the *Express*?

JC: I fell out with them on a matter of policy. It's too complicated a story to go into now, but I felt they behaved extraordinarily dishonestly over a certain political issue. I just felt I couldn't carry on any longer.

RP: Where did you move to?

JC: It took me some time to move anywhere, because Beaverbrook was a very powerful man in the Newspaper Proprietors Association, and I became pretty nearly unemployable for a while. Ultimately, I finished up with my very good friend Tom Hopkinson on *Picture Post*.

RP: Which, alas, sank with all hands towards the end of the 1950s.

JC: Entirely as a result of my misdoings. I wrote a piece from

Korea suggesting that the South Koreans were behaving in every way just as atrociously as the North Koreans, and that it was a great shame to see concentration camps with the United Nations flags flying on top. The proprietor thought that was an injudicious thing to say, and the editor refused to take it out – so the editor and I were summarily fired. So there I was – within two years I had been mixed-up in two quarrels involving moral issues – with the *Express* and with *Picture Post* – so I was in a total mess. But then I found my true home on *The News-Chronicle*, which was still going then, and which was the one paper where I really felt happy in comradely relations with everybody, and for which paper I travelled the entire world in perfect amity and peace.

RP: It was an excellent paper.

JC: A good paper – but it died. It has often been said that it was the first example of the ship that left the sinking rats.

RP: And then you moved into television which has been a whole new career. You must be one of the world's most travelled men.

JC: I think that, at some time or another, I've been to every place that is now a country – except New Zealand.

RP: Why is it that you've never been there?

JC: Well, it's not on the way to anywhere – unless you're going to the South Pole – and, an even better reason, nothing's ever happened there.

RP: You've even been to Albania. Now, that's a collector's piece. It can't be easy to get in.

JC: Very difficult indeed. I went in with an East German tourist group, pretending to be an East German tourist, if you can imagine. We touched down in Tirana, and I'd been there about three minutes when they rumbled me. They said, 'This is disgraceful, you're not supposed to be here, you can't come in – be gone, get out.' Their difficulty was that there was nowhere to get out to, because they had destroyed all the roads to Yugoslavia, there was no longer any railway, and the aeroplane came in only once every two weeks, and it had just gone. There was no way I could be expelled, so they kept me there. They sent me to a great big empty Russian hotel, at a place called Durrës on the Adriatic coast, which is really rather a nice place. This enormous hotel, which the

29

Russians had built just before they themselves had been kicked out, had about three hundred rooms, of which only one was occupied – mine. I wasn't allowed to leave it, but they wired off a little stretch of beach which I was allowed to gambol about on. It was really very dull indeed, and I didn't see very much of Albania.

RP: You've used a lot of your despatches as a basis for books, how many have you done now?

JC: A dozen or more.

RP: And they include an excellent autobiography called *Point of Departure*. That book achieved the unusual distinction of being reissued about ten years after it was first published.

JC: Yes, that was rather a nice thing to happen. Of all my books and writings, it's the only one I would like to be remembered by.

Arthur C. Clarke

Science has always been a closed book to me, and the hours I spent in the labs at school were a complete waste of time; but although the practical applications of bunsen burners, test tubes and foul smells were lost on me, I enjoyed the flights of fancy of the science-fiction writers of the day, and was a sucker for little green men and bug-eyed monsters. It has all grown up since then, and I find Mr Clarke's more sophisticated approach eminently readable. Not only does he have a delight in his subject, but it is a boyish delight.

RP: What part of England do you come from?
ACC: I was born in Minehead, in Somerset, a little seaside town. It was little in those days, it's quite large now.
RP: What was the first branch of science to interest you?
ACC: Originally, I think, palaeontology. I had a small collection of fossils, including a mammoth's tooth which a friend gave me. I also had a lot of flints. It was through that tooth that I got interested in dinosaurs – they still fascinate me – and then, for some reason which I don't recall, I switched quite suddenly to astronomy – and there I had found my metier.
RP: That led to dreams of inter-planetary travel?
ACC: That's right. I discovered that people were thinking of going out into space. I used to look at the moon through a home-made telescope – just a cardboard tube with a couple of lenses in it, and I got to know the moon and to map it. In fact, I knew the moon better than my native Somerset.
RP: In those pre-war days, were there already science-fiction societies?

31

ACC: Indeed, there was a great interest in science fiction.

RP: I remember there were all those American pulp magazines one could get at Woolworth's for 3d. each.

ACC: I used to haunt Woolworth's during my lunch hour.

RP: Were you bright at science at school?

ACC: I was always good at science and mathamatics. Oh, I was a horrible little swot.

RP: Did you start writing pieces very early?

ACC: My first pieces were published in the magazine of my school in Taunton, when I was fourteen or fifteen. Some of them have been reprinted lately, and I'm rather depressed to see small sign of improvement.

RP: When you left school, what was your first job?

ACC: I went straight into the Civil Service, locally at first and then in Whitehall. I must say I quite enjoyed it, with those long lunch hours' walking through St James's Park. I did much of my early writing in Civil Service time. When the war began, we were evacuated to North Wales, and from there I went into the Royal Air Force.

RP: Was there a chance to do scientific work?

ACC: I went in as an aircraftsman, and my training consisted of learning about electronics and wireless. I had always been interested in that sort of thing and had made my own radio sets. While I was still at school I made a light beam transmitter so that I could send messages along a beam of light – and that was pretty advanced stuff for those days. Of course, I thoroughly enjoyed learning about electronics. Nobody knew about radar at the time I went in; we still called it RDF – Radio Direction Finding. I became an instructor at the Radar School in Yatesbury, Wiltshire. In fact, I got my commission there, and went on to the first micro-wave blind landing system – the GCA – the talk-down system. We had a very complex and advanced radar system which detected where the aircraft was in the sky, and then you told the pilot what course to fly to get him down to the ground.

RP: This was real pioneer work.

ACC: Yes, we were working with the American scientists who had actually invented the system.

RP: In 1945, while you were still in uniform, you wrote an article about communications satellites.

ACC: Yes, that was the paper which started the Comsat business. I wrote it early in the year, and it was published in *Wireless World* in October, just after the war had ended. It laid down the principles which now determine the world's communication system – the idea that you would have satellites poised at such a height above the earth that they would remain stationary in the sky.

RP: Did anybody take your idea up and get excited about it?

ACC: A few people got excited about it; the Americans did first, and I have reason to believe that it was one of the stimuli which started the American satellite programme.

RP: Was the piece that you wrote complete enough for you to have patented the idea?

ACC: There has been some discussion about that. I might not have been able to do so because, although I described everything in the system, at that time it was not possible actually to build it, and that might have invalidated the patent. Of course, had I been clever enough, I would simply have incorporated the word Comsat, and done quite well out of that.

RP: What happened to you when you left the RAF?

ACC: I got an ex-service grant from the Government and went to King's College, London, where I took a degree in physics and pure and applied maths, and did some post-graduate work in astronomy.

RP: So now you were to be not merely an imaginative science-fiction writer but a qualified one.

ACC: Yes, I became a science editor and worked with the Institution of Electrical Engineers, as editor of *Science Abstracts*.

RP: Who were the pioneers of science fiction? There was H.G. Wells, of course ...

ACC: And Jules Verne – and, in this country particularly, Olaf Stapledon, who wrote a magnificent history of the future called *Last and First Men* which I discovered soon after it was published in 1930; and this book, the history of the next two thousand million years, had more influence on me than anything else I had ever read. It opened my mind to the possibilities of time and space, and directly influenced many of my early books.

RP: With scientific progress moving so fast, it must be a job keeping in advance of the real thing.

ACC: Well, it's almost impossible, of course, and many of the things I've described have become history. In 1948 I wrote a book about the first landing on the moon, which I put in 1978: I thought it was ridiculous putting it at only thirty years in the future, but in fact it beat my deadline.

RP: You commentated for American television on some of the Apollo missions, including the moon landing.

ACC: Yes, I was at Cape Kennedy for the launch of several of the missions, including the historic Apollo 11.

RP: Having predicted the landing on the moon, would you like to predict when the Mars landing will be?

ACC: Well, of course, this is not a scientific or technical matter, it's almost entirely a political matter – as indeed was the first landing on the moon. But assuming that there are no sudden discontinuities, either a war which wipes out civilization or the sudden discovery that there are Martians, I think there may be a man landing on Mars by the turn of the century.

RP: I presume that would be as far as we could go for a long, long time. I mean, we can't shut astronauts up in spaceships for years and years, without achieving some form of suspended animation or a medical discovery of that sort.

ACC: It would depend how large the spaceship is. In the next century we will be able to build very large space vehicles that could carry thousands of men: it could be a space colony in which they could live, in many ways, normal lives. They could go off for years, or even generations, and live in a little world quite happily. In fact, it could be a world larger than Athens in its heyday.

RP: Would the benefits justify it all?

ACC: Yes, space has already paid for itself many times over. For instance, tens of thousands of lives have been saved by weather satellites. A few years ago, half a million people were killed in the great Bangladesh hurricane, and most of them could have been saved if they had had accurate information from the weather satellites. We've mentioned communications satellites, and there's a whole branch of what they call application satellites, such as those which are examining the earth's resources from space, discovering new mineral deposits, new areas of fisheries and so on.

RP: How many fictional works have you written?

ACC: About a hundred short stories, which have now been collected in, I think, six volumes, and upwards of twenty novels of various lengths.

RP: One of my favourites is about the men on the first moon landing who insist on staying up there a full six months as it makes a difference to their income tax liability.

ACC: Needless to say, there was personal wishful thinking behind that; but in fact I have done better because the Sri Lanka government passed an act, usually known by my name, which means I can live in Sri Lanka without paying any income tax at all.

RP: You've been living there for a long time now.

ACC: Much of the time for the past twenty years, but I couldn't become a resident until they passed that act, otherwise I would have been paying British, American and Sri Lanka tax, and would have been instantly bankrupt.

RP: Surely your most celebrated work is 2001 - A Space Odyssy, the story of the film. How did that project start?

ACC: Stanley Kubrick wrote to me saying that he was interested in doing the proverbial good science-fiction movie, and did I have any ideas? Well, I did have one or two, and it so happened that I was going to New York to work for Time-Life on a book about space, and when that job was finished I went over full time with Stanley. We batted ideas back and forth to such an extent that now I can't remember who thought of what.

RP: Who reads science fiction?

ACC: It's extraordinarily varied. Schoolboys and schoolgirls, of course. There's quite a large feminine readership - and, in fact, feminine authorship. Science fiction cuts across all strata in all countries. It's popular everywhere, and I would like to think that its readers are intellectually more alert than readers of general fiction, because science fiction stretches and expands the mind. If it's escapism, it's escaping into the real universe.

RP: You've announced that you're giving up writing novels?

ACC: Yes, I just want to enjoy Sri Lanka, and my skin-diving, my books and records, my two mongeese – or mongoslings – and two German Shepherds and pet monkey, and a lot of other things.

Tom Conti

There is an ebullience about this lively and talented actor which doubtless stems from his Italian father, but he also retains an air of caution which one can ascribe to the Scottish side of him. He believes that enjoyment is an essential part of any job, and that an actor has not only to like the part he is playing but the audience he is playing it to.

RP: You were born in Scotland, Tom – whereabouts?
TC: In a little town called Paisley, which is famous for its patterns.
RP: Conti is not, of course, a Scottish name.
TC: No, it's an Italian name. My father came to Paisley because he knew someone who lived nearby. I think he thought he had been taken to America, but he was actually landed at Leith docks and told, 'You'll find the Empire State Building somewhere up there – up near Grassmarket.'
RP: And he married a Scottish girl, your mother. As a youngster, what was your ambition?
TC: To be an opera singer. It hasn't been realized, because God gave me a croak.
RP: Did you see much opera?
TC: Yes, a lot – and we went to many, many concerts. Those were the days when artists toured – artists like Gigli and Infantino and Joan Hammond and all those huge names of the past. They all came, doing one night stands round the country – and the place was always filled. St Andrew's Hall in Glasgow was always filled with Italians, and they were wonderful, happy occasions.
RP: In fact, what did you do when you left school?

TC: I went into my father's shop. He was a ladies' hairdresser, and he had a couple of shops. I just went in there to fill in time and decide what on earth I wanted to do. Then one day I happened to go out to buy a shirt, and it meant that I had to walk down Cannon Street. I passed the Music College, and all the windows were open and people were playing trumpets and fiddles and singing scales – a great, exciting cacophony. I thought, perhaps I should go there; maybe I should go and take the dust-sheet off the piano and have a go. Another part of the building was the College of Drama. Anyway, I went in there and said, 'How do you join this place?' And they said, 'Well, you do this and that and this and that – and talk to your parents.' And a week later I started.

RP: So it was a snap decision – and it was drama rather than music.

TC: Yes, it was taken out of my hands at the last minute. It was very weird.

RP: How long did you study there?

TC: Three years.

RP: And what was your first professional job?

TC: It was as an Acting ASM at the Citizens' Theatre, in Glasgow.

RP: The Citizens' Theatre, in the Gorbals – an adventurous theatre.

TC: It's adventurous in that it's stayed in the Gorbals, because it's not a good place to be. People were being carved up right and left, outside the front door. And it was an empty theatre; it was filled with actors, but no audience. My memory of the place is just empty seats and dark nights. One night, there were only thirteen people in the audience, and I think there were about fifteen of us on stage, but we didn't get the night off; the management made us play.

RP: And to be an ASM as well as an actor must have meant about sixteen hours a day.

TC: Oh, I never left the theatre. It was extraordinary. I went in on a Monday morning at half-past nine, and if there was a working weekend – if we were taking down one show and putting up another – I didn't come out until the following Monday morning. And all for a glorious eight pounds a week.

RP: How long were you at the Citizens'?

TC: A year, and then I messed around from rep to rep, and did some television. It was the beginning of a twelve-year spell in the wilderness.

RP: You also did some radio; I read that you met your wife, Kara, in a radio studio.

TC: Yes. I had met her once before, briefly; then, as luck will have it, we met again doing a play.

RP: When did you come south?

TC: About a year after we married. We happened to be coming through London on the way back from Italy, and we were offered a television play together, and we did it, and she said, 'We really ought to stay.' And I said, 'No, we must go back to Scotland. I've tried it in London; it's hopeless – we'll never get work.' And she said, 'Come on, we'll sit it out.'

RP: What sort of jobs did you do between theatrical engagements?

TC: All sorts of things. I played the guitar in restaurants, and I was a tour guide for a bit.

RP: Did you know London that well?

TC: I did by the time I had taken a few people round. I had to sit a little test, you know ... to make sure that I knew that Westminster Abbey was built by – er ...

RP: Well, go on.

TC: I don't know who the heck it was built by ... a bunch of monks, I suppose. If I'd said St Paul's, I'd have been able to say Wren.

RP: Was there any particular embarrassing moment that you remember?

TC: Of yes, there was one beaut. It was a sunny, summer day, and I was taking a family of Americans round in my car. We were walking down the left-hand side of St Paul's, inside the building, and there was a shaft of light coming down and hitting a crucifix on the wall. Now, the tourists like you to keep talking, you know; that way, they feel they're getting their money's worth, so I said, 'You'll see how the sunlight shafts through and hits the cross. Wren stipulated that there should be a window in that position and that there should always be a cross hung on the wall, so that at certain times of the year, at certain hours of the day ...' Of course, we all turned as one to see the sun coming through the window. And there were three spotlights behind a piece of wood. There was no window there at all.

RP: What was your first real break in the theatre?

TC: Breaks always start at an unexpected point. My break started when a man named Michael Rudman asked me to do a play by Cecil Taylor called *The Black and White Minstrels* at the Traverse Theatre in Edinburgh. It was a tiny little theatre – in those days it held about fifty people – and I said, 'I can't come here and work for £14 a week.' And he said, 'Well, I can only tell you that Nigel Hawthorne said exactly the same thing, but I talked him into it, and he came here, and he hasn't stopped working since.'

RP: So you took the chance.

TC: I took the chance and exactly the same thing happened; I haven't stopped working since.

RP: I suppose the play that gave the biggest boost to your career was the one in which you spent the entire evening in bed.

TC: *Whose Life is it Anyway?* Yes, that was by far the most exhausting thing I've ever done.

RP: You were a paraplegic patient in a hospital, and you had just your face and your voice to act with.

TC: It's easier than people think, actually, because you have things to help you – like being centre stage, dressed in a white gown in a white bed with a light bang on you. It's not too hard to hold the attention.

RP: But in bed, with the warmth of the lights, wasn't there a danger of dozing off during scenes which didn't concern you?

TC: Oh, I dozed off all the time. Oh yes, endlessly. I fell asleep in the middle of a line once, and Phoebe Nicholls, who was playing the nurse, had to wake me up.

RP: What happened if your nose itched or if you got cramp?

TC: I had a panic button in the bed, and there were various different signals I could make. If it just flashed on and off, then it meant 'help', and someone would come on, and I'd say, 'My nose is itching,' and she'd scratch my nose. If it was a continuous light, it meant 'Stand by the curtain'. And if I flashed in groups of three, it meant 'Bring down the curtain! Just anybody! Go to the curtain and bring it down!'

RP: A Mayday!

TC: Yes, it meant 'I'm about to throw up', or something like that.

RP: How many times did you play that part?

TC: Oh gosh, I don't know. About eight hundred, I suppose.

RP: You had a great success with it in New York, but when you left the cast an actress took over your part – which is unusual, to say the least.

TC: Yes, it was Mary Tyler Moore, and she was wonderful. You see they couldn't find an actor to take over from me: they wanted a star, but stars aren't too interested in taking over someone else's part; they want to originate things. The sex-change idea had come up early in the London run, only about a week after we had opened at the Mermaid Theatre. Jane Asher, who was my co-star in this country, said to me, 'I'm getting tired of playing this sodding doctor; why don't we change parts sometimes? You be in the bed one night, and I'll be in the bed the next.' And I thought this was an excellent idea. So we went to the management with it, and they said, wearily, 'Oh, yes. Ha, ha. Good night.' But Brian Clark, the author, thought about it, and when our casting difficulty turned up in New York, he did the rewrite.

•

Roald Dahl

He is a giggler: he sees the funny side in everything, which is probably why he writes so successfully for children as well as for adults. He believes that music can help a writer, and that to put on great music before starting work makes it impossible to write rubbish. He lives in Buckinghamshire and has four children.

RP: You're from a Norwegian family, I believe.

RD: Pure Norwegian, both father and mother – but born and educated in England. I speak Norwegian and have visited Norway nearly every year of my life, but I'm really very English.

RP: You went to an English public school.

RD: Where I was better at games than at work; there was certainly no sign of any ability to write. I was nothing at school; I wasn't even a house prefect.

RP: In one of your books, you quote your English report: 'indolent and illiterate'.

RD: I think 'illiterate' was a little unfair, because I used to read avidly. 'Indolent', yes.

RP: What did you read?

RD: Everything I could get hold of ... Dickens, Thackeray – and there was an American writer, a short story writer called Ambrose Bierce: at the age of eleven, I couldn't turn the light off.

RP: In your teens, you went off on a travelling adventure.

RD: Yes, it was something called the Public Schools Exploring Expedition, to Newfoundland. It was led by an intrepid and frightfully tough surgeon-commander who was on Scott's expedition to the South Pole. It was enormous fun, but it nearly killed us; marching across Newfoundland and back with a hundred and ten pounds on our backs. Of course, in those days the country was unexplored, and there weren't aeroplanes flying around.

RP: What did you want to be?

RD: I hadn't the foggiest idea. My father had died when I was three, so my mother brought us all up. She said, 'Do you want to go to Oxford or Cambridge?' – and in those days it was quite easy to get into them, if you could pay – but I said, 'No, I don't. I want to get a job that'll take me to distant lands.' So I went up for an interview with the Shell Company, for the Eastern staff. I remember my housemaster saying, 'I don't know what you're wasting your time with this for. There'll be the Head Boys of Eton and Harrow and God knows what there.' But that imposing board of directors, who were interviewing sixty boys for five places, all brightened up when I said I'd won the heavyweight boxing at school – and that got me one of the places.

RP: Where did it take you?

RD: To Dar-es-Salaam, in what was then called Tanganyika. It was marvellous, romantic, exciting. It took three weeks to get there on a ship.

RP: Was it an office job?

RD: It was a bit of everything. I was only eighteen, and it was rather marvellous for a chap of that age. I learned Swahili, and drove around and visited the sisal plantations and diamond mines and places like that, to see that the chaps had the right kind of lubricating oil for their machinery. You were miles from anywhere, and there were coconuts, snakes, zebras, giraffes, elephants, everything you could think of. I thought this was going to be my career, but after I'd been there about two years the war broke out. Obviously one joined up, so I drove a long way along rutted roads, fording rivers, up to Nairobi, and joined the RAF for flying training.

RP: Did you train in Nairobi?

RD: Our initial training, yes – and then we finished up in a ghastly place in Iraq where the temperature was 120° in the shade. You had to start flying at six in the morning and finish at nine – and that was it, because it was so hot.

RP: You served in the Middle East. You were rather badly shot up.

RD: Yes, I finished up in a pile of flames on the ground, but I recovered from that and went on flying for a bit.

RP: Then to the United States as Assistant Air Attaché, which sounds rather a glamorous post.

RD: I didn't last very long in it, because I'm a tactless sort of fellow, and that's the one thing a diplomat mustn't be. I got shunted out of that job, and then I was working for the Quiet Canadian, Sir William Stevenson.

RP: Intelligence?

RD: Yes. Much more fun.

RP: It was while you were in Washington, I believe, that you began to write.

RD: Yes, I'd never thought about it before. At that time America was hardly in the war, and we were doing everything we could to get help from the Americans. One morning, I was sitting in my room in the Embassy, and a door opened and a little round face with thick glasses poked in, and said, 'May I come in?' I thought this little man was going to ask for a job of some sort – not that I could have given him one – but he said, 'My name is C.S. Forester,' and I said, 'Oh, go on!', and he said, 'No, honestly.' I was an avid reader, and one of my gods was walking into the room. He said, 'Look, will you come out to lunch with me and tell me your most exciting adventure in the war, and I'll write it for the *Saturday Evening Post*, and it'll be good for Britain.' So we went out to lunch, and ordered duck. He was trying to make notes of what I was saying and shovel duck into his mouth at the same time, and it was difficult. So I said, 'If I scribble all this down this evening, and send it to you, then you can put it into proper shape. Would that help?' He said, 'Well, that'd be marvellous.' So I did. A week later, I got a lovely letter from him, and a cheque for a thousand dollars: he said he hadn't touched it, and he'd sold it to the *Saturday Evening Post* for me, and they wanted some more.

RP: A thousand dollars for an evening's work. Not bad.

RD: I said, 'It can't be as easy as all that' – but it somehow worked. It was.

44

RP: I know you wrote a number of RAF stories to follow that, and they must have been very useful for the British war effort. You're credited with inventing the word 'gremlin'.

RD: Well, it may be true, and it probably is, but I don't like to take too much credit for that. Just after the Forester thing, I wrote a little story about creatures, and it was called 'The Gremlins'.

RP: And those were the original gremlins? The ones that used to get in the machinery, and climb out on the wings of aircraft and do all that damage?

RD: Yes.

RP: They bred very fast; they began turning up in broadcasting almost immediately. What happened to you when the war ended?

RD: I was managing to sell more or less everything I wrote to big American magazines, and it seemed that as a single man I could earn a living, so I resigned from the Shell Company and offered to give them back all the gratuities they'd paid me during the war, and they were extremely nice and said, 'You'd better keep them, because we think you'll need them if you're going into the writing racket – and good luck.'

RP: You were writing short stories; you didn't tackle novels?

RD: If you get on to something you find you can do, I think you're a bit of a silly ass if you try something else which may be a flop.

RP: They're very ingeniously constructed, often very funny, and sometimes rather gruesome. Because of the gruesome quality, they seem to pair rather strangely with the children's books which have been your other major output.

RD: I don't think they're gruesome at all; I only write really what I think is funny. One is an entertainer.

RP: Do you think they are all funny?

RD: I've probably got a warped sense of humour, but I think it's terribly funny if somebody gets killed by being hit on the head with a frozen leg of lamb or something like that. You can't really call it tragic, can you? It's the old story about the man slipping on a banana skin; it's jolly painful, but we all roar with laughter, don't we?

RP: It depends which side you're on, really. You've done a few scripts for the big screen – one of the James Bond films, for example.

RD: *You Only Live Twice* – that was fun. That's the only one I've had any real fun doing. You live in such luxury when you do a Bond film. We went to Japan and we went everywhere in helicopters – tops of mountains and everywhere.

RP: And you wrote *Chitty Chitty Bang Bang*.

RD: Yes, but that wasn't much fun.

RP: Wasn't it?

RD: I'd better not talk ... you see, I'll start calling people horrible names. I'm not in love with cinema directors – let's just put it that way.

RP: You lived in the United States for a number of years ...

RD: Well, back and forth between there and here.

RP: While you were in America, you had the good fortune to become married to that excellent actress, Patricia Neale. Have you written any screenplays for her?

RD: One. There again, I think I'd rather not talk about it too much, because – er ...

RP: It was one of those?

RD: Yes, it was one of those. I don't think it was a bad screenplay, but things happen to films; that's why it's so much nicer – if you're an ordinary writer – to stick to writing books and stories, and then nobody can screw around with them, can they?

RP: Are you disciplined? Do you work set hours?

RD: Yes, I am a disciplined writer. I don't think any writer works particularly long hours, because he can't – he becomes inefficient. I work from ten to twelve, and from four to six. It's time for a drink at twelve, and it's time for a drink at six, so I hotfoot it down from my little hut in the garden and have one.

RP: Do you work fast? How long does a short story take?

RD: Anything up to six months. I'm a very slow worker. Very slow.

RP: Now, we know that your wife had a serious illness; she had more than one very serious stroke, and you did marvellous work in getting her to recover. As a result of this, you built up a foundation – a group of treatment centres ...

RD: I didn't build it up; it was simply my original small idea of how to treat a stroke patient, by giving her very intensive therapy.

RP: Immediately?

RD: As soon as possible. As soon as you can get the patient out of bed – or even in bed. The first few months are vital. Amateurs are called in to help, because English local hospitals are all overworked and understaffed. In our case, my wife was offered half an hour's speech therapy a week, and I said, 'That's no ruddy good, she's going to need six hours a day.'

RP: And you gave her six hours a day?

RD: Yes, we called in chums and they popped in and out regularly, and it was very fierce and intense. The final teacher we had, who lives in our village, is an extraordinary woman named Valerie Eden Griffiths; she has taken this whole scheme up, and allied herself with the Chest and Heart Society – which is now, I think, called the Chest, Heart and Stroke Society – and there are now about thirty branches in the United Kingdom, each one with a hundred amateur volunteers who are ready to rush to a stroke patient who has been discharged from hospital. The scheme's working well. Another great thing, you see, a stroke patient doesn't want to be left alone, staring at the ceiling – and what can the poor husband or wife do unless he or she has got help?

RP: That's marvellous work.

Les Dawson

Les is the only man who has ever made me dry up completely in a studio. There I was, talking to him about his career and asking him reasonably intelligent questions, and suddenly he went off into a superbly surrealist routine about his concern for the horned whelk in Morecambe Bay – you can read it a few pages further on – and I found myself quite rigid with suppressed laughter and unable to utter a word.

RP: Les, I know you were brought up in a fairly run-down area of Manchester. Did you know actual hardship as a child?

LD: We lived in a road called Miracle Road, and the reason it was called Miracle Road was because if the houses stood up it was a miracle. No, it wasn't easy; it was a very harsh upbringing really. My father was superstitious; he wouldn't work if there was a Friday in the week.

RP: What were you good at when you were at school?

LD: Essays.

RP: Were you, at that age, a comic? Were you the school jester?

LD: Yes, because I was fat, and when you're fat you can't run and you can't fight, so you have to be merry with people, and pleasant – and so we fat people are the great philosophers. Every philosopher that ever was has been fat, did you know that? There's never been a thin philosopher. Descartes was fat, and Kant was fat, Engles was fat – and Nietzsche.

RP: But they weren't all funny.

LD: Oh, I don't know ... have you read philosophy?

RP: Did you go to the music hall a lot when you were a boy?

LD: Yes, I used to go to the northern theatres. I saw some pretty good acts.

RP: Who were your heroes?

LD: The people I really liked, who were a big influence in my life, were people like Robb Wilton, Norman Evans and W. C. Fields.

RP: As we know to our cost, somebody taught you to play the piano. Whose idea was that?

LD: Well, it's a long story. You see, I used to play the piano when I was a child, and the neighbours loved it; they used to break the windows to hear me better, and my father used to help me to keep time by banging the lid up and down on my fingers. From there, I progressed and I did my first concert, which is always a salutory lesson for any child entering the music business. It was a school concert, and when I had finished playing the children stamped their feet and clapped their hands – all over me.

RP: What was your first job when you left school?

LD: I was an apprentice electrician.

RP: What had you got in mind?

LD: Anything, except being an apprentice electrician.

RP: Despite what you said earlier on, you were pretty good at boxing.

LD: Yes, I was a boxer. In fact, I was the only boxer ever to be carried into the ring as well as out. I was carried out of the ring so often that I had handles sewn on my shorts. My father said to me one night, 'Give it up, son.' I said, 'We've not left the dressing-room yet, Dad.' I knew then that my career had come to an end, because I'm basically a coward.

RP: The time for National Service came along. What did you opt for?

LD: Desertion. They wouldn't wear that, so I went into the Tank Corps. I became a tank driver.

RP: And your impressions of Al Jolson at regimental concerts are still spoken of by your comrades in hushed tones. Was that the first time you faced an audience?

LD: Do you want the full story about this? Do you want the truth on this programme? Are we being man to man – face to face?

RP: Yes, yes.

LD: The absolute truth is I got forty-eight days' detention for going absent without leave.

RP: Where did you go?

LD: I didn't go anywhere, I was caught just as I went out of the wire of the perimeter. There was a big fellow there, much bigger than I am – in fact, he had shoulders like the Cotswolds – and he bundled me up into a small heap and took me back again. Because of that small demeanour, I got forty-eight days. Luckily for me, it was Cambrai Day, which means a lot in the Tank Corps because it's the anniversary of the very first time tanks were ever used in warfare – at Cambrai in 1915 – and there was nobody to play the piano ... so they dragged me out of the guardhouse, and I never went back.

RP: And when you came out of the Army?

LD: Well, I couldn't settle. I suffered a very upsetting revelation in the Army: the fact that I couldn't get up in the morning. In fact, I was court-martialled; the officer said, 'Don't you hear the bugle?' and I said, 'No, sir, they play it when I'm asleep.' So, when I came out of the Army, there was nowhere to go, my parents disowned me – so I thought I'd go to Paris. I wanted to be a writer, I'd always wanted to be a writer, so I gravitated to Paris, which I thought was the absolute Valhalla of the arts in those days.

RP: Had you done any writing?

LD: Yes, in the Army – for *The Soldier*. One or two bits and pieces.

RP: So you took a room in Paris and started to write.

LD: Well, I had to work up to a room. But the thing was, Paris was the wrong place to write – because of the smell of Paris, the very vitality of Paris.

RP: What were you trying to write?

LD: Essays.

RP: Still? You weren't going to make much of a living writing essays. How did you live?

LD: Playing the piano.

RP: Where?

LD: In a brothel.

RP: Successfully?

LD: The brothel was successful. I wasn't. I must be perfectly honest,

I didn't know at the time that the place was a brothel. I was engaged to play the piano from three in the morning until six. I thought I was being successful until Madame told me one day that she hired me to get rid of people.

RP: How long did the Paris experiment last?

LD: A year. Then I couldn't take the starvation any more. So I lived in London for a while, and had a succession of jobs.

RP: What sort of jobs?

LD: From professional babysitting to washing pots in cafés, but I could get three meals a day.

RP: Had you started comicking yet?

LD: No, oddly enough, I really hadn't got down to the comedy field. I tried playing the piano and singing a few songs and getting a few laughs – mainly when I sang and played the piano. I did one or two clubs in London, and it didn't get me anywhere at all. And I caught the tail end of the music halls and – one thing I'm very grateful for – I worked with Robb Wilton.

RP: Where was that?

LD: That was at the Chiswick Empire. He was top of the bill.

RP: What sort of material did you use?

LD: Well, it wasn't doleful, it was sort of 'Hi there, I just love you people.' It sounded American, because I thought you had to be like that, and tell wonderful funny stories. I died very successfully.

RP: So that was the pattern for a few years . . . club jobs when you could get them, and uninteresting jobs to keep yourself going?

LD: Oh, very uninteresting. I sold babies' potties, for instance, round the shops. There was one particular company where the advertising claimed that you couldn't spill this potty – it was a non-spill potty – and they booked me as a rep for this, and I proved beyond a shadow of a doubt that you could spill the potty, so I didn't last very long. I was signing on for the dole so often that they asked me to MC the staff dances.

RP: There's a story about a job you had in a club in Hull which had a traumatic effect on your career.

LD: Yes . . . there was a man called Al Heath, and if he's listening, I still bless him. He invited me along to an audition at the Max Rivers studios, which was a sort of Belsen with lights, and he offered me about £18 for a week to play a series of clubs in Hull. I don't think any comic in the business has gone through what I went through ... I mean, I didn't just die, I was resurrected nightly. By the Thursday night I had had quite sufficient, so I went to a place in Hull which is very old and steeped in history called The Land of Green Ginger, which is where Wilberforce and the Slave Business all began and ended – and I got completely and utterly stoned. Then I went to this club, and the curtains opened, and I slumped on the piano and I couldn't rise – I was incapable of it – and I said the first thing that came into my mind, which was, 'It's a great pleasure to be in this reconverted kipper depot,' – and they had just spent £25,000 on this club. The odd thing was, instead of being hooted off, as I had been before, the customers started to laugh – and I began to realize that what I'd done actually was to be myself. It was a moment of truth. I began to sort myself out.

RP: What was the breakthrough? When were you able finally to become a full-time professional comedian?

LD: It was about 1964. There was a television show called *Big Night Out in Blackpool*. I went very well, and it really started from there.

RP: And you've had two or three books published. Which way do you want your career to go? Do you want to go on doing the clubs? Do you want to write?

LD: I don't know. You see, there's something that nobody knows about. I think I can confide in you, because we've been friends for a long time, Roy. I am very much concerned with the conservation of natural wildlife, and we do have a problem on our hands now, particularly with the horned whelk of Morecambe Bay.

RP: I'm worried about that too. I'm so glad you've raised it.

LD: Thank you. You know, I'm finding indifference, like a wall, everywhere I go. The problem is that the whelk, one of the natural denizens of our shores, is in danger of extinction because of silt which is raised from the seabed because of people drilling for oil. This relentless search for minerals is destroying every aspect of our life.

RP: Theatres are closing too.

LD: The theatres are closing because you can't get whelks. What is happening is that the horned whelk has a very small nasal passage, so in its search for a mate it relies on its eyes. Its eyesight is all important. But the silt causes astigmatism, and in some cases the whelks are cross-eyed.

RP: What can we listeners do about this?

LD: This is a very serious subject, and I feel very strongly about it. We found the other day in Fleetwood that one whelk was trying to mount a discarded yoghurt carton, and we can't permit this. It shows, of course, that its eyesight is no longer keen. We are planning to open a chain of clinics, from Devizes to the Wash, where whelks can be fitted with contact lenses and be reintroduced to natural nautical life.

RP: I'm very happy to hear this.

Lord Denning

Even after all this time, I occasionally feel nervous in approaching an especially distinguished castaway: I did so in the case of the Rt. Hon. Lord Denning, our most distinguished man of law. There seemed to me a reasonable chance that England's Senior Civil Law Judge and Master of the Rolls would tell me, sternly, to go away and not bother a man whose responsibilities are so heavy. But it was not like that at all: he was friendly and relaxed and, speaking in a soft voice with an attractive Hampshire burr, he told me how sad he had been that he had not been selected for the church choir, and how, in writing, he tries to emulate John Bunyan, with his short, easily understood sentences.

RP: First, Lord Denning, what are the Rolls?
LD: They're the old parchment rolls on which, many hundreds of years ago, all the records of the courts and the government were kept. These were the Rolls of the Realm, and the Master of the Rolls was in charge of them. Many are now in the Public Record Office.
RP: You were born in a small town in Hampshire. I believe your father kept a draper's shop?
LD: Yes.
RP: You went to the local school first of all?
LD: I went to our own little school, yes – and then I got a little scholarship to the grammar school at Andover, where I went by train.
RP: What were your best subjects at school?
LD: Mathematics and English literature.

RP: Did you have any particular ambition as a schoolboy?

LD: My mother remembered that when I was a little boy, I said, 'I think I'm going to become a barrister.' That was at about the age of ten – but I had no idea what a barrister was.

RP: When you left the grammar school, the First World War was on. You joined the Army.

LD: I went for a little time to Oxford – and then I was in the Royal Engineers. In due course I was commissioned as a second lieutenant, and we were rushed out to France in March 1918, when the Germans had forced the Allies back to Amiens, towards the gates of Paris. All us youngsters of nineteen were rushed out to hold the line. You know Lord Haig's words: 'There must be no retirement. Every position must be held to the last man. With our backs to the wall, and believing in the justice of our cause, we will fight on to the end.' As you know, we did fight on, and we went on to victory.

RP: When you were demobilized, did you go back to Oxford?

LD: Almost at once. We were demobilized on a Thursday, and I started at Oxford again on the Monday.

RP: You were reading mathematics; is that right?

LD: Yes.

RP: You took a first. What happened when you came down?

LD: I taught mathematics at Winchester for a year – but I didn't want to stay at that all my life.

RP: Was it then that you went back to the ambition you had had at ten years old, the law?

LD: I suppose it did go back to that time.

RP: So, back to Oxford. How long did it take you to get your law degree.

LD: Oh, I got through it quickly – I think about eight months.

RP: To take a first in law, from scratch, in eight months! That must be rather unusual, Lord Denning.

LD: It is unusual.

RP: You were one of five brothers. Sadly, two were killed in the First World War; one became a general, one an admiral, and you, sir, have done rather well. Is there any one quality in your early upbringing to which you can attribute those achievements?

LD: It was a combination of both Father and Mother: Father was

rather a dreamer, very good at literature and something of a poet –
and Mother was the active, keen intelligence, very anxious for her
boys to get on, and making sure that they kept on the right paths
and did their work.

RP: Now, your own story: a young law graduate. What next?
Some dinners to eat?

LD: Oh yes – and, of course, I had to be in chambers as a pupil –
and try to get some briefs when I was called to the Bar. In those
days, there was quite a long time to wait.

RP: Do you remember your very first brief?

LD: I think it was in the West London County Courts – for two
guineas. Then I'd have the little briefs, the dock briefs.

RP: You would sit in court and wait to be briefed?

LD: Yes, the accused would pick one of us out. There was no legal
aid in those days; we might have a day or two days for one pound
three and sixpence.

RP: Can you remember any particular great characters among the
judges before whom you appeared as a young barrister?

LD: Ah yes, there were characters who could be rather frightening
to a young man. I remember Mr Justice Swift, a very robust judge
– and Lord Justice Scrutton. They seemed to be greater, robuster
characters then: we're all too polite nowadays. If you did anything
wrong in the County Courts, you could be rebuked most severely,
and lose your client.

RP: You were appointed a judge yourself in 1944. Am I right in
saying that you've been a judge longer than anyone in English
legal history?

LD: So far as I can discover, yes. I started quite young, as English
judges go, and now I've been a judge for over thirty-six years.

RP: And, of course, you have a freehold.

LD: Ah yes, the newer judges – those appointed since 1959 – have
to go at seventy-five. I was appointed so many years ago that I can
go on indefinitely.

RP: You were promoted to Lord Justice of Appeal, and then Lord
of Appeal in Ordinary, and you remained in the House of Lords
until 1962, when you elected to retire, and become Master of the
Rolls.

LD: I don't know about retire. I went back because it's not nearly so much fun in the House of Lords – to be one of five, and dissenting . . . well, nobody takes any notice of a dissenting judgement there. So, in 1962, I went back, and the Lord Chancellor invited me to be Master of the Rolls.

RP: But the Master of the Rolls runs the Court of Appeal, and the judgements of the Court of Appeal can be overturned by the Lords, so in a way you were demoting yourself.

LD: Yes, you can call it that, but, mark you, I'm in charge of the show, and we have many, many more cases in the Court of Appeal than the House of Lords which are not appealed at all, and, in that way, we can influence – and do influence – the working of the law far more than the House of Lords. They may reverse us, but that doesn't worry us.

RP: In fact, you have had a number of your judgements rebuffed by the Lords in recent months.

LD: Maybe – but that doesn't mean their Lordships are right, you know.

RP: There's a story about you which I admire very much: you are, I believe, the only judge ever to have reversed one of his own judgements. You reassembled the court and announced that your previous judgement should be considered interim. That is unique, is it not?

LD: Well, perhaps so. But I don't mind saying I'm wrong and starting again. Everyone is wrong from time to time.

Mark Elder

Let us no longer think of the music director of an opera company as autocratic, bewhiskered and elderly; the 1980s style is more likely to be young Mr Elder, who holds the post with the English National Opera Company. When I asked him which record above all others he would like on a desert island, he chose Fred Astaire singing 'I Used To Be Colour Blind'.

ME: I auditioned at Covent Garden, and they asked me to join for the coming season. I started on *The Ring* with Solti, and in the course of the eighteen months that I was on the staff there was a terrifically varied repertoire. I did a lot of prompting, which in Italy is a very highly paid and highly skilled job, but in this country it's not so widely accepted or understood. At Covent Garden in those days there was hardly an opera that wasn't prompted, and it was a great training and a marvellous way to get to know unfamiliar works. For instance, I prompted Richard Strauss's *Der Rosenkavalier*, *Salome* and *Arabella*, an opera which I was later to conduct. I knew nothing about them, and it was a great chance to explore them.

RP: How does a prompter work? Does he wait for an artist to dry up before he feeds the line, or is he singing along the whole time?

ME: I think the purpose of prompting is to take some weight off a singer's back because, in such a complicated thing as opera, anything can go wrong. As you know, the prompter sits in the middle of the front of the stage, underneath a little curved box, which you sometimes notice in opera houses. He, or she, gives the first few words of every single musical entrance, accompanied by an appropriate gesture, so he not only has to be conversant with several different languages but also with the productions, so that he knows where the singers are going to be.

RP: I suppose he's anticipating the conductor slightly.

ME: Yes, I had a closed-circuit television with me in the prompt box and it gave me a picture of the conductor all the time. Before the days of television, it had to be done with a driving mirror. There are slightly different styles of prompting for the Italian school of opera and the German school: the German style tends to need more work, but the Italians use it like a trigger. I shall never forget, in my inexperienced days at Wexford Festival, before I went to Covent Garden, I gave an early cue to an Italian singer and as soon as he heard my voice he bounced in off me and sang an entire aria one beat in advance. The next time I delayed it by one beat and he got the whole thing right. It's really quite extraordinary the control and effect the prompter has on the singers. I'm told that in Parma, and some other Italian opera houses, the singers ask, not who the conductor is but who the prompter is; they know that in the heat of the moment the prompter is going to be the one of more value to them.

RP: Working at floor level, it must be a very dusty job.

ME: I remember a dress rehearsal of Puccini's *Turandot* in which James King, who was singing the tenor part, had been rather put off in the course of the proceedings, and in the Riddle Scene he was down on one knee and putting so much into his acting that his fur hat fell off. He muttered a curse and with one swift gesture tossed the hat right at me in the prompt box, just as I opened my mouth to give him a cue – so I got a mouthful of fur.

John Fowles

Mr Fowles is, as he admits, one of those for whom writing is an obsession, but it is not his only obsession – he has been helping to edit John Aubrey's *Monumentum Britannica*, the great seventeenth-century text about antiquities in Britain, and he is also the honorary curator of the museum in Lyme Regis, where he lives. Among his distinguished novels is *The French Lieutenant's Woman*, which is set largely in Lyme Regis, so he had the unusual experience of seeing his story being filmed within a hundred yards of his home.

RP: You were at Bedford School during the war. The BBC Symphony Orchestra was there then.

JF: That's right – and I have the unique honour of once having hit Sir Adrian Boult on his bald head with a fives ball. He was rather fond of watching us play fives, and one day a ball got through a hole in the netting.

RP: I believe they rehearsed in the Great Hall; did you get in to rehearsals?

JF: Well, for a time I was head boy and was lucky; I heard some marvellous music there.

RP: Head boy! So you knew power and glory as a youngster.

JF: Yes, and it put me off it for the rest of my life.

RP: In wartime, I suppose there was no point in having ambitions for later life; you were automatically going into one of the services. Is that how you felt?

JF: Certainly one knew one had to do National Service, but I was vague about what I would do afterwards. Head boys were supposed to go into the Foreign Service, or something like that. In so much as I had any ideas, it was that.

RP: You went into the Royal Marines and took a commission; I suppose you'd taken Cert A and all that stuff while you were at school.

JF: Yes.

RP: What did you do during your time in the Marines?

JF: I didn't enjoy it. I went through recruit training of course – but my last year I did enjoy, because I was on Dartmoor training Marines who had been picked to go into the Commandos. It meant that I could spend most of my time wandering over Dartmoor, which was fine.

RP: And because of your Oxford place you got out quite early when the war was over.

JF: Luckily. One day, the great Lord Mayor of Plymouth, Isaac Foot – Michael Foot's father – came to our camp, and I was appointed his ADC for the occasion. I told him that I didn't know what to do – that I could go to Oxford or I could stay on in the Marines. His answer was that anyone who was so stupid as to think there was a choice deserved to stay in the Marines. Coming from a famous lord mayor that was a very valuable piece of advice – and I took it.

RP: So, up to Oxford. Why did you read French?

JF: Mainly because I'd done it at school; in those days, that kind of choice was decided for one very early. We took Higher Cert at the age of fifteen then, I think, and I have never had much aptitude for mathematics, so I did French and German, but when I got to Oxford I was allowed to drop German.

RP: What were your extra-curricular interests?

JF: Cricket. I've always had a mania for cricket, and I still watch it a lot – and I was a keen amateur natural historian. I didn't do very much work, but very few of us did in those days – in the late forties. I began to have the idea that perhaps I might one day write books, but that was almost commonplace – certainly in the arts faculties at Oxford.

RP: And in the meantime?

JF: A position fell open at the University of Poitiers, in France, so I went off for a year to teach English.

RP: Enjoyable?

61

JF: Very. I wasn't competent at all. I must have been the worst university teacher of English in France, but I made some good French friends there, and I enjoyed it.

RP: After that?

JF: I took a job in Greece, at a famous public school which called itself the Eton of Greece. I was there for nearly two years.

RP: Whereabouts is it?

JF: On the island of Spetsai, which is off the Peloponnesus. It's about six hours by boat from Athens.

RP: Is it a cosmopolitan school, or were they all Greek boys?

JF: They were Greek boys. Then I came back to England and taught at an adult education college, and ended up at a college in Hampstead where I taught English to foreign girls.

RP: Had you begun to write?

JF: I began when I came back from Greece.

RP: Was it really a vocational feeling? Or was it just to get out of teaching, or to make money?

JF: Well, I couldn't not write. Nowadays, I get letters from would-be young writers who say, 'I want to write,' and I always answer that that's not enough. It's not a business of wanting, it's having an obsession – it's not being able not to write.

RP: And it was novels that appealed to you.

JF: In fact, I did try a travel book – about Greece. I sent it to a then well-known agent, Paul Scott, who later became a very good novelist, and he felt that the book wasn't good enough as a travel book, but there was one section which was written in fictional terms, and he said, 'This is good, you're a novelist, try fiction.' Once again, that was a very useful piece of advice.

RP: I believe you showed some humility in submitting your first novel.

JF: I think I knew somebody would publish it, but that it became a best-seller did come as a surprise.

JF: What was that first novel?

JF: *The Collector*.

RP: An international success. Was it taken by the first publisher to whom you sent it?

JF: Yes, it went to Tom Maschler, at Jonathan Cape, who has an excellent eye for novels, and he took it at once.

RP: A first impression is that it's a first-rate psychological thriller about a rather retarded man who kidnaps a girl and keeps her locked up in a cellar, with tragic results. In fact, it demonstrated some philosophical beliefs.

JF: It was reviewed largely as a thriller, but of course I never intended to write one. It was about what I see as a biological problem with the human race, which is the enormous variety of intelligence and culture that our societies and, of course, genetics bring about. It was really the conflicts between stupidity and intelligence - but not meaning that stupidity is to be entirely blamed and that intelligence is necessarily always right. There are faults on both sides.

RP: You published your beliefs in your second book - a book of - what - aphorisms?

JF: That was a little bit naughty because, if you publish a best-seller, you can more or less tell your publisher what you want to publish next. I'm grateful I did it in a way, because I have always been interested in sociology and philosophy, and that book allowed me to get a lot of things off my chest - things not easy to fit into a novel.

RP: You called that book, *The Aristos*. What does that mean?

JF: Well, it has nothing to do with the French expression 'les aristos', meaning the aristocrats: it simply means, in classical Greek, the best for a given situation. The book tried, over-ambitiously, to propose a best course of conduct for the late twentieth-century individual.

RP: Your next book was a very long novel, *The Magus*.

JF: It was really my first novel, but it took me years and years and years to write - I had all sorts of problems with it - so I stopped at one point and wrote *The Collector* and published that, and *The Magus* came next.

RP: It was about an Englishman teaching on a Greek island: that sounds as if, as with most novels, there was a fair amount of autobiography in it.

JF: There really wasn't in this case. It was an attempt to blend fantasy and realism, and it was a didactic book in a way - a teaching book. It was a kind of long sermon told in terms of an adventure story.

RP: A complex book which, eleven years after its publication, you decided to revise. That's an unusual step.

JF: Well, as I said, I was on it for years and years and years, and in the end I more or less said, 'To hell with it. I'd better publish it, or I'm going to spend the rest of my life fiddling about with it,' and eleven years later I felt it still wasn't right, and it would be fun to go back to it and try to re-melt it; to try to get back into the spirit in which I wrote it, and alter it. I think of it as a piece of furniture: the joints were all bad, so I took it to bits and rejointed it and polished it.

RP: This seems a very good thing to do. I'm surprised more writers don't go back to early work and rework it.

JF: Money's the answer. More writers would do it if they could afford to take two years off. Henry James revised a lot, but very few other writers have. You have to have the money and the leisure.

Brian Glover

The first occasion on which I met the actor and ex-wrestler, Brian Glover, was in the bar at the Cottesloe Theatre, where he was playing God in a mediaeval Mystery play. He made a minor mistake, when greeting me, of leaving his glass unattended: he saw it was missing, and he turned with a roar to shout, 'Who's got God's Guinness?' At Barnsley Grammar School, he had been for two terms in the same class as Michael Parkinson, whom he remembers as a very good cricketer and a rotten footballer, whereas Brian was a rotten cricketer and a very good footballer. Later, he worked for the *Barnsley Chronicle*, while Mr Parkinson was down the road at the *Mexboro' Times*. Both gentlemen have done all right since.

RP: When you left Barnsley Grammar School, what did you want to do?
BG: Lads like me were always going to be schoolmasters, or in the Civil Service keeping the Empire going . . . we still had an Empire in those days. My mother wanted me to be a draughtsman.
RP: You moved on to Sheffield University; what did you read there?
BG: Geography.
RP: Why geography?
BG: We had a wonderful geography teacher at school, so everybody wanted to read geography at university.
RP: You'd taken up wrestling on the side; how did that start?
BG: My dad was a wrestler – he used to wrestle as The Red Devil. He ran a gymnasium in Barnsley and I was always there. First of

all, it was amateur boxing, but I was the wrong shape for a boxer, being a short, round guy, so it was a natural progression to wrestling.

RP: What did you call yourself?

BG: Initially, I was Erik Tamberg, the Blond Bomber from Sweden, but then I became Leon Arras from Paris, France.

RP: Why did you change?

BG: One night in Wilmslow I substituted for a Frenchman who hadn't turned up, and I was introduced in the ring as Leon Arras, straight from Paris, France, and I hung on to the name – except that, after a time, I became Leon Arras from Barnsley. Then years later, in a big cycle-drome in Rouen, the dressing-room door opened one night and in loomed this giant wrestler with cauliflower ears and bent elbows, and he said, 'Où est Leon Arras?' and I said, 'Ici,' and he said, 'Moi aussi,' and I said, 'You didn't turn up in Wilmslow.'

RP: You'd been using his name; was he cross?

BG: No, I think he was quite flattered. Anyway, he'd got a bar in Liège by this time.

RP: Was it because of wrestling that you quit university after the first year?

BG: Actually, I did a year and a half there – but I was just earning so much money. I didn't go to the university, and that was it; in those days, if you didn't go you didn't get a grant.

RP: At one time, you were a tea-blender.

BG: I was a tea-blender's assistant; it was a vacation job in Barnsley Co-op. When I saw the advertisement, I thought it would be little china cups, and I'd be sipping tea and saying, 'A little more Darjeeling,' but when I got there I found this guy who sat on one end of a weighing scale, and he said, 'Right, lad, two shovelfuls of that and one shovelful of the other, and when I go up in the air it's right.' I shovelled the stuff all day long, and my grandmother said, 'Since you've been a tea-blender's assistant at the Co-op, Brian, the tea's improved no end.'

RP: Going back to wrestling, tell me how the game works. Are you booked for a single bout or for a tour?

BG: Promoters would book you for their halls for a week, more or less; so if you were working for Scottish promoters you'd do a week up in Scotland – but you'd still have to do Edinburgh to Cardiff overnight occasionally. In wrestling, you're a long time on the road.

RP: How long do you rehearse?

BG: We don't rehearse at all.

RP: But surely all those acrobatics that you see on the box on Saturday afternoons can't be completely spontaneous. People would get hurt.

BG: People do get hurt. I was a good-looking fellow before I joined the wrestling game. Do you want to feel my Boston Crab?

RP: Your what?

BG: My Boston Crab. If there's a shriek, listeners, you'll know that Plomley's just had my Boston Crab – and it hurts.

RP: I'll take your word for it. Now, you'd thrown up university in order to be thrown about in the ring; what did your mother say?

BG: She never approved, of course, but I did become a schoolmaster to try to appease her slightly – a lot of teaching, a lot of wrestling.

RP: But in those days, teachers had to be respectable: weren't you ever rumbled?

BG: Leon Arras was not the schoolmaster who was in front of 3B on a Monday morning. I just masqueraded with these two wonderful careers at the same time. I kept off the telly, of course – but I remember going back to school after a summer holiday, and the headmaster saying he'd been to the wrestling at Clacton, and he'd seen a man wrestle Randolph Turpin, who'd been a celebrated boxer ... and that man had been me! I'd seen the headmaster in the front row, and I'd wrestled the whole bout with my back to him.

RP: You could go and wrestle on the Continent at weekends.

BG: Oh yes, I used to go to Paris a lot. Many, many times I went to Paris. I became a bit of a star there; they used to call me La Grande Vedette Britannique.

RP: Weren't you still Leon Arras?

BG: But I was the British Leon Arras. My gimmick was to get my French wrong. When my opponent got hold of my arm, I'd say,

'Let go of my leg.' *'Oo! ma jambe!'* I'd say, when he was pulling my *bras* off. The French thought that was hilarious.

RP: Could you do more than one bout in a weekend?

BG: Indeed I could. I used to leave school in Barnsley at four o'clock on Friday afternoon, drive to Leeds airport, catch the five o'clock plane to London, and there, if you're in the know, you can do a standby quickly in half an hour, and I could be in Paris by half past seven or eight and wrestle there. After the bout, I'd have a wonderful meal. Saturday morning, I was pushed on to a train to Basle or Geneva for a contest that evening. Then back to Paris on the night train, and wrestle on Sunday afternoon at the Elysée-Montmartre, rush to Orly Airport, fly across to London, then up to Leeds, get into my car, and I'd be in my local pub in Barnsley before closing time. People would say, 'Been wrestling this weekend, Brian?' and I'd say, 'Yes, I've done a couple in Paris and one in Switzerland,' and they used to look at me and think 'Liar!' But it was true.

RP: So you were busy leading this double life: how did acting come into it?

BG: Well, I was always the guy who wrote the school play, and I'd been in a few amateur dramatic societies when I was at college, and wrestlers are on the fringe of show-biz all the time and I'd done a few parts in commercials. Then, at this school I was teaching at there was a fellow called Barry Hines who was a games master, and he wrote a book called *A Kestrel for a Knave*. He arrived one day and said, 'They're making a film of my novel,' and I said, 'Try and get me a part.' Well, *A Kestrel for a Knave* became the film *Kes*, and I had quite a successful little role – as the games master!

RP: What happened next?

BG: I had a telephone call from H. M. Tennent's to come down to London to audition for a play called *Bequest to the Nation* by Terence Rattigan, and they asked me to play Captain Hardy to Ian Holm's Nelson and Zoe Caldwell's Emma Hamilton.

RP: At the Theatre Royal, Haymarket.

BG: Yes, it was a very respectable West End debut.

Helene Hanff

Miss Hanff is small and dark and talkative. I recorded an interview with her in her suite on one of the top floors of a high-rise London hotel, where her hosts had put her on the theory that being high up would remind her of New York, and besides it would be quiet up there. In fact, it wasn't at all quiet, because it was impossible to persuade the people on the telephone switchboard that, just for an hour, Miss Hanff did not require any calls, and because the hotel was staging a fire drill, and because there was some form of demonstration going on outside, and because there were friends knocking at the door asking if she were ready to leave for the airport. The night before, Miss Hanff had seen a play, based on a book of hers called *84 Charing Cross Road*, staged at a London theatre, and she was very happy

HH: I had two elder brothers. My father had run away from home to go on the stage as a song and dance man, and when I decided to go to New York to crash the theatre, he was overheard to remark to my mother, 'I have two sons, and the ham has to come out in her!'

RP: How long had he lasted as a song and dance man?

HH: Two years. He got stranded in Montana, and wired for the fare home, which my grandmother sent him. When he got home he had lice or fleas or something, so she threw him into the bathtub, burned all his clothes and said that was the end of the theatre.

RP: What did he go into afterwards?

HH: He became a Willy Loman, he sold shirts. This was during the Depression, and since box-office men had empty seats and no shirts he used to swap shirts for passes, so every Monday night during the Depression our whole family went to the theatre.

RP: You're from Philadelphia which is, or used to be, a good theatre town.

HH: It was a great try-out town; we got everything before Broadway did.

RP: As a schoolgirl, what was your ambition?

HH: I wanted to be a writer – and I got stagestruck. That was through going to the theatre every Monday night. They didn't have baby-sitters in those days; when they went out, you went out.

RP: Did you go to college?

HH: I had one year of college, and then I had to quit, learn typing, and get a job.

RP: What sort of job?

HH: I worked in a diesel-engine basement. Ten dollars a week and all the grease I could carry home on me.

RP: You made a pretty good job of educating yourself; at any rate so far as English literature's concerned.

HH: I was haunted by the fact that I had no education and that I wanted to be a writer. So I just went down to the library and told the lady I wanted to learn something about English literature and, God bless her! she steered me to a shelf where I found Sir Arthur Quiller-Couch's lectures at Cambridge. So I lugged them home. He had been teaching Harrow and Eton students, who knew English literature, and, every time he referred to something he knew they knew, I had to say, 'Wait here,' and go out and get it. One of the things I went out to get was *Paradise Lost*, and all of Milton's sentences end in Latin, so I had to say, 'Wait here', and I went out and got a teacher to teach me Latin for free, so I could get back to Milton and then get back to Quiller-Couch. So it took me thirteen years to get through first-year Harrow, I think.

RP: How long did you stay in the diesel-engine business?

HH: I was only there a few months, and then I got a nice quiet situation as secretary jointly to a dance band leader and a saxophone teacher. The dance band leader played at sub-debutante

70

parties, and to do these parties he had to know when the best boys' schools had their vacations, because he wanted the sub-debs to have a good stag-line. So my job was to write haughtily condescending letters to the headmasters of Hotchkiss and St Paul's and Andover and Exeter, and I signed them 'Baroness von Hanff'. Now, I was a short, dumpy eighteen-year-old with straight hair and glasses, and I had to lope to the Ritz-Carlton desk, where they had a mailbox, every morning, and announce that I was Baroness von Hanff and ask for my mail. It was so unnerving that it was a pleasure to go back to type my third act through a three-hour saxophone lesson. I was writing plays all the time.

RP: This playwriting thing ... there was a playwriting contest that you entered.

HH: That was the great mistake. I won it.

RP: How many plays did you submit?

HH: To the contest, four.

RP: Specially written ones?

HH: Oh, specially written – one every two weeks. Writing a three-act play takes no time at all, if you haven't got any idea what you're doing. I never had any idea what I was doing.

RP: Who was running this contest?

HH: The Theatre Guild was behind it – or at least the Theatre Guild had undertaken to train the winning playwrights.

RP: The Theatre Guild was very important in the New York theatre at that time.

HH: It was the only theatrical producing company that was not really out to make money; it was out to discover American dramatists and European dramatists. I believe they produced the first O'Neill. I'm not sure how many by Shaw they produced, but they were his favourite producing house.

RP: Was this the Guild's first playwriting competition?

HH: It was the second.

RP: Who had won the first?

HH: Funny you should ask. They had picked two winning dramatists the first year, given them fifteen hundred bucks to live on, and sent them on their way. Now that first year the contest had really been run by a place called the Bureau of New Plays, but now the Theatre Guild had stepped in, and the Theatre Guild said to the Bureau of New Plays, 'You're doing this all wrong. It's a very bad thing to give playwrights money and no training, and just let them fritter it away.' So we second-year winners were trained to death. I mean we went to seminars, we went to rehearsals, we went to openings, we were trained by playwrights whose plays invariably flopped, directors whose plays flopped, and the Theatre Guild, which was teaching us, had seventeen straight flops in the next two years. Not one of the twelve of us they trained ever became a playwright: the two young men who'd been given fifteen hundred bucks and sent wandering off on their own were Arthur Miller and Tennessee Williams. It does not pay to educate playwrights.

RP: So the pattern for a few years was you writing plays –

HH: – which nobody produced –

RP: – and doing various odd jobs. You had a system for seeing every Broadway production at a minimum of expense.

HH: Well, we had no money. My friend Maxine and I would wait in a cheap drug-store up the street from the theatre. When the interval started, and people came out on the sidewalk to smoke, we'd mingle with the smokers, and we'd mingle our way into the theatre. Maxine, who had 20/20 vision, could spot the seats that had no coats on them, and we saw the second and third acts of everything. We found out that nothing ever happened in the first act anyway, because they know you're coming late.

RP: How many plays did you write altogether?

HH: Twenty. One a year.

RP: And did you ever see one on a stage?

HH: None ever got as far as a rehearsal. Lots of options though.

RP: Well, options are handy.

HH: An option means that a producer takes it for three months and has you rewrite it completely and then he drops it ... then another producer picks it up and has you rewrite it completely, and *he* drops it. Most of them give you money. Now and then you run into one who forgets to send the cheque – and, after you've rewritten the play he's found somebody else's – and he sends his best regards to you through his secretary.

RP: Tell me about the various odd jobs.

HH: The best was reading scripts for the New York offices of Hollywood studios.

RP: How did that work?

HH: There were outside readers and inside readers. The inside readers sat in a dungeon and read all day long. They never came out. We never saw them. An outside reader came in at four o'clock, picked up a play or a novel, took it home, read it that night, did a synopsis the next morning before breakfast, and then was free to write all day. You brought it in at four and took home another one.

RP: You had begun writing for television.

HH: Well, no. When I began writing for television, I walked into Paramount and said, 'I quit.' I'd just got my first hour television script commissioned for more money than they'd pay me in three months, and I said, 'That's it!'

RP: That was the Ellery Queen show?

HH: That was 1952 – *The Adventures of Ellery Queen*.

RP: Live television.

HH: Indeed. If an actor had the last line in one scene you couldn't give him the first line in the next, because he needed ten seconds off-camera to walk from the living-room to the bedroom.

RP: How many characters were you allowed?

HH: I was allowed five full parts – Ellery, his father, the murderer, the corpse, and one suspect. It would be very difficult to do a murder mystery on less.

RP: You also wrote some historical programmes.

HH: Oh yes, I graduated to a show called *The Hallmark Hall of Fame*, in which Sarah Churchill was the mistress of ceremonies. Now, there were taboos on the Hall of Fame, one of which was that we were not allowed to write about those who fought in the American War of Independence – because Mr Hall, of the Hallmark Greeting Card Company, would not insult Churchill's daughter by suggesting that the British had lost it.

RP: You could run into trouble with the Ancient Greeks, I seem to remember.

HH: Well, yes. I blame that on an Englishman named Walter

73

Savage Landor – you can't blame the Greeks. Walter Savage Landor wrote a lovely, lovely dialogue between Aesop, in the days when he was a slave, and an innocent young slave-girl named Rhodope, and I took off on Aesop and Rhodope and wrote a lovely uplift script. It was to be broadcast at 2 pm Hollywood time on a Sunday afternoon, and at ten o'clock in the morning I opened the *Times* Book Review section, and there was a full-page review of a book called *A House is Not a Home* by a madam called Polly Adler, and in the middle of the page was the sculptured head of a Greek girl, and under it in italics it said, 'Rhodope, the most famous prostitute in Greece'. This was back in the 1950s. Mr Hall was so pure you couldn't even say 'darn' on his show. Now he lived in Kansas City, Missouri, and Ethel Frank, my story editor whom nothing fazed, said, 'Don't panic, don't panic.' She called Kansas City, and she got the advertising agency representative out of bed, and he drove out to the suburbs and took the book review section out of the *New York Times* on Mr Hall's porch. It saved the show.

RP: Now all the time you were slaving away in your New York apartment, writing for television, you were conducting a correspondence with Marks and Co., Booksellers, of 84 Charing Cross Road, London, WC2.

HH: With Frank Doel, of Marks and Co.

RP: He was the man who used to answer your letters?

HH: He was the man who tracked down all the books I wanted. And I wrote him outraged letters when he sent the wrong one, and I needled him by calling him Frankie when he was still writing, 'Dear Miss Hanff'.

RP: Very generously, in those immediately post-war days you used to send food parcels to the staff.

HH: Well, I was appalled. I mean, you were living on one egg a week and one orange a month, and I couldn't bear it. I had a catalogue which dealt with food parcels, and I used to go crazy because the packages were really food parcels for one family, and I was sending them to a bookshop where every one of six people was going home to a separate family ... one dozen eggs in one parcel, with sweet biscuits? Or two dozen eggs and no sweet biscuits? One dozen eggs meant everybody had two eggs to take home to a family of six. It drove me crazy.

RP: Nevertheless, it was very sweet of you. It was a correspondence that went on for twenty years – you made these friends whom you never met. You hadn't visited Britain?

HH: No.

RP: What did you want to see most in Britain?

HH: London, London.

RP: You had this resolve to see the scene of your literary heritage.

HH: I wanted to see the corner where the Globe Theatre stood – and St Paul's, where Donne preached – and the Tower, where Elizabeth sat on the step in front of Traitor's Gate, and refused to go in because she wasn't a traitor.

RP: Well, you were to see it, but you had to wait. There was a change in your career as a writer. American television left New York and went to a new headquarters in California.

HH: Packed up and moved to Hollywood, where I didn't want to live, and left me without a profession. I mean, I'd never written anything in my life but dialogue – in bad plays and mediocre television. I said to myself: You're going to have to write something else; I mean, people do write prose. So I got down one of my old plays and turned it into a magazine article and sent it off to the *New Yorker*, which promptly sent it back. Then I sent it to *Harper's* and they bought it, and asked, Did I have anything else? So I said, 'Wait there', and I wrote another one and sent it to them, and they sent it back, and I sent it to the *New Yorker* and the *New Yorker* bought it. Of course, I then wrote thirteen pieces nobody bought, but never mind. After twenty years, I had finally got off the theatre.

RP: Who was it suggested that you should write an autobiographical book about the trials and tribulations of being a playwright?

HH: The article that I wrote for *Harper's* was a little spoof, a story of the production of *Oklahoma!* and how it came to be.

RP: Was that a Theatre Guild production while you were working for them?

HH: Right. It was my reminiscences about those days. And the *Harper's* editor wrote me, 'Dear Miss Hanff, do you have a book in mind?' and I wrote back, 'No, I don't, but I'm thrilled ... it's a very high class question.' And she wrote back and said, 'Well, let's have lunch' – and as soon as she saw me, she said, 'I've got a great idea for your book. Why don't you write a funny book about everything that's happened to you since you came to New York? And something told me not to tell her it wasn't funny. So I went home and I wrote a book, and that was *Underfoot in Show-Business*.

RP: A very funny book. Then you had a quite brilliant idea of making a book out of your correspondence with Marks and Co., the booksellers. Do you ordinarily keep all your letters?

HH: I don't keep anything, no. I live in a one-room flat. God knows, my old plays went down the incinerator twenty years ago. I kept Frank's letters because they were a record of the books I'd bought which my accountant wanted when he did my income tax. He said, 'You're building a professional writer's library, and we make periodic deductions for depreciation,' and so forth. So I kept them by accident. When I got the letter telling me Frank was dead, I had to write something about it. And I wasn't sure I still had the letters; I went hunting. When I finally found them, I started to cry, I was so relieved.

RP: And those letters became *84 Charing Cross Road*, a very short book, and somehow a very unlikely book to be an international success.

HH: It couldn't seem unlikelier to me, that's for sure.

RP: And it brought you, at long last, to London.

HH: It did indeed. It did indeed.

RP: You've seen it all – and, sadly, you visited the empty premises of Marks & Co., who are now out of business.

HH: But it was wonderful just to be there. It was empty and dusty and the shelves were on the floor, but at least I was in London. I remember thinking, walking down the staircase, 'How about this, Frankie? I finally made it.'

RP: Your first visit to London, and that was another book for you to write – *The Duchess of Bloomsbury Street*.

HH: Yes, I kept a diary, because I thought I wouldn't remember it all, and when I got back to New York I turned it into a book, and

André Deutsch brought it out in London, and it got me back here again.

RP: You're quite a regular visitor now.

HH: Oh, now I run back and forth like it's nothing.

RP: And, at long last, you have your name on the billboard outside a theatre, and it's a London theatre.

HH: Unbelievable. Just unbelievable. It's all due to James Roose Evans, who wrote me that he wanted to dramatize *84 Charing Cross Road* for a summer theatre in Salisbury, where it got marvellous reviews, and the next thing I knew he said it was opening in London, and I came over.

RP: And it's a great success, and when you're back in New York, it'll still be going on every night.

HH: Unbelievable. It's Flanagan's Law.

RP: What's Flanagan's Law?

HH: It was explained to me by a stage manager named Bill Flanagan. Flanagan's law of the theatre is: 'No matter what happens to you, it's unexpected.'

Russell Harty

We were required to present a live programme at Olympia, the London exhibition centre, during the run of the Ideal Home Exhibition, and obviously we had to pick a castaway who was, in professional parlance, 'rock-solid', meaning an artiste who was unlikely to be upset by alien conditions. We did very well in picking Mr Harty, because it needed unusual concentration to broadcast a seemingly relaxed interview while sitting on a small open stage surrounded on three sides by a staring populace, most of whom were eating fish fingers. It was hot, crowded, noisy and smelly, but Mr Harty faced up to the ordeal like the true-blue broadcaster he is. Immediately opposite the BBC's stand was a stand tenanted by the Royal Navy, and we were both very grateful to be invited into their wardroom afterwards to drink a very large gin-and-tonic indeed.

RP: What did you do when you graduated from Oxford?
RH: All my friends applied for jobs at the BBC and went into broadcasting so, sheep-like, I applied for a job at a new television firm called Granada. They said, 'You can become an Assistant Floor Manager for £420 a year, but for three months only.' Now, all my life I'd been taught that I should get a sound and sensible job with a pension – I mean, at the age of twenty-three I used to lie awake at night worrying about my pension – so I turned down Granada Television and went to become a schoolmaster, than which there is nothing safer.
RP: Where?
RH: For a short period of time I taught at a school in Blackburn

78

which was very, very rough indeed. We had to use a cane to keep
any kind of silence, and a lot of boys, as an end-of-term *jeu d'esprit*,
used to poison each other with bits of rat poison that lay around
the school hall to get rid of the odd rodent. It was quite a jolly
experience, but it was a tough school.

RP: You felt you should move on to something quieter?

RH: I felt I had been wafted to a kind of nirvana when I went to
work at the school improbably called Giggleswick, which is in
North Yorkshire. Boys backed away when I appeared in my
shining bombazine gown, and people said good morning and
stood back against the wall, and bowed.

RP: You taught English and drama there. Was there a drama
tradition in the school, or did you start it?

RH: I started it. It was a very hearty school, and drama was
considered to be a very sissy occupation, so I had a fairly tough
fight to get it onto the syllabus.

RP: What did you do during the holidays?

RH: I came to London nearly every holiday. I spent a lot of time
pretending I was a member of the BBC, sitting in the canteen with
all the mates I had been at Oxford with, who had moved on to
greater things. I pretended I was part of the establishment and
nodded at Stratford Johns a lot.

RP: Did he nod back?

RH: No.

RP: What a shame. You taught for a while in the United States.

RH: That was a very odd thing. Some friends of mine from
America came to watch me teaching at Giggleswick, and one of
them said, 'You'd be rather good in America, because you're
slightly dotty in the classroom. Why don't you go and teach in
America for a while? You must have a year off and go there.' It
was a very wild experience for me because I was teaching
twenty- and twenty-one-year-old people in a sharp, bright Jewish
community in Manhattan, and if I said something like, 'Virginia
Woolf walked into the water with stones in her pockets', they
would say, 'Excuse me, Professor Harty, do you know this was an
actual fact? Were you on the scene? Are you telling the truth?'

RP: You had this obsession with the BBC; in fact, you did walk the
hallowed corridors of Broadcasting House as a Radio 3 producer.

RH: Yes, but a very frightened producer. We used to have the most awful meetings every Wednesday morning, where we were each required to comment on the other producers' programmes. Everybody criticized and attacked the work other people had done. I remember one morning the Chairman – who was Howard Newby – said to me, 'What did you think about Devlin?' Something called the Devlin Report had just come out, and we were all supposed to be very up-to-date and to know about these things. 'Do you have any views on Devlin?' he asked – and I said the only line I could think of at the moment, which was, 'It's his mother I feel sorry for.' People didn't know whether to laugh or resign, but it put my stock up by half an inch.

RP: Well done. What was the very first broadcast you did yourself, uttering at the microphone?

RH: Reading letters from pained husbands in *Woman's Hour*.

RP: *Woman's Hour*?

RH: When Marjorie Anderson wanted a letter from a pained husband read out, they sent down to the bowels of Broadcasting House for me, and I read out this letter from 'Pained' of Basingstoke.

RP: You didn't stay in radio very long.

RH: I was wooed out of radio by Humphrey Burton, who was starting a new arts programme for London Weekend Television.

RP: Was that *Aquarius*?

RH: Yes.

RP: A general arts programme in which you began doing interviews.

RH: Yes, but I did them from behind the camera; no viewer could see me, they would just hear a piping voice.

RP: Was that modesty, or were you doing as you were told?

RH: I was doing as I was told – and it was modesty too.

RP: In due course you were allowed into vision, and you achieved considerable success, and you were offered your own interview show. In fact, you were put into the field in opposition to the BBC's Mr Parkinson.

RH: Yes.

RP: Same sort of show, but you ask more piquant questions.

RH: Well, I read that I ask more piquant questions, but I'm never aware of it.

RP: It's a dangerous trade ... there was a Miss Jones, who clouted you about the head.

RH: It was more dangerous than even Miss Jones knew about, because if we'd gone on for another four minutes I would have clouted her about the head too.

RP: And there was a Mr Stardust, who refused to shake hands with you. Have you found out why?

RH: Afterwards, he said to me privately, 'It was nothing to do with you personally, it was to do with the fact that I wear these knuckle-dusters, and it would have hurt you had there been an electrical discharge in the studio.'

RP: And Miss Hayworth wouldn't talk to you.

RH: Well, she would talk to me. She said Yes and No for fifty-five minutes. I don't mean non-stop.

RP: Just when required.

RH: When required. She said Yes and No and that was all ... which left me with a lot of egg on my face.

RP: Earlier than that you had an ordeal with a group called The Who. Did you realize at the beginning that you were heading for trouble?

RH: Not at all. I thought they were a group of well-behaved lads who would answer every boring question that I gave them, and I had a clipboard and a list of questions, and I started to go through them. About half-way through, boredom was written all over their faces, and I heard behind me the sound of shirts being ripped and torn – expensive silk shirts, too. I turned round, and saw that Pete Townsend was ripping the late Keith Moon's shirt, and Roger Daltry was ripping somebody else's shirt, while I was persisting in those lunatic questions, like, 'Which one of you writes the music and which one of you writes the words?' ... When they'd finished ripping their shirts, they all stopped, and there was a dreadful silence in the studio, and they all looked at me, and one of them said, 'There's one person here whose clothes are still intact', and of course I foolishly looked over my shoulder to see who the person was, and then they got me. They threw me on the floor, took a lot of my clothes off, threw my shoes away – and, half naked, I was still holding on to my clipboard and saying, 'What do you think has been your most successful concert?'

Earl Hines

There's no way to describe Earl Hines except by using the cliché 'a legendary figure in the world of jazz'. I had previously interviewed him twenty-three years before, and he did not seem to have put on a single pound, but then he has always looked after himself and taken plenty of exercise. He made his first disc as long ago as 1922 or 1923, in Richmond, Indiana, when he was touring with Lois Deppe's band. He remembers that they went into a kind of steam room, with towels hanging on the walls to deaden the resonance, and it was so hot that everyone took his shirt off. Then they had to wait fifteen or twenty minutes until the wax was soft enough for them to record.

RP: You were born in Pittsburg, is that right?
EH: Yes. Pittsburg, Pennsylvania.
RP: Was there a lot of music in your home?
EH: I was surrounded by it: my father played cornet and had a brass band, and my mother played organ, and my uncle played all the brass instruments, and my auntie was in light opera.
RP: Did your mother give you your first piano lessons?
EH: Yes, she did.
RP: You played the organ in church yourself for a while.
EH: That's right – for three dollars a month.
RP: And you took up the cornet.
EH: I fooled around with all of Dad's instruments. The reason I selected the cornet was because he did a very good job on it, and it didn't seem a heavy instrument to carry around, and I thought it was the kind of instrument I could stand out front with, see. I

liked the tone of the cornet too, but when I tried to play it, it used to hurt me behind my ears, so I put it down and I learned the piano.

RP: How old were you when you had your first job?

EH: Sixteen.

RP: In a band?

EH: Yes. We were playing in halls where there were upright pianos and no amplification, and they'd give me a solo, and I was still trying to play a little fingering, like I used to do on my classical tunes, and I couldn't be heard. So I thought of the trumpet style – I thought of what my father was playing to lead the band with – so I used trumpet style and octaves on piano and I cut through the band. That's why all the pianists began to use the same thing.

RP: From Pittsburg, you went to Chicago.

EH: Well, the gentleman who owned the club in Pittsburg had decided to open a club in Chicago, but he had a lot of trouble with the musicians' union there, so he said, 'I'll go back and get my band from Pittsburg.'

RP: Was it at about that time in Chicago that you met Louis Armstrong and became great friends with him?

EH: Yes, it was during that time.

RP: There's a story that you and he used to fill in bad patches by playing in a cinema for silent movies. Is that true?

EH: Yes. We were working in the Sunset Café at night, and we'd leave there around four in the morning, and we'd have to open in the theatre about eleven – just five hours later. It was terrible.

RP: I would love to have heard you two playing 'Hearts and Flowers'.

EH: To tell you the truth, it was so much fun. We were trying to watch the director and trying to look at the movies too. When they got a good picture in there we were running all over the place, and the director said he had to let both of us go.

RP: You were still in your early twenties – I think twenty-three – when you formed your own band in Chicago.

EH: At the Grand Terrace Café.

RP: That was a big club, wasn't it, with a big floor show, radio broadcasts and all the rest of it.

EH: That's right.

RP: Chicago in the twenties – a tough era. I believe Al Capone owned a piece of the Grand Terrace.

EH: Al Capone came in after we were open about two years. He said, 'We're going to take twenty-five per cent.'

RP: Just like that?

EH: Just like that. The gentleman that owned the club was a guy who couldn't talk very good English, and he says, 'What do you mean, take twenty-five per cent?' So Capone says, 'We're going to take twenty-five per cent and we're going to give you protection,' and the owner says, 'I don't need no protection. For two years, I've been here. For one year, I had to suffer, but I just now begin to realize that I'm making a living for my family.' Capone says, 'You've got two children, and you like them, don't you?' and the owner says, 'You wouldn't do that,' and Capone says, 'No, I wouldn't, but unless we get twenty-five per cent ...' So every night there would be two men come in the back door, and there'd be one on the front door and one at the cash register, and they took just twenty-five per cent. One day, Capone's lieutenant – his name was Fosco – called a meeting. He said, 'I want to meet everybody that's in the organization – the show people, the band musicians, the waiters.' And at the meeting, he said, 'I want all of you to be like the three monkeys; you hear nothing, you see nothing, and you say nothing.' And that's what we did, and that's why we got along.

RP: Did you ever see a gun in use?

EH: Everybody in the place – waiters and everybody – carried a gun ... and there was never a gun fired.

RP: Was there any trouble with Capone when you wanted to leave the club?

EH: No. Capone was a very congenial fellow.

RP: Was he now?

EH: People say the worst things about him, and I have to say the good things. He used to say, 'Everything that happens in Chicago, they blame it on me – but I got a big shoulder, I can carry it.' I remember the time when Chicago had so much snow that you had to dig a path to get to where you were going, and the real-estate men were putting people out of their homes, and throwing their furniture out in the snow – and Capone used to bring a truck round and pick up the furniture and get them a place to live until they could find a spot. And he had a restaurant open there twenty-four hours a day for poor people. They didn't have to pay nothing – but just go in there and eat. These are some of the things he did that I thought were very nice, and naturally I didn't dwell on the things people said he did, because we were working all the time, and we never did see any of these things happen. On St Valentine's Day, I was about a block away . . .

RP: St Valentine's Day – the massacre in the garage.

EH: Al Capone said, 'They blamed me for that, but I was nowhere around.'

Freddie Jones

When we were recording, it was a nice change to see Freddie with his own face, because he wears so many disguises in the theatre or in films or on television that few people know what this first-rate character actor really looks like.

He is astonishingly thorough in his work, and when he was playing Claudius in the television series, *The Caesars* – a role for which he won an international award at Monte Carlo – he walked for three months with a stone in a shoe, to get into the habit of walking with the same kind of limp that Claudius had.

FJ: My first love of music came from my mother, who was a pianist with the old silent movies, and later in pubs. Indeed she still plays occasionally in a pub now that she's eighty, which I think is marvellous. She plays the piano like most people play rugger, as though she's got a grudge against it; but, nevertheless, over the decades she's given a lot of people a lot of pleasure. She used to play the Rachmaninov Prelude in C sharp minor, the second Hungarian Rhapsody and Rhapsody in Blue. She pointed out their virtues by breaking them down into little pieces and explaining them, just as Dobson and Young did so brilliantly and successfully during the war. She inculcated a great love of music in me, so I'm indebted to her for that – and for many other things, of course.

RP: You were born and brought up in the Potteries, weren't you?

FJ: Yes, I was born in the late twenties, and lived through the Depression.

RP: Did you have a family connection with the pottery business?

FJ: Yes, my father was dealing with very heavy pottery all his life. It broke his body in the end. He had very large heavy weights of clay to deal with.

RP: Did you go to work in the Potteries yourself?

FJ: I worked with the British Ceramic Research Institute.

RP: Was that your first job?

FJ: Well, I did a job here, a job there. I didn't really know what I wanted to do. From my background it wasn't possible to become a professional poet or traveller or writer or actor, which I fundamentally felt is what I wanted to be.

RP: You've always written verse, haven't you?

FJ: Yes – very bad.

RP: What side of the pottery business were you concerned with?

FJ: Things like urinals and lavatories, doing research on the glazes and so on.

RP: You had this nagging feeling for the arts; what pushed you in the right direction?

FJ: It was a girl I met who suggested that we should do a drama course at a Workers' Adult Education Centre. They'd built a new Centre near Tamworth, which is where we had moved to from the Potteries, so we went along. Then one evening the lecturer, who was a producer and lecturer at the Birmingham Repertory School, one of the best schools in the country, asked if I would stay behind so that she could have a word. She said to me, to my total astonishment, 'Don't think me impertinent, but why is a man of your huge talent working in science?' I said, 'Please would you say that again slowly, so that I can carry each word in my head.' Thereafter, by a series of negative actions, I was asked to resign my job. This girl started sending for prospectuses of drama schools, and I applied for a scholarship and got one.

RP: Which school was it?

FJ: The Rose Bruford College at Sidcup in Kent.

RP: Did you arrange with the pottery firm that they'd take you back if anything blew up, or did you cast right adrift?

FJ: I understand that the shares went up four points when I left.

RP: How long did you stay at the college?

FJ: Three years. Each year we did one play in London, as a showpiece, and at the end they asked me to play *Peer Gynt*, three hours and twenty minutes of blank verse. I had lots of enquiries from all sorts of people, and I was absolutely thrilled. I made a tactical error, I think, in accepting the first concrete offer, which was a six-month contract with the Arts Council to tour Great Britain with Shakespeare's *Romeo and Juliet* and Ustinov's *Romanoff and Juliet*. By the time we got back, I was completely forgotten and as dead as last year's kippered herring.

RP: In those days, the rep companies were still going; did you work in rep?

FJ: I did indeed. Among them, I worked for Harry Hanson, who at one time had no fewer than forty-eight companies in various parts of the country.

RP: Harry Hanson and his Court Players. That was weekly rep, of course. Where did you play for him?

FJ: Stockton-on-Tees and Bridlington.

RP: In those early days, where did you enjoy working most?

FJ: I think at the Theatre Royal, Lincoln, which is a beautiful little theatre. And for a while I was at the Bristol Old Vic.

RP: And, of course, there must have been times when there was no work about at all.

FJ: Of course. The next record that I'm going to choose was part of a very hard time in my life, but a very happy time. I lived in a house in Notting Hill, off the Portobello Road, and it was full of writers and actors. In the basement was Tom Stoppard, typing his nights away on nothing but scripts for *Mrs Dale's Diary* and promptly getting them rejected. On the ground floor was a man named Derek Marlow, and he spent all his time leaning back on a chair looking out on this little street, all day and every day until it grew dark, all day and ever day. He said he was going to write, but I never saw him even write his name. One sterile morning, I went downstairs and I knocked on his door, and he said, 'Come in,' and we chatted. He said, 'I have formed a great love for Vaughan Williams. Do you know Vaughan Williams?' I said, 'I love his work very much indeed.' He said, 'Well, when I last had a bit of money, I bought two or three of his records: do you know his Overture to The Wasps?', and I said, 'Not only do I know it, if you'd care to put it on, I shall conduct it for you.'

Now, I don't know a minim from a minute, but he put it on and I conducted. It was an actor's impersonation of a conductor, but if you know where the various sections of the orchestra come in and out, it can be very effective. He sat open-mouthed, and applauded at the end. Now, we were so poor that a packet of cigarettes was an issue; you would need to go round the house and see if somebody had threepence or twopence to make up the amount of money required. None of us took the dole, or anything like that; I don't know why, but we never did. Anyway, it was in this climate that the following beautiful thing happened. Derek said to me, a few days later, 'My girl-friend's coming round, and I can manage a pot of tea because a couple of quid has come in from a repeat of a walk-on I did on television. Will you come and conduct The Wasps Overture for my girl-friend?' I said 'Certainly I will; I'm open for engagements.'

So I went down and we had a cup of tea and I met his girl-friend, who was very sweet. Suddenly I felt a bit inhibited. Then Derek said, 'Before you conduct, I've got a little present for you,' and I thought, he can't have a present for me, because nobody's got any money. But he handed me a brown paper bag. I opened it, and he'd bought me a baton. I have to confess I was moved to tears. It's a bit like an O. Henry story, isn't it? The moment was so important that nothing else mattered, and I conducted magnificently.

There's a pay-off to the story. I hadn't seen Derek or heard from him for years and years, and then one day I met a mutual friend and we began asking each other about people from the old days, and he said, 'You've heard about Derek Marlow, haven't you?' and I said, 'No, what's happened to him?' and he said, 'Well, I should think at the moment he's swimming in Moët and Chandon in Hollywood.' Apparently he'd come up with a novel called *A Dandy in Aspic*, and sold the film rights for a fortune. Subsequently I saw in *Radio Times*, on one of the colour pages, pictures of a magnificent Tudor mansion in the Vale of Evesham, with rolling lawns, and with Derek and his beautiful wife and his children and his dogs, and I later visited him there. That was beautiful, wasn't it?

RP: So all that staring into the street had produced results.

FJ: Indeed.

RP: It's time that you chose another disc, and I suspect that you're going to conduct for us The Wasps.

FJ: Yes. I'll just move my chair. Do you mind moving back a bit?

Tristan Jones

If I had to choose a desert island companion of my own sex, I think it would be Tristan Jones. He is surely the most resourceful of all my castaways, and I am sure that, within a few months, we would be homeward bound in a seaworthy craft, with ample supplies of everything we needed. My only worry would be that, in mid-voyage, Mr Jones might decide that sailing home was too routine a proposition and that, while we were at it, we might as well circumnavigate the globe, or set course for Murmansk, on the off-chance that a lady of his acquaintance was still entertaining friendly thoughts about him.

RP: After your back was hurt, when the hydrographic ship was blown up, you had trouble getting a job, didn't you?

TJ: I tried to join the Merchant Navy as soon as I was walking again, but they wouldn't accept me because I couldn't be insured. Then I met someone that was involved with the Dutch yacht industry, and he needed crews to deliver yachts to other countries, mainly in South America – so I made several transatlantic voyages down to Brazil, down to Rio. There was a sort of cachet about a yacht that had been sailed from Europe, you see: the price went up – and anyway it was cheaper than putting it on a cargo boat.

RP: I know you did a few years of that, but you still hadn't got your own boat. May we mention how you set about getting the money to buy one?

TJ: Certainly. I don't consider there's any criminal activity in taking some Scottish Sunshine across the Channel. Anyway, they accused me of 500,000 bottles and that was wrong – it was 472,000 exactly.

RP: Bottles that found their way from this country over to France?

TJ: Right. They sent us eau-de-Cologne and frogs' legs and the metric system, so why not send them something back?

RP: It seems fair.

TJ: And I was probably helping some poor Hebridean island, I hope.

RP: So one way or another you had the money to buy your own boat. What sort of craft was it, and what did you want to do in it?

TJ: I couldn't afford a lot of money, so the best hull I could find was a Royal National Lifeboat Institution ex-beach-launched lifeboat, built in 1908 at the Thames Ironworks, here in London. I was looking for a hull that would be tough enough to be set in the ice – that is, to be frozen into the ice of the Arctic. The ice cap is not just a flat plain, as a lot of people imagine it is; it's a jumbled-up mass of movement and noise. Very frightening at times. I wanted to set the boat in and try to get a little bit further north than Nansen got in the *Fram* in 1893.

RP: To break the record? Further north than anyone had ever sailed before?

TJ: Well, I thought, if eighteen Norwegians could do it, one Welshman could do it, you see. I've always been fascinated by the Polar regions.

RP: How far north did Nansen get?

TJ: The ship got within ninety miles of the Pole. Nansen wasn't on board at the time. I failed miserably. I did it all wrong.

RP: Which route did you take?

TJ: First, I went up the east coast of Greenland. I spent the winter in Scoresby Sound, which was near an Eskimo village.

RP: Scoresby – that was named after the Yorkshire scientist, wasn't it?

TJ: That's right. All along that coast is a long trail of British names.

RP: Where was it that the polar bear came aboard?

TJ: That was on the ice-floes to the east of Greenland. I'd got stuck up a lee about eighty miles long, and I finished by hauling the boat up on to the ice by hand. A tremendous job. It was while I was on that floe, floating south, hoping to escape when the ice broke up, that the bear appeared. He was about twelve feet tall. A tremendous thing. They're very, very dangerous animals out on the floe. They're the kings of everything. Whether they look upon us as competitors for food or as food itself I don't know, but they will attack anything that moves.

RP: Did he attack you?

TJ: No, he attacked the boat. One swipe of his claw and those one-inch-thick guard-rails were just bending over like putty. I was in a panic at first. I dived down and got my Verey pistol – my signal pistol – and fired it at the bear, who was roaring away. He turned round towards me and the flare went straight in his mouth. He jumped away and dived into the sea, over the edge of the floe. I don't know whether he died. I think he must have done, because phosphorus doesn't go out under water, you see. I hate to hurt any kind of animal, but it was a matter of life and death.

RP: You had a dog with you on that trip, didn't you?

TJ: Yes, a labrador. For several reasons. One, obviously, is that he's a spare food supply in case everything else runs out. A second thing is that a labrador is the best animal you can have on board a boat in a fog. He's better than a radar set. If he hears a noise, he'll point straight at it. If you're off a coast in a fog and you've got a labrador on board and he's trained to point at the noise, you'll know exactly where the shore-line is. They've a very acute sense of direction and hearing.

RP: You were frozen in for just over a year: you must have been very glad of the company of that dog.

TJ: Oh, I was, yes. Nelson and I were great friends, and it's a comfort just to have something living around you in those circumstances.

RP: Did you have a radio?

TJ: I had a radio. It was an old-fashioned type which broke down. You know the old-fashioned types with the glass accumulators? It was one of those, and once it had gone I was absolutely alone. I didn't think I'd get out. I thought I was dead. Then I thought, well, I'll play it out and see. Maybe the ice will break; maybe I can get out of this corner.

RP: The floe that you were frozen into was drifting, of course?

TJ: It was drifting and moving; that's how I got trapped, you see. I took shelter behind an ice-berg and the whole thing moved around in a clockwise direction and trapped me, and I couldn't get out.

RP: Wasn't there a nasty moment when the ice-berg began to capsize?

TJ: Well, you see the north-east wind was blowing rain and sleet and snow on top of the berg, and it was getting top-heavy. They do that continually. It's very dangerous. It's only the flat Antarctic bergs that don't tip over.

RP: How long did that trip take altogether?

TJ: Two and a half years. And by the time I sighted England again it was three and a half. Originally, I set off for Canada, but I got dismasted off Cape Farewell and wound up in Norway. Then I made my way through to the Baltic to find a girl-friend, but by that time she was well and truly married.

RP: Bad luck.

TJ: Then I got arrested by the Russians as a spy, and I finished up by being sunk by Dutch cheese in Holland.

RP: Tell me about that.

TJ: Well, I'd got as far as Holland, and I was trading around and I'd filled the boat, and I met this warehouse watchman who asked me if I liked cheese. So I said, 'Yes, I like anything I can eat.' I thought he would bring three or four cheeses on board for me. But no! I heard this rumbling noise, and there he is ... he's a one-legged guy and he's pushing a railway truck, and it's full of Dutch cheese. So I loaded two hundred Edam cheeses on board the boat, not realizing that the canal was so shallow and that the cheese weighed so much. In fact, the two tons of cheese just sank the boat on to the bottom of the canal. Now, a sailor has to keep his priorities right, and the police were looking for the cheese and I was stuck there and couldn't move.

RP: How did you get out of that?

TJ: I decided that instead of ditching the cheese I'd ditch the engine, because it hadn't worked for eight months anyway. Then the boat just floated enough for me to pull her off the mud and sail off out of Holland.

RP: And you lived on cheese for quite a while?

TJ: I did – but I exchanged half of it for a brand-new little diesel engine.

Ronald Lockley

Mr Lockley is one of the few who have lived on a lonely island from choice. I doubt if he is quite as resourceful as Tristan Jones, but I am sure he could settle down comfortably while waiting for rescue, and that he would find ways of logging his observations on wild life.

RP: What was your ambition, Ronald? When you left school, how did you think you were going to earn your living?
RL: Well, I failed matriculation. I wanted to get out on the land, and I started thinking I'd grow herbs. That was impracticable, so I became a poultry farmer – but all the time I was looking out for my ideal island. And at last I found one.
RP: Why an island? How do you think this desire to be solitary came about? Was it a kind of retreat from society?
RL: Yes, I always was and always have been an escapist; and after reading Thoreau's *Walden* I thought, well, there's a man who expresses everything I really want in life; I want to get away, live simply, find my own food. And I was fortunate, when I was about twenty-three, to find the little island of Skokholm, off the coast of Wales.
RP: Where is it exactly?
RL: Right off the extremity of the coast of South Wales, right in the Irish Sea, or St George's Channel.
RP: How far off the coast?
RL: Four or five miles, through a very difficult tide race.
RP: Skokholm – where did the name come from?
RL: It's Viking. The Vikings ravished the whole of the coast of Wales. It means the Woody Island, I think.

RP: How big is it?

RL: About two hundred and forty acres. It's one mile long and half a mile at its widest point.

RP: Any buildings on it?

RL: There was a tumbledown farm without a roof, and there's a lighthouse, which is manned by three keepers, at the far end.

RP: Had previous tenants made a go of it?

RL: A long time ago, in the last century; but in the present century I don't think people want to live in such isolation. There was no harbour there, so the little farmhouse was used in the summer by fishermen, and eventually, of course, the wind and the weather took the roof off. I saw there was a potential living there. I'd catch lobsters, crabs, crayfish. I'd keep sheep. There were a lot of rabbits there. But primarily I wanted to go there because of my love of birds. There were something like three hundred thousand birds nesting there, and two species especially hadn't been studied – the sheerwater and the storm petrel. They were there in hundreds, all around the house. In fact they'd taken possession of it.

RP: You formed there the first bird observatory in Great Britain.

RL: I began in 1928 and 1929 by studying the shearwaters, these extraordinary birds which come into burrows at night. Nothing was known about them. Next I studied puffins and storm petrels. What was also interesting was the mass of migrant birds, passing up and down the coast in the autumn and spring. I was trying to ring all these birds, but it was really getting too much of a task, then because I was writing articles for *The Countryman* and some scientific papers, people began to ask if they could come and help. So in 1933 I organized the first British bird observatory, and I'm glad to say it's gone on ever since.

RP: You did a lot of tests and experiments about migration.

RL: Well, we'd been ringing these shearwaters, and found they'd been going right down across the Equator to the coast of the Argentine, and we also found other marked birds making long migrations. So I did some homing experiments by taking shear-waters from their breeding holes, where they had an egg or a chick to come back to – I'd take one only, leaving the partner – and send them to various far-off places, the Faroe Islands, Venice,

Boston, where they were released, and a certain proportion came back at such a speed that it was obvious they knew their way. But how did they know their way? We don't know. We think that they're guided somehow by the heavenly bodies, the stars by night and the sun by day.

RP: One fortunate event in your early days in the island was the shipwreck of a schooner.

RL: Yes, that was marvellous. It happened only three months after I had arrived there. I had very little money, because I had spent a lot on a boat, and I was wondering how I could ever afford to repair the farmhouse. Then, suddenly, a schooner in full sail ran into the island, with nobody on board, and settled down at high tide.

RP: Your personal *Marie Celeste*.

RL: Yes. Her name was *Alice Williams* – and her figure-head is still used as a mark for people going to the island. If you're coming in the boat – and you can stay at the observatory, if you like – there's the figure-head marking the landing steps.

RP: And you became the owner. How much did you pay for her?

RL: That first year I had a very good fisherman helping me, because I didn't know anything about boats, and – a good old wrecker he was! – he said, 'She's ours, but you've got to go ashore and ring up the underwriter. And you must say that the ship is a total wreck, and offer to buy it. But don't give 'em anything.' Well, I rang up the underwriter, who by extraordinary coincidence happened to be an old sweetheart of my mother's, and I think he gave in a little bit. He said, 'I want several hundred pounds for the ship.' I said, 'Well, you'll have to come and get her, because she's settled down and broken her back.' And after a lot of haggling, he said, 'All right, all right, what's your offer?' I said, 'One pound.' He said, 'You can have her for five pounds, but I'm going to collect the anchors.' Of course, he never did.

RP: How big was the schooner? What was her length?

RL: She was about seventy feet long.

RP: You had all that gorgeous wood and metal ... and canvas.

RL: Yes. She was lying against the cliffs and we just stripped her. We had forty or fifty tons of coal, as well, which lasted us many years.

RP: I suppose the war brought your island experiment to an end.

RL: Yes, when the war broke out, the Army commandeered it and were going to fortify it, because it covered the entrance to Milford Haven. Luckily they never did.

RP: I know you spent part of the war in Naval Intelligence. Can you tell us anything about what you were doing?

RL: Well, I went to the Naval recruiting station at Milford Haven and out walked a friend of mine, a birdwatcher named Commander Wilson, who was head of Naval Intelligence there. He said, 'What are you doing here?' and I said, 'I thought I'd try to do something useful in the Navy.' He said, 'You're the very man I want. I want you to go round the coasts of Wales and Ireland, disguised as a fisherman, and report on places where German submarines are coming in. We know they're doing it. They're putting in at night and getting information, and landing people, especially in south-west Ireland.' So I had three summers going round the coasts, disguised as a fisherman, making a list of places where the Germans might come in. I want to tell you about one rather fascinating occurrence. On the south-west coast of Ireland we came across a herd of seals. Seals were very common during the war because the fishermen weren't killing them. I had a partner with me; his name was Gerald and he was an Irish-speaking Irishman in the British Navy. I had him with me because we had to be in touch with the Irish coastguards, so somebody had to speak Irish. We were in a little wild bay and we saw a young girl swimming, as we thought, among the seals. Well, now I think back on it, she must have been nearer the shore really, and she'd swum out towards the seals. When she saw us she swam back ashore, and ran up into a narrow cleft in the cliffs. That night, after we anchored our boat there, we walked up a lane, and came across a thatched cottage with an old couple in it who could only speak Irish. Gerald found out from them that the girl was their granddaughter. She had lost her parents when she was very young, and couldn't remember them, she was far from any school, and she was out of control. 'She's quite wild; we can't do anything with her,' they said. I went away, thinking how fascinating it was, this girl swimming with the seals. Well, after the war I went back there, the Nature Conservancy had invited me to find out how many seals were breeding round the coast of Ireland, because the fishermen complained that they were taking all the salmon. The first thing I did was go to that spot, to find out what had happened to the girl, but the cottage was in ruins and she had disappeared. Later I did something I don't normally do: I wrote a fictional story about a girl who thought she was a seal, and I was the hero, of course; I was the Naval officer who came back and tried to take her away from the sea after the war. I called it *Seal Woman*. My publishers think I shouldn't write fiction, but I like doing it as a relief from non-fiction.

RP: Especially when you get an idea like the girl who swims with the seals. I wonder what happened to her. You never found out?

RL: No, but everybody who has read the book has asked me to find out.

Paul McCartney

In 1963, I interviewed the enterprising young entrepreneur, Brian Epstein, who had found a sweat-stained, leather-clad group bashing away in a Liverpool basement and turned them into the biggest show-business sensation of the century. I asked him if he would arrange for the Beatles to appear on *Desert Island Discs*, each member choosing two records. He shook his head and said that it would be virtually impossible to get them to take the procedure seriously, and that I would have great difficulty in controlling them. I offered to take a chance, but he could not be persuaded.

Nineteen years later, to celebrate the fortieth birthday of the series, Paul McCartney made an appearance on his own. He was quiet, relaxed, and looked only about half his age, which was thirty-nine. One of the richest men in the country, he divides his time between his music and his business interests. He did not choose a Beatles recording, but included a song by John Lennon who, just a few months before, had been shot down in a New York street. It was a song called 'Beautiful Boy', which Lennon had dedicated to his infant son, Sean.

RP: Paul, I don't think it's news to many people that you come from Liverpool, from a Liverpool Irish family. Your mother was a nurse, I believe.
PMCC: Yes, she was.
RP: And you had the extreme misfortune to lose her when you were in your early teens. Your father was a salesman.
PMCC: Yes – a cotton salesman.
RP: And, more important than that, a musician.

PMCC: Yes, he used to bang about; he had a little band of his own called Jim Mac's Band.

RP: Was he trained, or did he play by ear?

PMCC: He played by ear – his left one.

RP: As a youngster, were you interested?

PMCC: Yes, I was very interested. I used to say, 'Well, why don't you teach me?' But he was one of those fathers who said, 'If you want to learn, you should learn properly.'

RP: Could you pick out a tune?

PMCC: By the age of fourteen I was picking out a tune. Before that I was just listening. He'd teach me and my brother little things like – we'd be listening to the radio and he'd say, 'Can you hear that deep noise there? That's a bass.' He'd teach us to differentiate between instruments, and teach us what harmony was. Not in a technical way, just, 'This is a harmony to that' sort of thing. It was all thirds and very simple stuff. But I think he was very influential on my love of music, because he was always tinkling away – things like 'Chicago', 'Lullaby of the Leaves', 'Stairway to Paradise' and all that. I think he was a great pianist. I mean, he wasn't technically good, but he used to tell me, 'It's handy to be able to play the piano, because you get all your drinks bought for you and you're the life and soul of the party.'

RP: What was the first impact of rock and roll?

PMCC: I think probably Elvis was the first. The first record I actually bought was 'Be-bop-a-lula', by Gene Vincent, and that set me off buying a lot. 'Rock Around the Clock' was another. To me, it was a whole new direction of music. Pretty respectable people had been singing until then, but now there was all these people in crazy clothes, with slicked-back hair. Lonny Donegan was the other big influence; he's what made all the kids buy guitars.

RP: When did you get one? Did you have to save up, or did somebody give you one?

PMCC: Well, my Dad bought me a trumpet, because he'd been a trumpeter till his teeth gave out. You know, there was a big fad, everyone wanted to be a trumpeter; the star thing was to be Harry James, or Eddie Calvert, The Man With The Golden Trumpet. But I worked out that I couldn't sing and play trumpet. So I swapped the trumpet for a guitar, which I've still got – it's a Zenith. I took it home, and I couldn't play it at all – couldn't even begin to play it. Then I worked out it was because I was left-handed and the guitar wasn't. So I strung it the other way round.

RP: Obviously, you started looking round, watching what there was of guitar technique. Which local groups impressed you?

PMCC: There was a group called Cass and the Casanovas, and I knew Cass – I went to school with him. Round about that time, they had a lot of skiffle contests; in fact, Jim Dale, who's now playing *Barnum,* used to host them, and a lot of my mates went into that. They did very well, but that was before I'd got into a group. I was just sort of beginning to look the part, and beginning to research the whole thing. We started to look for Mr Carroll Levis, who shall be nameless, who ran Carroll Levis and his Discoveries. We went on one of those.

RP: How did you do?

PMCC: We failed miserably. We got beaten by a woman who played the spoons.

RP: There was a group called, rather unglamorously, the Quarry Men. How good were they?

PMCC: That was John Lennon's group. John went to a school called Quarry Bank, so that was why the group was called the Quarry Men. I went to this other school, and one of my friends from there was called Ivan Vaughan, and Ivy, as we called him, was a neighbour of John's and knew him. So Ivy invited me, one day, to Walton village fête, and the Quarry Men were playing there. It was all a bit skiffly, but John held the show very well. So I went backstage in this church hall, and we got talking. He'd finished his shows and he was sort of getting a bit drunk. I think I must have been about fourteen and he was about sixteen, something like that. And I knew the words to Eddie Cochran's 'Twenty Flight Rock', and that meant I was in. That was me.

RP: So you began to sit in with the group?

PMCC: So I sat in. I wrote the words out for them, like everyone was very impressed that I knew the words, and I knew a couple of chords. I thought no more of it really, and went away, and then, a couple of weeks later, one of the fellows out of the group said

'We'd like to ask you to join. It's pretty good that, knowing all the words to "Twenty Flight Rock". Very impressive.' And I sang a bit of Little Richard stuff as well, which I used to do at that time.

RP: Do you remember the first date for which you had a fee?

PMCC: I think it would have been a place called Wilson Hall, in Garston. I don't know how much we got. It wasn't much, you know; we'd be on a maximum of about two pounds for the whole band. And we split that into about five.

RP: You changed to a more up-market title, Johnny and the Moondogs. Did that make any difference?

PMCC: None at all. I mean, like my Dad's band – he used to keep changing the name of his group because nobody wanted them back. It was a bit like that for us. We did an audition for Larry Parnes – he had a stable of people like Billy Fury, Marty Wilde – all virile, gutsy names. Clint Thigh! All that stuff. He had some auditions in Liverpool for groups to back these people. He wanted a backing group for a singer called Johnny Gentle, and we auditioned for that. We were the Moondogs, but someone at that audition persuaded us to change it to the Silver Beatles.

RP: Why Silver?

PMCC: Well, they wanted to make John the leader of the group, so they wanted to call it Long John Silver and the Beatles – because we'd just discovered 'Beatles' and we weren't really secure with it, so we kept trying to change it. We ended up with Long John and the Silver Beatles. Then we dropped the Long John bit, and eventually it got honed down to the Beatles.

RP: You had a bit of trouble hanging on to a drummer.

PMCC: We had lots of trouble with drummers; they're a notoriously difficult bunch.

RP: Well, nobody likes carting all the stuff about.

PMCC: They could never get on buses, you know; them and bass players. Then there's trouble with the girl-friend: 'It's me or your drums!'

RP: What was the first taste of glory? Did you get the job as support group with Johnny Gentle?

PMCC: Yes, in Scotland. It really went to our heads, you know; we went mad, and we sent postcards home about how people were asking for our autographs. We changed our names. It was great. I changed mine to Paul Ramon.

RP: Did you come back from Scotland with any money?

PMcC: None at all, but it really didn't matter. I mean, we were just over the moon.

RP: You were going to be a teacher at one time. Had you junked that idea completely, or were you keeping it as a safety-net?

PMcC: I was sort of keeping it in reserve. I thought, well, at least until I'm twenty-four I've got the option of going to the art school, and not having to get a job. I was always going to go to art college – but things took off before I ever had to resort to that.

RP: So, the Beatles had played for a real management, and they'd toured, and they were now playing gigs. More or less by chance, you got an overseas engagement.

PMcC: Yes, some overseas promoter had come to Liverpool, and he wanted a bunch of Liverpool groups – I think he wanted them on the cheap – some cheap rock and roll to put into his clubs. So we were asked. It was fifteen pounds a week, which at that time was quite good actually. This was to work in the Kaiserkeller – the King's Cellar – in Grosse Freiheit, which is a street just off the Reeperbahn, probably the toughest area in Hamburg.

RP: Accommodation provided?

PMcC: If you can call it accommodation. It was pretty dingy. Other groups that came couldn't believe the sort of squalor we were living in. But at the time we were lads. I mean, it was great with fifteen pounds in your pocket. We managed – never saved anything. Spent it all.

RP: How many hours a night did you play?

PMcC: We'd actually play eight hours, but it totally wrecked us. I remember getting home to England, and my Dad thought I was really half dead. I must have looked like a skeleton, but I was having such a ball, you know, staying up late and everything – and I was just a young kid.

RP: Was it helping the group? Providing you were trying, the more you played, the better you were going to get.

PMcC: Our ambition became not to have to repeat a tune in those eight hours, and we finally got it.

RP: That was good.

PMCC: When we came back to England, it gave us a huge reper-toire. Later in our career, we'd come to BBC shows and stuff, and producers would say, 'What do you want to do?' and we'd say, 'Well, what do you want to hear?'

RP: Was there anybody to pull you together, to smarten you up, provide showmanship?

PMCC: When we first arrived in Hamburg, we were a very green bunch; we just used to stand there and go through the tunes, which would have been enough in Liverpool – but the manager in the club was a fellow called Willy, and he used to say to us, 'Mak' shao, Mak' shao' – you know, 'make a show'. People would come to the door of the club, and they'd poke their heads in and look at the beer prices, and they'd vaguely see a band there – so we'd have to go, 'Whoops! Hey! Look at us! Come on in!' – and it was really good for us. Good training. Getting pulling power. So immediately anyone put his head round the door, we'd 'Mak' shao'.

RP: So back to Liverpool as 'The International Favourites! Direct from Continental Success!!'

PMCC: 'Direct from Hamburg!' All the kids in the dance halls thought we were German; they were surprised to hear us speak English.

RP: Was it then that you started at the Cavern?

PMCC: I'm pretty hazy on chronological order, but it would be about then.

RP: From what I hear, it seems to have been something of a claustrophobic hell.

PMCC: I loved it. I think it was great. It was a claustrophobic hell, but it was a great one. We started to build the crowd there with this Hamburg experience of pulling people, and once we had them there, holding them. When you packed them all in, the problem was that the walls began to sweat, and that would fall into the amps, which would then blow all the electricity. So then we had to even learn how to hold an audience with no electricity! We used to keep them entertained by singing commercials at them.

RP: To what extent were you and John Lennon working at com-posing and arranging? Had you started seriously?

PMCC: Yes, we had. In the very early days of the Beatles, John and I used to take time off school and go home to my house – 'sagging off', as we used to call it – and I used to prepare a pipeful of Typhoo tea. My Dad never left any tobacco around, but he left empty pipes around, so we used to smoke Typhoo tea. And we used to sit around being very arty, and think of ourselves as Dylan Thomas or someone. We started writing together then. We wrote quite a few songs before we ever got one published – and we used to work in Hamburg.

RP: Did you sit down and work together, or did one of you get an idea and bring it to the other for a second opinion? How did it happen?

PMCC: It used to happen every way. We never got a formula. That was probably one of the good things about it. We used to sit down with two guitars, and if neither of us had an idea, we'd just start to look for one, just strumming and waiting till one came out. Quite often one of us would have thought of a first line or a second line or a chorus or something. We were learning the job. Eventually one or two started to come out which were quite decent.

RP: The Beatles were getting a good local reputation. What you really needed was a manager to look after things – and there was one right to hand in Liverpool.

PMCC: Yes, there was a fellow, Brian Epstein, who had a record shop, and he'd been asked for a record that we'd made in Hamburg, when we'd backed a fellow called Tony Sheridan. Brian hadn't heard of it or of us, and somebody said, 'Oh, they're just down the road at the Cavern.' So he came in one day and looked at us, and apparently thought there was something there. We were all leather and sweat at that time, and he cleaned up the act a little bit, and said, 'Well, we've got to try for London, so you're going to have to get suits', which no one was very keen to do, but we went that way.

RP: He tidied you up, and got you auditions for record companies, which was the important thing.

PMCC: Yes, none of which was interested in us. Everyone turned us down.

RP: And they've been eating their hearts out ever since! Did the company that eventually accepted you allow you to record the Lennon and McCartney numbers, or did they want the Tin Pan Alley stuff?

PMCC: We said, 'We've really got a feeling we don't want to use other people's stuff; we really want to try and write our own stuff.' So, after much humming and ha-ing, George Martin let us do our own record, which was a minor hit. I think it got in the Top Twenty – or Thirty.

RP: Was that the first intimation you had that the Beatles were going to take off – that something was going to happen?

PMCC: That was really the big start of it all.

RP: I don't think there's any need to tell the Beatles story again, Paul – of the films, the world tours, money rolling in in fantastic sums. Do you remember it as a physically frightening time?

PMCC: No, I was never really frightened at all. Even when we were getting death threats and stuff on American tours, we just used to take it with a pinch of salt. Mind you, it was Ringo who got the death threat, and I don't think he took it with a pinch of salt! There were a couple of dodgy moments, you know. There was a woman who had predicted the death of J.F.K., and she said that on the flight from Denver to Indianapolis our plane would crash, and we'd all die. And we had to get on that plane – because they wouldn't move the schedules just for her. So we all got pretty merry that night. That was pretty frightening, but you just had to go through all of that.

RP: The crowds must have been frightening.

PMCC: I never really used to get frightened of the crowds at all. People used to say, 'Wow! you can't go anywhere', but I actually used to get to most places I wanted to. You couldn't go down Oxford Street in the rush hour, because you'd attract a crowd there, but you could go round the little back streets. You get a speed of movement, and once the crowd's about ten, you say, 'Thank you', and you move quick and get out.

Fitzroy Maclean

Sir Fitzroy would be at his best if he discovered that his deserted island had, in fact, an indigenous population. Within a short time he would have taught them the advantages of democratic government and arranged for their integration into the British Commonwealth. He would then write a memorable book about his experiences, and probably follow it with another which told the history and origins of his new friends.

RP: As a youngster, what was it your ambition to be?
FM: To be a diplomat.
RP: Was it the prospect of travel which attracted you?
FM: Not really – no. I thought it would be the most interesting and exciting thing I could do.
RP: In fact, you did join the Diplomatic Service when you came down from Cambridge. What was your first posting?
FM: Paris.
RP: A plum job right away.
FM: Well, I had been in the Foreign Office for a few months before that, and they did something they'd apparently never done before, which was to send round a form to fill out asking, 'Where would you like to be sent', and I thought there's no harm in aiming high, so I put down Paris. A month later, they said, 'Your going to Paris.'
RP: That was in the mid-thirties – the days of the Popular Front. There was a lot going on. How long were you there?
FM: Three years. Then they said, 'Where do you want to go next?' and I said, 'Moscow.' They said, 'You must be out of your mind.' But I said, 'No, I want to go there,' and they said, 'Well, nobody else does, so it's the easiest thing in the world.'

RP: One of the drawbacks must have been that the Russians weren't permitted to meet foreign diplomats.

FM: It's true it was nearly impossible, but not quite. I went there with the firm determination to meet as many Russians as I could and, in fact, I did meet a few, mostly in trains and buses and places like that. The further one got away from Moscow, the easier the atmosphere was. But it was very difficult indeed. They were terrified. And rightly so.

RP: In the thirties there were trials going on, and there was tremendous unrest. Was it a reign of terror?

FM: It certainly was a reign of terror, but I wouldn't say there was unrest, because people weren't given the opportunity to be restless. It was total control, total autocracy, total power concentrated in one man's hands - in Stalin's hands - such as had never existed in the world before ... At any rate, you would have to go back to somebody like Genghis Khan to get that sort of thing. And, of course, a terribly oppressive, and repressive, atmosphere.

RP: By sheer persistence and a lot of cheek, you went to a lot of places in the Soviet Union where you weren't supposed to go. These were unofficial travels, just out of curiosity?

FM: As you say, unofficial. What I found when I got to wherever I was going was, of course, interesting, to say the least of it, but I was really on local leave at the time.

RP: You got to, among other places, Turkestan and Afghanistan - sometimes by showing meaningless but impressive looking documents to people who couldn't read anyway.

FM: That was it. Sometimes it worked, and sometimes it didn't.

RP: You got over the border into China once, I believe.

FM: I wasn't so lucky there. They put me straight into jail and then expelled me. But then the Foreign Office had insisted on my warning the Russians what my intentions were, which rather enabled them to take steps in advance, as they were in control of that part of China. 'You won't enjoy yourself there,' they said when I crossed the frontier, and when I came back twenty-four hours later, they said, 'We told you so.'

RP: After a while, surely, the Russians kept an eye on you.

FM: Oh, they kept an eye on me from the word go. By the end of

111

my time there, I had four full-time followers, who sat in a motor-car outside my house. When I went for a walk after dinner they followed me. And they followed me to Central Asia, and they followed me up a lot of very, very uncomfortable mountains in their tight black shoes.

RP: You took the golden road to Samarkand, and to Bukhara. How did you manage with languages? You spoke Russian, but not everybody else did.

FM: Almost everbody spoke a little Russian, and when it comes to getting something to eat, and you haven't had anything to eat for a long time, it's remarkable how you make yourself understood.

RP: You travelled for a while on an old medical certificate.

FM: I travelled at one time on an old bill from some shop in London that had By Royal Appointment on it – you know, they were by appointment to the Duke of Connaught or Queen Mary or someone – and it was covered with impressive coats of arms. That took in everybody. It was a marvellous bill, that. I paid it in the end, too.

RP: You had been in Russia about three years, I believe, and then the war started. At that point you suddenly decided to become a politician. Why?

FM: What I had decided to do was to get out of the Foreign Office and into the Army, but I found this wasn't easy because I was frozen in the Foreign Office by the Defence Regulations. Then I discovered that under one of the rules of the Foreign Office anybody who stood for Parliament, or even thought of standing for Parliament, had to resign first. So I went along to the Permanent Under Secretary of State and announced that it was my intention to stand for Parliament.

RP: Did that get you out?

FM: Yes. I handed in my resignation immediately, went to King's Cross and took a train for Inverness, and I'd arranged with a friend at the War Office that I should get straight into the Cameron Highlanders as a private soldier. Winston Churchill was very amused by this stratagem. He once introduced me to Field Marshal Smuts as 'the young man who made a public convenience of the

Mother of Parliaments.' All I can say is that the Mother of Parliaments made a public convenience of me for the next thirty-odd years.

RP: Very quickly you were transferred from the Cameron Highlanders to a specialized unit.

FM: Well, I met a friend, David Stirling, who a few weeks before had raised the SAS, the Special Air Service Regiment, and from what he told me about it, it sounded the sort of thing I should enjoy. So I got into that.

RP: What was your first enterprise with the SAS?

FM: A raid on Benghazi, which was then several hundred miles behind enemy lines.

RP: Demolition and sabotage?

FM: Demolition and sabotage.

RP: One of your exploits was to kidnap a Persian general.

FM: That was in Isfahan. General Zahedi was the army commander, and it had been discovered that he was in touch with the Germans. It was the time when it looked as though the Germans were going to break through the Caucasus into Persia, and if that happened my job was going to be to stay behind the German lines. Meantime, the powers-that-be thought it would be a good idea to remove General Zahedi. The Germans were apparently going to do an airborne landing on our headquarters, and he was going to join in on their side. I was given the job of taking him away, which went off extremely smoothly, with the help of a platoon of Seaforth Highlanders.

RP: That General afterwards became very important in Persia.

FM: He afterwards became Prime Minister and did a very good job. I remember feeling at the time how lucky it was that I hadn't shot him.

RP: Did you ever visit his country during his term of office?

FM: I did indeed, and I also became a friend of his son, who was later Foreign Minister and Ambassador here in London and in Washington.

RP: So you must have treated the General right?

FM: I don't know about that - but he was certainly one of the nicest people I ever kidnapped.

RP: A later wartime exploit of yours was to parachute into Yugoslavia. I believe the Yugoslav enterprise was Mr Churchill's scheme. He sent for you.

FM: It was his personal idea. Very much so. I had asked to be parachuted into Greece, because I knew Classical Greek and I could understand modern Greek. By then the war in the desert was over and I wanted to get back to Europe and stay there – not just make occasional darts behind the German lines. So I put this idea forward, and the answer came back, 'We don't want Maclean for Greece, but we do want him for Yugoslavia.' I assumed I was going to General Mihajlovic and the Cetniks, but when I saw the Prime Minister he explained to me that he had begun to have doubts about what was happening in Yugoslavia, from intercepted enemy signals – intercepted by what was known as the Ultra Secret, now no longer a secret. He had come to the conclusion that there was some other resistance movement who really were fighting the Germans, and he said to me, 'I want you to go in and find out what is happening there.' And that is what I did a few weeks later.

RP: So you were dropped into Yugoslavia, and you met Tito.

FM: I met Tito immediately. He was a shadowy figure in those days, and very little was known in the outside world about what was really happening in Yugoslavia. Of course, the Germans and the Italians knew much more about it than we did: they'd found out the hard way. Well, when I met Tito I was relieved to find a very sensible, hard-headed individual. He made no bones about being a Communist, but in spite of that he had a sense of humour, he was ready to discuss any question on its merits and he took his decisions there and then, without referring to higher authority. I thought this was the sort of man that one could do business with. I also found that his resistance movement was infinitely more important than anybody outside had imagined. He was containing a score of enemy divisions which could otherwise have been used on other fronts, and it was also, of course, politically much more significant than people outside realized.

RP: So what was really proposed was that you, a Tory MP, should promote a Communist revolution.

FM: Winston put it rather brutally. He said, 'Your job is to find out who's killing the most Germans, and see how we can help them to kill more. Your mission is, therefore, primarily military, and only secondly political.'

RP: Tito was a rather independent kind of Communist, wasn't he?

FM: That was what I noticed. On the military side, of course, there was no doubt at all that this was a very formidable movement indeed, as the Germans had known all too well for the last couple of years. Politically, I found him very unlike any Communist I had met before and, having spent three years in Stalin's Russia, I had met a lot, and in other places as well. The Russians, I thought to myself, are going to have trouble with you after the war. And indeed they did. In my first major report to the Prime Minister, I said, 'Much will depend on Tito and whether he sees himself in his former role of Moscow-trained Communist, agent of the Communist International, or as the potential ruler of an independent Yugoslavia.' That, of course, was the question which came up in acute form once he was in power in Belgrade, and very soon led to the break with Moscow that we all know about.

RP: I believe you still have a house in Yugoslavia.

FM: I have a little house there, which I bought ten or twelve years ago, and where we spend many happy weeks every year.

RP: And you continued to see Tito?

FM: I saw Tito right up to the time of his death, pretty well every time I went to Yugoslavia.

V. S. Naipaul

Mr Naipaul, an Indian born in Trinidad, did not visit this country until he came as an Oxford undergraduate. The process of absorbing enough of our way of life to be able to write about it was a long and sometimes difficult one. When he is not travelling, he lives in the Wiltshire countryside.

RP: You were born in Trinidad to an Indian family. Are there many Indians there? And when and why did they go there?

VSN: I suppose we were a community of about a hundred thousand, but in fifty years it has grown considerably. The Indians went there to work on the sugar estates after the abolition of slavery. I think the first migrants went over in 1845, so we're a very old community. My own family went over there about a hundred years ago, so I can claim a grandfather who has come from India, but for the rest I was very much a man of the New World.

RP: Your father was a journalist.

VSN: Yes, on the local daily paper. I don't know where he would have got the literary urge from – or how a man who would have heard only Hindi when he was a child would have wished to learn English and then try to write in English, but he did. Having become a journalist, he also began to write, and from the sight of him trying to write, and then writing, and the memory of him reading to me, I myself developed.

RP: It's said that at the age of twelve you swore an oath that you would leave Trinidad within five years, and that you wrote that oath in a school book.

VSN: That's true – because I was aware that I was born in a place that was very far from civilization ... and by civilization I mean a way of life where the mind and the activities of the mind would be given due regard; because I thought that unless I got to a place where the mind was regarded, I would be crushed and extinguished, and this fear of extinction was the great driving force in my early life.

RP: In fact, you won a scholarship to Oxford to read English. What was the first impact of Oxford? Was it as wonderful as you thought it was going to be, or was it a disappointment?

VSN: I had come from this curious background. I was among strange people with strange social manners, and I was in no position to appreciate their manners. I was in no position to appreciate the complexity of English society. I was in no position to appreciate architecture. I was applying the very simple standards of a colonial, doubly colonial, people, and I was a bit at sea. Also, I never really had enough money at Oxford.

RP: Could you manage any extra-curricular activities? Did you get mixed up in drama or sport or politics?

VSN: No, I was entirely submerged. I so much wanted to go to Oxford, and then having got there I really felt let down. I suppose I had expected something that really didn't exist.

RP: What happened to you when you graduated?

VSN: I had to make a living, and I also had to be a writer. It was very hard to be a writer because at the age of twenty-one or so one isn't very good. I don't think there are any prodigies in writing – it's something that has to be developed. You have to practise. I had just a few pounds, and I couldn't get a job anywhere, so I spent about six months with a cousin who was studying law in London, and at the end of that time I got a little job with the BBC.

RP: Doing what?

VSN: Well, I had a contract to edit a little programme on the Caribbean Service. It was a literary programme, and while I was rejecting people's manuscripts and making rather grim comments on people's work on the radio, I was writing absolute rubbish in my cousin's basement flat in Paddington. This went on for a little while and then I asked Arthur Calder-Marshall, who'd appeared on the programme once or twice, to look at what I'd written, which was now a great pile of manuscript. He wrote me a two-page letter, beginning 'You should abandon this, it's very bad', and went on to give me a little advice. I was very distressed for a couple of months, but then one day in the BBC – in the freelances' room which they gave us – out of a wish to turn my back on this profound rubbish I'd been writing and which Mr Calder-Marshall had told me to give up, I began writing quite differently, simply and directly, and very nice people in the room with me looked over my shoulder as I wrote this and, because they knew I wanted to be a writer, said, 'That's good'; and then I wrote the next day and the next day, and it went on, and so I wrote my first book with people looking over my shoulder.

RP: In fact, you wrote three novels, which you said were your 'apprentice novels'.

VSN: Yes.

RP: Two of them won very distinguished literary prizes.

VSN: They were picked up, they were picked up. After a year of nothing happening, one was picked up.

RP: You were playing safe at the start by writing about a background you knew, about Trinidad.

VSN: When you are young, you can't write. You have the material that you will write about, but you haven't been able to put sufficient distance between the experience and yourself. You're too much a part of it. So all this early experience, which was meaningless to me at the age of eighteen or nineteen when I had *tried* to write, by the age of twenty-three had a lot more meaning. So I wasn't playing safe, I was using what I had. Later, the English experience, the outer experience, the experience of a more fractured, difficult, many-sided world had to be coped with, but at that moment it was a fairly easy business of dealing with the one-culture society that was my background. I wasn't playing safe.

RP: You went on to write *A House for Mr Biswas*, another Caribbean book, which was possibly your best-seller of those early days.

VSN: Caribbean is again a difficult word; I would say it was a book about an immigrant family in Trinidad. Was it a best-seller? I've never written a best-seller. My books have ticked over and, very pleasingly, have given the impression of being best-sellers.

Jeffrey Archer

Lauren Bacall

Opposite
Above Picking up John Blashford-Snell for *This is Your Life*. Derek Drescher, producer of *Desert Island Discs,* is on the left
Below left Mel Brooks directing *Blazing Saddles*
Below right James Cameron

This page
Above left Arthur C. Clarke in Sri Lanka
Above right Tom Conti
Right Roald Dahl

Lord Denning

Les Dawson

John Fowles

Mark Elder

This page
Above left Brian Glover
Above right Helene Hanff
Left Russell Harty

Opposite
Above Earl Hines
Below Freddie Jones

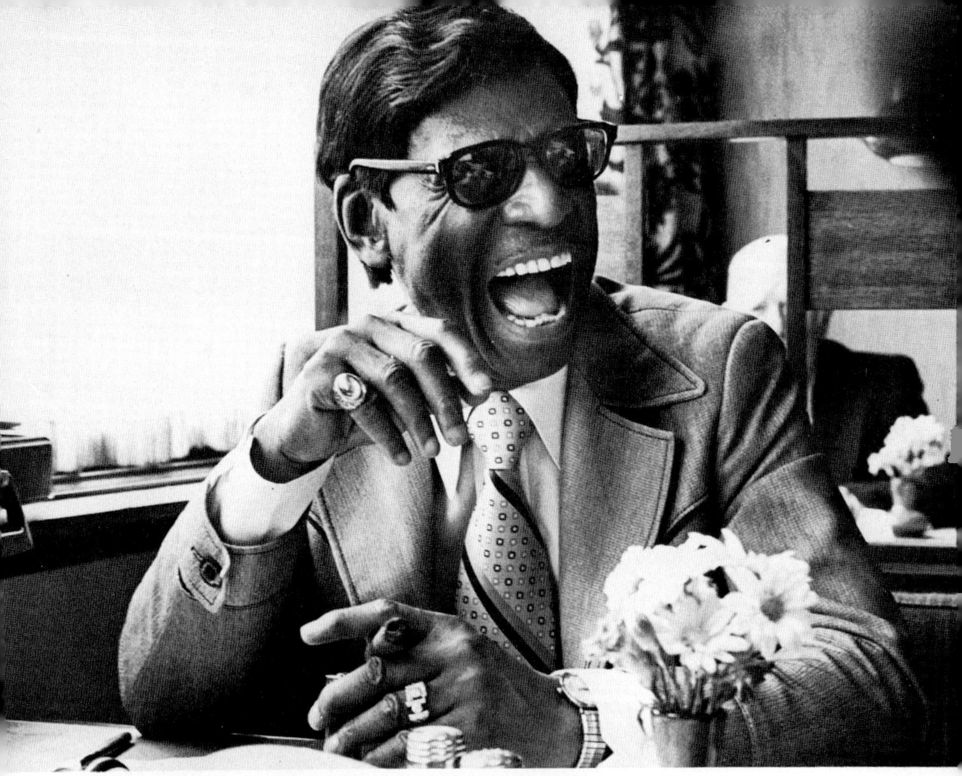

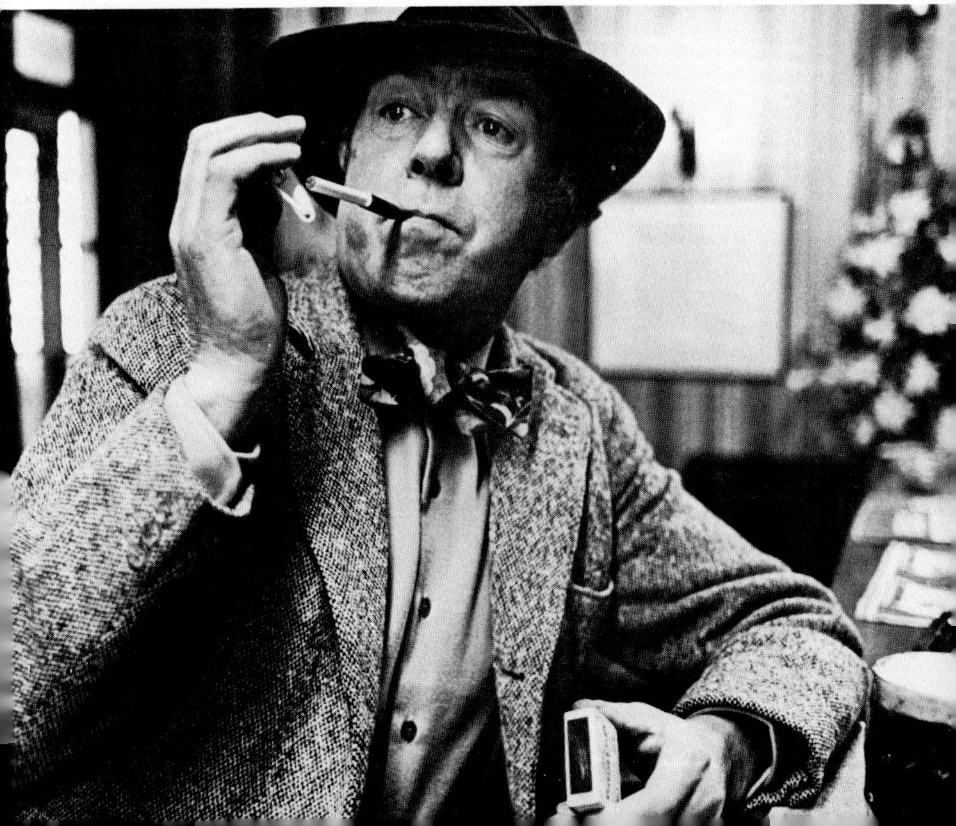

Above left Tristan Jones
Above right Ronald Lockley in his island days
Left Sir Fitzroy Maclean

Above Paul McCartney and Roy Plomley keeping quiet about Paul's record choice
for the fortieth anniversary programme
Below left V. S. Naipaul
Below right David Niven in 55 *Days in Peking*

Above left Gregory Peck
Above right Donald Pleasence
Right Robert Powell

Left Otto Preminger
Below Preparing the
1,500th programme with
Sir Ralph Richardson

Right Dr A. L. Rowse
Below With Dr Edmund
Rubbra in his home in
Buckinghamshire

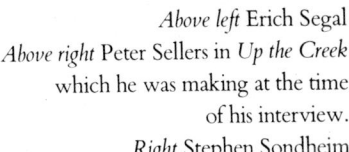

Above left Erich Segal
Above right Peter Sellers in *Up the Creek*
which he was making at the time
of his interview.
Right Stephen Sondheim

Left Derek Tangye
Below With Margaret Thatcher

Above left Baroness Maria von Trapp
Above right P. L. Travers
Left Fred Trueman

Above left Peter Ustinov
Above right Natalie Wood
Left Barbara Woodhouse

RP: From now on, I don't think any two of your novels had the same background. You spent a year here, a year there.

VSN: In 1960, when I was twenty-eight, I was asked by the Trinidad government to go back, and the Prime Minister, Dr Williams, asked whether I'd like to travel and to write a book about the Caribbean and about the Colonies. I had a lot of diffidence, because it was outside my experience to write this kind of work, and because I never had any views. If you come from my kind of background, you don't have views as a young man; you just accept and you experience. I was very neutral, very easy, so this business of writing as though I had views was new to me. It was a great strain, but I was very glad I did it in the end, because it released another side of one's talent, exercised it and extended it.

RP: Now let's stay with your novels, Mr Naipaul. *Mr Stone and the Knight's Companion* was about an Englishman. Was it set in England?

VSN: Yes.

RP: Did you write it in England?

VSN: No, I wrote it when I was in India. I went to India to spend a year, but I had to write another book to prove to myself that I could write, that it wasn't all over, that one had a talent.

RP: Is it generally your rule that you write against your surroundings? If you wanted to write a book about France, would you write it in France, or go elsewhere?

VSN: Until recently, I've always moved out, so that memory would do the selection, but on my recent travels I have actually done the writing on the spot. I don't take notes. I think memory heightens and selects, so I've always preferred to add distance.

RP: Apart from your travelogues, how many countries have you settled in long enough to write a book?

VSN: I haven't worked it out; one just moves around by association. You go to Argentina, and you feel, yes, Argentina was opened up in 1881, but surely the Belgians were opening the Congo at the same time. Shouldn't I go and see what happened there too?

RP: Three of your recent novels seem to have a theme in common, although the settings are very different. The three I'm talking about are *In a Free State*, which won the Booker Prize, *Guerillas*

119

and *A Bend in the River*. They are about rootless people who are caught up with violence or political turmoil.

VSN: Yes, you might see them as being linked in that way; to me, they presented quite different problems. One is writing in these books about people who inhabit entirely separate cultural worlds, and they come together and they misunderstand one another and they lie to one another and some kind of unhappiness ensues. The material and the people are different and, to me, they're entirely different books. That's why I needed four years between each to get the energy.

RP: While we're staying with fiction, one thing you've done, which was a splendid and admirable thing to do, is collect your father's stories, some of which were never published and put them into a book.

VSN: Shortly before he died, when I was still at Oxford, he sent me those stories. I read them with the eye of a man of twenty-one, and I just thought, Well, these things can't be published. Who'll publish them? The experience was so limited; no one will be interested. And I kept them by me for twenty years, and then I looked at them, and time had ripened them and matured them, had given them an historical interest in addition to their literary quality. So I spent a lot of time putting them together and writing the foreword. Writing that little foreword was a very painful thing to do, emotionally very demanding.

RP: Your younger brother is also a professional writer, of course. It would have delighted your father that his ambitions had been fulfilled by both his sons.

VSN: I hope so. I've often thought, you know, that perhaps, if my father had lived it might have damaged me. I would have felt, here was another person. As it was, when he died I was free. So probably all family relations have an element of oddity, malice, reverence ... all these things come together.

RP: You were still at Oxford when he died?

VSN: Yes, it was part of the blackness of those years at Oxford.

RP: You talked about the gap that you leave between your novels; this is the time, of course, when you write your travel books. One was about India, *An Area of Darkness*, and you sought out the village from which your grandfather set out for Trinidad. Did you find relations there?

VSN: Yes, the whole village was related. Yes, the village has the name of the caste and the group, and it's that kind of village.

RP: Could you relate to the way of life?

VSN: I was very touched and found it very attractive, but I couldn't be there. They're physically very attractive, the women were pretty – but my life is much more consciously the life of the individual, the intellect, learning, history, appreciation.

RP: What is your writing discipline? Do you set yourself so many hours a day, or so many words a day? How do you operate?

VSN: It's become a very messy process of late, with age and with insomnia. When I was young, I had the gift of sleeping. I would go to bed at about eleven and sleep for nine hours, and get up at eight and work right through the morning, and then work in the afternoon and, if I was really pushed, I could also work in the evening. I divided my day into three parts, usually worked for two – but most effectively in the morning. Now, after thinking what I have to do and getting up very late and drugged, I can start writing at about 4.30 pm and write until about 7.30 – perhaps, on some occasions, eight o'clock – and then, if I've written well my mind becomes very active and I just stay awake, and so this good day of writing is followed by a day of stupefaction. My dream is to get up and to work about three hours, give it all that one has, and then to cool down. I am entirely involved and consumed by whatever I'm doing, however small and however short. I live with the whole thing, I carry it in my head, and I am restless until it's all on paper.

RP: How many drafts do you ordinarily write of a novel?

VSN: Only three really, not more. One's very rough and fast until it becomes hard, until I know where I am going, which is when I begin to write very carefully; then I go back and rewrite the rough bit up to where it became good, and that is re-creation; and then I have a final oversee.

RP: Have you ever abandoned a book?

VSN: I have abandoned nearly every book I've written. I don't

121

know where one gets the drive to take this very artificial thing to the end, to get to the stage where the words do have a feeling of inevitability and reality. It's always slightly miraculous to me.

David Niven

The late James Agate, surely Britain's most entertaining, if ego-
tistical, drama critic, used to refer to embellishments and exagger-
ations put in to make a good anecdote even better as 'heightened
truth', and I suspect that David Niven sometimes resorts to it.
None the less, he is a brilliant story-teller. To our great regret, as
he was leaving the studio after our recording, he turned and said,
'I've had second thoughts about the Japanese story: will you be
very kind and cut it out?' We did so with regret, because the
description of his experiences while making deodorant commercials for Japanese television was superbly funny. I hope, one day,
he'll include it in a book.

RP: Let's talk about your early life, David. Are you a Londoner?
DN: I'm a Scot but I was born in London, because my mother
came down from Scotland to see a specialist and dropped me right
in his consulting room, almost.
RP: You should have been born in Scotland?
DN: I was intended to be, but there it is.
RP: Now, you recovered quickly from the early setback of being
expelled from your prep school . . .
DN: Well, not very quickly. I was indeed expelled, but for nothing
very awful. Then I went to a crammer to try to get into the Navy
– but I failed there because I got only eight marks out of three
hundred in mathematics, and the Navy thought I wasn't the sort
of man they wanted to steer battleships.
RP: You were at Stowe after that, and there you showed a lack of
conventionality because, when other boys would invite their

mothers and sisters to cricket matches and so on, you would have on your arm a charming young lady whom you'd picked up in Piccadilly.

DN: That was a rather peculiar episode, but I think I was a little ahead of my years. We had a house in Sloane Street, but there wasn't room for me in it, so I was farmed out and I slept in a miserable room with a tin po under the bed up in St James's Place. I had to go there every night, and it was tuppence on the bus – a no. 19, I remember, or a 22 – and I got off at the Ritz Hotel. After a while, I got bored with going straight to my room every night, and I used to wander along Piccadilly and look at the lights. Well, I noticed these girls walking about and I thought they seemed very friendly, and indeed they were – and I got to know one.

RP: And she contributed to your education at Stowe.

DN: She was very much responsible for it.

RP: Why did you opt to go to Sandhurst and become an Army officer?

DN: My father was killed in the First War and my mother married again, a perfectly dreadful man, and really they wanted to get me off the books, because we were very broke. Well, there was a master at Stowe, Major Howarth, and he suggested that I became a soldier. The next thing I knew I was taking the exams to go to Sandhurst. I was in the Highland Light Infantry for four and a half years; I was in Malta, and then in the Citadel Barracks, Dover, which is now, quite rightly, a Borstal.

RP: During your service in this country, as many young Army officers used to do in those days, you did a day's work as a crowd artist in a film. Did that job make any particular impression on you?

DN: There was a girl in my life – not the lady I met in Piccadilly – who knew a man who ran a small studio called Sound City, and she thought I should become a movie actor, so she arranged a job for me one day as a crowd artiste in a racing picture called *All the Winners*.

RP: Did you ever see it?

DN: No. I don't think anybody else did either.

RP: Why did you leave the Army?

DN: Because I hated it, and because I saw no future in it. Obviously, it was peacetime and in my regiment lieutenants had sixteen years' service before they became captains, and as a Second Lieutenant I was getting nine shillings a day. Also, I went to America on a holiday as somebody's guest, and I feasted on the fleshpots. I felt I couldn't face the discipline any more. I couldn't wait to get out. I was rude to a general, among other things.

RP: So you went back to America.

DN: I emigrated via Canada.

RP: What did you do there?

DN: Odd jobs. Then I went to New York and sold whisky – it was just after Prohibition – and I ran an indoor pony race in Atlantic City – then wound up in Hollywood, broke, and became a film extra.

RP: Why did you head for Hollywood?

DN: I had done some amateur theatricals, and I had a feeling I might be able to do films. Fatal mistake. After a struggle I finally registered as an extra, and there were twenty-two thousand of us scratching around for eight hundred jobs. Well, I did numerous pictures as an extra. I did twenty-seven Westerns among other things. Obviously with this voice – the English accent, as they called it – I wasn't allowed to open my trap anyway.

RP: Were you usually on the goodies' side or the baddies' side?

DN: I was a baddy, because I photographed dark. I was always standing behind the villain and pushing up my hat.

RP: How did you keep going when you weren't in demand at the studios?

DN: I worked as a deckhand on a swordfish boat.

RP: You were a deckhand – and yet you had crewed in a sailing race representing Great Britain.

DN: Yes, I had, you know. I was in Great Britain's amateur crew in a race for something called the Cumberland Cup – for eight metre craft.

RP: And you'd got a Rugby blue at Sandhurst, so all that makes an impressive athletic background. What was the first film in which you were entrusted with a line?

DN: A picture with Elissa Landi, and I had to say, 'Goodbye, my dear,' in a railway-station scene. I was such a smash that I was

125

hired to say, 'Hello, my dear,' to Ruth Chatterton in another film.

RP: The contract system was operating then; were you given one quite soon?

DN: Quite soon, yes. I was incredibly lucky, I was given one by the great Sam Goldwyn – at minimum money by California State law incidentally, but a bonanza for me.

RP: Because you were under contract to Goldwyn, that didn't mean you didn't work for other studios: you were hired out.

DN: Oh, all the time. The thing was to get you trained and get you to learn the business and then you were loaned out. When you got fairly popular, then Goldwyn could charge another studio an immense amount of money while continuing to pay me my normal tiny salary. He could pay for me for the next five years by loaning me out for one film.

RP: Did you have any freedom? When you were given a really terrible script could you turn it down?

DN: You could always turn it down, but then you were suspended – quite rightly, because if you refuse to work you shouldn't be paid – but the iniquity was that you were suspended for the duration of the film, which was probably four months, plus half that again as a punishment, making six months – and the whole six months was added on to the end of your contract.

RP: Was there a large British colony in Hollywood at that time?

DN: There was indeed. We're now talking about the thirties – the late thirties – when Hollywood was in love with British history: they were making films like *The Charge of the Light Brigade* and *Mutiny on the Bounty* and Dickens and all that.

RP: Which do you think is the best film you've been concerned with?

DN: I thought *Around the World in Eighty Days* was very good; it was fun.

RP: And the worst?

DN: I should think *Bonnie Prince Charlie* – unfortunately.

RP: A British film!

DN: Oh dear, yes. It took six months to make, and it was very peculiar. We were never more than one day ahead of the writers. It was the most awful thing I've ever been through.

RP: Nowadays, cinema is recognized as a director's medium. You worked with many of the great Hollywood directors; how many of them really were great?

DN: Well, I worked with Lubitsch and John Ford, and they were sensational. For example, Ford was such a sensational director that he never bothered to see what we call the 'rushes'. He knew exactly what he had shot the previous day, without looking at it, and there was nothing else for the editor of the film to do except stick it together. And Carol Reed – he was a great director.

RP: Your Hollywood career was interrupted for five or six years when you rejoined the British Army during the war. When you went back to the West Coast, was there any appreciable change? Had the war years added depth, do you think?

DN: I think they had. A lot of the nonsense had gone – the rather lovely nonsense of people believing their own publicity. It was more down to earth, and there was a whole new breed of actors – people like Marlon Brando and Jimmy Dean and Paul Newman had appeared, which was marvellous for the business.

RP: You were awarded an Oscar for your performance in Terence Rattigan's *Separate Tables*: now that was a subject at which there would have been raised eyebrows before the war.

DN: And in the early years after the war, too. I did a picture with Loretta Young just after the war – we did eight pictures together – and we were married in this film and we were having breakfast in bed, both in pyjamas and eating from trays – and the man from the Hays Office said, 'Stop! Cut it! Niven must have one foot on the floor.' Can you imagine? That was in 1947.

RP: You've done very little stage work. You were in one production at the Pasadena Playhouse ...

DN: And one play on Broadway. I love the theatre, but as part of the audience; I loathe performing on the stage.

RP: Tell me about the play on Broadway. That was with Gloria Swanson, wasn't it?

DN: Yes, it was called *Nina*: it had been a great success in French, but was a total disaster in English. Gloria had a clothing company, and wore clothes she had designed herself. On the opening night, in the first scene, I had to kiss her. I grabbed her, and there was a loud report and a sort of twanging noise, and four and a half inches of white whalebone shot out of her chest and right up my nose. In the morning, Walter Kerr, the drama critic of the *Herald-Tribune*, said in his review: 'We understood from the programme that Miss Swanson designed her own clothes: like the play, they fell apart in the first act.'

Gregory Peck

The early life of Gregory Peck had two similarities with my own: the fathers of both of us were pharmacists, and the sport we both favoured was rowing. He has a considerable interest in music, and plays the guitar. In his early days in the theatre, he played in a musical, and he hoped that one day he would be invited to play in a musical film. When the movie version of *The Man from La Mancha* was planned, he spent some months with a vocal coach and then proposed himself for the leading part. Regretfully, the producers declined his services and gave the role to Peter O'Toole. 'I've great love and affection and respect for Peter O'Toole,' says Greg, with comic indignation, 'but I tell you here and now that I can sing better than he can.'

RP: Your father was a pharmacist; did you have any medical ambitions?
GP: I did for a while – I think because it would have pleased him – but I wasn't much good at it, and I soon switched to literature and history and psychology and such things as that.
RP: You were in military school, and then you went to Berkeley. You were a rowing man, I believe.
GP: Yes, I'd started in San Diego Rowing Club. I was long and lean, and that seemed to suggest that I might be able to pull an oar. I continued in the University of California, where they had very respectable crews.
RP: And you rowed at Poughkeepsie, which I suppose is the equivalent of our Henley.
GP: Yes.

RP: How did acting come into your life?

GP: During my last year of college I was approached on the campus. I was striding about in my longness and leanness, in my crew sweater with a great golden C on my chest, and the director of the college theatre came along, and he said, 'I need a tall actor, I've nothing but short actors.' That was the first time in my life that it ever occurred to me that I might go on a stage in front of people.

RP: It's unusual for a rowing man to double in theatricals at university.

GP: Yes, I was the only one that I knew of, and I don't know why I said yes, but I'd been to some of the plays and I'd taken note that the girls were pretty and attractive, and something in me, some instinct for playing the game of pretend, made me agree. During that final year, I think I appeared in five plays, and I wasn't any good in any of them, but I thought I detected a slight improvement. Well, I had previously thought I might write or be a journalist, but on an impulse, more or less, I took off for New York to become an actor.

RP: What did you do for money?

GP: I had very little, but then I didn't know anyone else who had any, so we were all quite cosy together. We borrowed from one another, and I did odd jobs. I guided tours at Radio City, and I was a barker at the World's Fair in 1939, and I did a bit of modelling. I'm not proud of that, but I modelled for mail order catalogues, and used to get $25 a day for leaping in and out of two or three hundred outfits from long underwear to overcoats. None of them fitted, but there was a man behind me who was very handy with safety pins, pinning me up so that I could jump in front of the camera.

RP: What was your very first paid engagement in the theatre?

GP: I went to a very strange place in Virginia for the summer, and the pay was room and board. The board, such as it was, had been handed in at the box-office, because it was towards the end of the Depression and the locals were mostly farmers and, instead of money, they bartered things that they grew.

RP: Ah, the famous Barter Theatre!

GP: They brought in piglets, quarts of cottage cheese, bales of spinach, fresh corn – and that's what we ate. When you've had spinach and cottage cheese for a week at a stretch, you can't appreciate what an exotic meal it can be. Nevertheless, we did eat and we did work, and I played in ten plays in ten weeks, which was good experience.

RP: What was the first engagement when you were paid in dollar bills rather than spinach?

GP: It was another summer job in New York State, where I played bits and pieces for $25 a week. I remember I had a line or two in a play called *The Male Animal* with José Ferrer and Uta Hagen.

RP: You then had a couple of years with Katherine Cornell and Guthrie McClintic.

GP: Yes, I did. They came to see the final audition play at my drama school – I was still studying, at a place called the Neighbourhood Playhouse – and it was the custom that agents and producers and professionals would be invited to see the final production of our two-year training course. The next morning, we all gathered by the telephone receptionist to see if anyone would get a call. Well, the telephone rang, and the receptionist covered the mouthpiece and nodded at me. 'Guthrie McClintic wants to see you this morning,' she said. Well, I knew where Guthrie McClintic's office was, because I had been in there and registered to let them know that I was in town and available for work, and it was exactly six blocks from the school. So I took off and I ran down four flights of stairs, and I ran half a block across 46th Street to Sixth Avenue, and I ran four blocks up Sixth Avenue to 50th, and dashed into the RKO building. There was an elevator waiting, I pressed the button and shot up to the eighth floor, and ran down the hallway. Mr McClintic's office door was open: it was a Saturday morning, and he was there alone. I skidded into his office, and he was still talking to the receptionist on the telephone. He saw me, and he began to laugh, and he slid right off his chair on to the floor, still laughing. When he'd pulled himself together, he said, 'You've got the job.' It was a small part in Shaw's *The Doctor's Dilemma*, with Miss Cornell, and it was a nationwide tour, so I was able to get some experience with very, very good people.

RP: And your first Broadway appearance?

GP: It was a play by Emlyn Williams called *The Morning Star*, which was about London in the Blitz and which had been a success in the West End, but the sentiment and the humour of the Blitz didn't register with the New York audience, although we got good reviews.

RP: Very speedily, you became much in demand as a Broadway actor, and inevitably that led to interest in Hollywood.

GP: Well, I did make a test in New York after my first few plays, and I don't know why I agreed to do it because I had absolutely no interest in pictures. I wasn't taken up and no offer was made, and I forgot about it. Then, thirty-five years later, Danny Selznick called me one day and said, 'We've discovered an early test of yours; would you like to have a look at it?' I said, 'I'm not sure that I would', and he said, 'Well, we want to get rid of this old stuff, so we'll send it over', and then I knew why I hadn't had any offers. It was ghastly.

RP: There was a time when you turned down an MGM contract.

GP: I did later on, yes. Louis B. Mayer wanted me to join his Family of Stars, and although I'd come round to the idea that I'd like to make films, I was determined not to be signed exclusively with anyone, so I was fortunate enough to witness L.B.'s great crying act, which he put on for my benefit, in his grief that I wouldn't let him look after my career. He did actually cry.

RP: Convincingly?

GP: Very convincingly. At least, I was convinced. When I left his office with my agent, I said, 'I haven't seen a performance as good as that since I saw the Lunts,' and my agent said, 'Oh, he does that every day. He loves to do it.'

RP: What, in fact, was your first film?

GP: It was called *Days of Glory* and it was with the ballerina, Tamara Toumanova. Someone had the bright idea of making a feature film with unknowns – people who had not been on the screen before. It didn't turn out to be a very good idea, or a very good film.

RP: Your second film was *The Keys of the Kingdom*, and for that you were nominated for an Oscar, which was good going.

GP: I played that story with utter, overwhelming sincerity, although with very little skill, and it seemed to make an impression on people. I believed in the character and in the story, and I threw myself into it; I enjoyed the whole procedure and began to drop my prejudice against films.

RP: At one time, somehow or other, you managed to get yourself signed up to make fourteen pictures.

GP: That was a kind of masterstroke of Leland Hayward, who was probably the best-known agent in Hollywood. He had such illustrious clients as Garbo and Ingrid Bergman and Joseph Cotten, but he was married to Margaret Sullavan, and she took a dim view of his being an agent and thought he ought to climb up another rung on the social and theatrical ladder and become a respectable Broadway producer instead of a flesh-peddler - and I believe she called him that to his face. So I think it was probably a final stroke of hyper-activity and the total synthesis of his genius as an agent that he signed me up for fourteen pictures with four different studios, and then left town.

RP: Didn't you make two at once at one point?

GP: Well, they overlapped. *The Yearling* was a film in which I was a Florida cracker, a backwoods farmer, and *Duel in the Sun* was a Western which Mr Selznick had decided to make, and as *The Yearling* ran over schedule and *Duel in the Sun* was ready to begin, for a few weeks I found myself bicycling from one studio to another, and switching from my Southern cracker accent to my Texas/Oklahoma twang as a cowboy. They were very different pictures; *The Yearling* was something of a tear-jerker, and *Duel in the Sun* was rather steamy, and came to be known as *Lust in the Dust*.

RP: An early film of yours which I remember with pleasure was *Spellbound* with Ingrid Bergman, which you made for Alfred Hitchcock. How did you get on with him?

GP: I got along very well with Hitchcock. People say that he browbeat actors, and he's often quoted as saying, 'Actors are cattle, and the real work is done in the planning stage before we go on the floor', but, you know, Hitchcock had a particular gift for making himself quotable. In fact, he was always considerate and gentle with his 'cattle'. I never heard him humiliate an actor, quite the contrary.

RP: You were to work for him again in *The Paradine Case*.

GP: Yes.

RP: A film for which you got very serious consideration from the critics was *A Gentleman's Agreement*, which was one of the early films of social significance.

GP: That was the first film to deal with anti-Semitism. It was produced by Darryl Zanuck who, incidentally, was not Jewish; he was a Swiss, born in Wahoo, Nebraska. He told me that he had many telephone calls from Jewish colleagues who ran the other studios, and they said, 'Why do you want to deal with that subject? Why do you want to rock the boat? We're doing fine as we are.' But we went ahead and, since it was new, we all felt something of a pioneering spirit. Darryl got a group of very talented people together, Moss Hart to write the screenplay, Elia Kazan to direct, Dorothy McGuire and John Garfield to play leading roles, and the picture came out well and won an Academy Award, and it did, in a small way, break an old and foolish taboo.

RP: You still kept a foot in the theatre. You couldn't often get to New York, so you brought your own theatre to the West Coast.

GP: Yes, with a couple of cronies, Dorothy McGuire and Mel Ferrer, we began a summer repertory operation at La Jolla, which is my home town. They happened to have a nice little theatre there and, for six years, we went down, and we'd produce all the plays ourselves, and we'd each appear, at least once, each summer.

RP: I'm told there were some very distinguished productions.

GP: The opening bill, in 1947, was dear old Dame May Whitty in *Night Must Fall*, and she was extremely good.

RP: She had played the part many times, in London and New York. Getting back to films, you were collecting a number of Oscar nominations, for *Keys of the Kingdom*, for *Gentleman's Agreement*, and yet another for a war film, *Twelve O'Clock High*, which created quite an impact – but you get no credit at all for turning down *High Noon*. How did that happen?

GP: It was an error of judgment on my part. I had made a film called *The Gunfighter*, which even today remains one of my favourites, and several weeks later a producer by the name of Stanley Kramer sent me a script of *High Noon*. I recognized that it was a fine script, there was no doubt about that, but in my mistaken sense of youthful idealism, I thought, Well, I don't want to repeat myself; they're too alike. It had to do with the traditional loner, who faces the whole town alone and puts his life on the line for what he considers to be right. I turned it down and Gary Cooper immediately accepted, and went on to do it with enormous success and won an Oscar doing it, as well he should, because he was perfect in it. I could have played the role, but no one could have played it any better than Gary Cooper played it.

RP: Have you enjoyed Westerns?

GP: Up to a point. I made ten or twelve and, believe it or not, back in 1950 I was voted the Outstanding Western Star of the Year, and somewhere in my basement I have a pair of silver spurs to prove it. But I didn't want to go on and on doing that. For one thing, they don't talk much; they're always taciturn and they don't have much to say; and for good reason, because most of those Western characters were only semi-educated and they weren't very conversational. It gets a bit monotonous to be out on location somewhere - let's say in Gallop, New Mexico - and have only two or three lines to say in a week.

RP: Do you enjoy riding?

GP: I like the riding part of it, that's always been a part of my life. The Western is a classic American film form; it's a bit out of style now, but maybe the cycle will come round again.

RP: You've made several good sea stories. *Captain Horatio Horn-blower, RN* was an excellent film.

GP: I enjoyed making that. It was my first film in England, back in 1950 out at Denham, with the great Raoul Walsh directing.

RP: And *Moby Dick*. There's a terrifying story about you being adrift on a rubber whale.

GP: It's true enough. We were attempting to film Ahab in the last throes on the back of the great white whale, entangled in the ropes of many harpoons that had been plunged into this beast, and the whale was actually eighty-five feet long. It was made of some kind of dirty grey-white rubberized material, and underneath was the hull of an old potato schooner. Well, a sudden gale blew up, and the waves were perhaps twelve or fourteen feet high, and the tow-rope broke. The fog rolled in, and suddenly I was alone – Moby Dick and I were alone in the Irish Sea, and it was rather dicey there.

RP: How far off the coast?

GP: We were eight or nine miles out, and it was so foggy that I had no idea which way to swim, whether to go for Ireland or for Wales. And it was very slippery on that whale. I didn't have a very good hold on him, and it actually crossed my mind that I might die there, and I began to get a queasy feeling in the stomach, and a kind of lassitude, which I'm told comes along with physical fear, began to overtake me. But then the thought of the newspaper headlines really overcame the fear – 'Movie Actor Dies on Rubber Whale in Irish Sea'. So I began to shout and yell, and finally from the direction of my voice they were able to find their way through the fog to the whale, and I gratefully slid down the side into a motor-launch.

RP: Another film of yours that looked highly dangerous was *The Guns of Navarone*. Was that risky?

GP: Now and then you have a narrow escape, or a little brush with danger. I've broken a leg while making a Western, and I've wrenched this and that and torn a ligament here and there, but for a very good and practical reason our doubles do most of the really dangerous things, because you can't set up a seven-million-dollar film and have your star carried off to the hospital or the mortuary in the middle of it.

RP: After all those nominations, you did get your Oscar, for a film called *To Kill a Mockingbird*. That was one I didn't see.

GP: It's a very American story, set in the 1930s in a small town in the South. I played the only lawyer in town, a widower with two children, and he risks his standing in the community and even his safety and that of his children by defending a black man who is falsely accused of rape. In the early 1930s it was, I'm sorry to say, totally impossible and unknown for a black man to be acquitted on such a charge. It was a dramatic trial and I gave him a spirited defence, but inevitably he was found guilty. There was one mar-

vellous moment, when I was leaving the courtroom, having lost
the case, and my two children were in the gallery where the black
people sat, and as I walked down the centre aisle of the courtroom
by myself, a black man in the gallery said to my children, 'Stand
up, children, your father's passin'.' That was a nice moment.

RP: Would you say the most profitable film you've ever made was
The Omen.

GP: By far, by far. At the box-office, it was a phenomenon, and I
don't think anyone anticipated it. I knew it was a well-crafted
paperback, a horror-thriller. I'd never done anything like it, and
I thought, Well, it's a commercial film and we can do something
with it. I liked the idea of playing with Lee Remick, and she and
I put our heads together and decided that the way that we could
bring credibility to these events, a lot of which, I must say, were
nonsensical, was to try to create a believable love story between a
man and his wife, so that the audience would care and be concerned about the terrible things that were going to happen to us.
So we played it in that way and that seemed to help to put it over.
Much to our surprise, it became a fantastically popular film; people
lined up round the world and it brought in about a hundred
million dollars. It was the first of many films dealing with the
occult.

RP: You set up a production company yourself. Did you enjoy
handling that side of things?

GP: Not much. I found that to produce a film takes about a year
out of your life. I enjoyed the creative side of it, working with the
writers and the editors, and the director and the actors – but the
business side, what they call the 'below the line' side, I found
terribly boring. There were long, long days in the office, and I
missed the excitement of being on the floor, with the camera and
the crew and the actors. I produced a couple of films, not particularly successfully, and I was off the screen for three years, and
then I decided I'd rather get back where the real fun is.

Donald Pleasence

I don't know why Donald Pleasence is cast in so many sinister roles, because he is not a bit like that; in fact, it seems that what really interests him are the children's books he writes. He has five daughters and lives by the Thames in London.

DP: I was born in Worksop, which is near Nottingham, but I lived there only a few days. I came from Sheffield, sort of, and lots of other places around there.

RP: And you were one of the railway children.

DP: You could say that; my father was a station master, a roving station master – in Grimaldby, in Lincolnshire, in Conisborough, near Doncaster, and at Ecclesfield, near Sheffield.

RP: It must have been wonderful to have a railway station to play in.

DP: It was really nice. Sometimes they'd leave a whole train behind for my brother and I to play with. Once they left a steam-roller and we managed to get it started up. It's very difficult to stop a steam-roller once you've got it going.

RP: Was it going downhill?

DP: No, it was going along the goods yard. We nearly knocked the station house down. But my brother was very clever and he found the right handle to pull to stop it.

RP: If you played your cards right, was there free travel?

DP: Oh yes, there was always free travel in those days, and you don't half miss it. We had what we called PTS – Privilege Tickets.

RP: There weren't a lot of theatres around in those parts. How did you get hooked in the first place?

138

DP: There were two theatres in Sheffield. I used to go regularly and sit in the gods for a shilling or something. Sometimes I used to go to Leeds, and occasionally I would go to London.

RP: On a PT?

DP: Yes. I might go with my father, or both my parents. Later on, I would go by myself, to go to the theatre in the gallery.

RP: When did you make up your mind that you wanted to work · in the theatre?

DP: When I was about seven years old. I used to go and stand up in those music festivals in places like Cleethorpes and Scunthorpe and Sheffield, and I won prizes – silver medals and things like that. I thought this must be the life, really. You stand up there, and nobody interrupts you: I decided from that moment on that it was the only way to live.

RP: What did you recite?

DP: 'I wish I lived in a caravan,
    With a horse to drive, like a pedlar man.'
That was my first effort at the age of seven, in Scunthorpe.

RP: You got a prize for that?

DP: First prize, yes. Then I went on to the 'The Highwayman' by Alfred Noyes, and all those things.

RP: You had this ambition firmly in your head to go to drama school?

DP: I didn't go to anywhere like the Royal Academy of Dramatic Art – I couldn't get in, actually. I went to a very nice gentleman called Edward R. Broadhead, who ran a kind of drama school in Batley, in Yorkshire. That was while I was still at school.

RP: And when you left?

DP: For a couple of years I worked on the railways as a clerk, until I could get a job in a repertory company.

RP: What sort of clerking did you do?

DP: I was in charge of a small Yorkshire station called Swinton, the main export of which was maggots – for fishing. There was a maggot factory just down the road, and I used to book these maggots in, and do whatever one used to do with waybills and things like that, and then lug them on to the guard's van as the train came in. That was my main occupation.

RP: So you were in charge of the station.

DP: I absolutely was. I had two porters under me. That was the whole staff.

RP: Plus some trainloads of maggots. What was that first job in a repertory company?

DP: It was in the Channel Islands. I wrote to them and got a job at thirty shillings a week.

RP: Where?

DP: The Playhouse Theatre, Jersey. It was run by an actor named Laurence Naismith.

RP: What was your very first appearance?

DP: I had a small part in *Wuthering Heights*, Hareton Earnshaw. At least, my accent was right.

RP: How long did you stay at the Playhouse in Jersey?

DP: The war came after three months, and that kind of put an end to things. On a Sunday morning I was putting up the set for the next week's play when that famous speech of Chamberlain's came over the radio, and that was it. I went in the RAF.

RP: Air crew.

DP: Yes.

RP: What was your job?

DP: I was what was called a Wop AG – a Wireless Operator/Air Gunner.

RP: What sort of aircraft?

DP: I flew in Wellingtons and Lancasters. I got shot down in a Lancaster.

RP: How many missions did you fly?

DP: Nineteen, I think.

RP: Where were you shot down?

DP: In France – Pas de Calais. On a daylight raid. I landed by parachute.

RP: Then what happened?

DP: I got caught immediately, by lots of Germans. They stuck me in a prison in Abbeville, and then I was marched up to Germany with the retreating German army, and that was not very pleasant, and eventually I was in a German camp on the Baltic.

RP: Any drama shows in the camp?

DP: Yes, we did quite a bit. They were all flyers, of one kind or another – mostly Americans. I did a production of *The Petrified Forest* in which I played the Leslie Howard part opposite a six-foot American Army pilot. I made him sit down all the time.

RP: He was playing the girl's part?

DP: The Bette Davis part, yes. We had some really good actors.

RP: How long were you in the bag?

DP: Just under a year.

RP: So presumably to London, climbing the staircases to the agents' offices in Charing Cross Road. Was there much work about?

DP: I think I was lucky. I was supposed to be suffering from malnutrition or something, so I was about to be demobilized; I was splendidly dressed in a flight lieutenant's uniform. Somebody told me that Peter Brook was holding auditions for a play called *The Brothers Karamazov* at the old Lyric Theatre, Hammersmith. So I went along, and I got a tiny walk-on sort of part for £7 a week, which was not very much even in those days. Alec Guinness starred in it, and had adapted it from the Dostoevsky novel. I went along to the first reading, and an actor who was playing one of the brothers wasn't able to be there, so I read his part, and the young Peter Brook, who was all of eighteen, I think, and Alec Guinness were very pleased, so they gave me a nice part that wasn't cast, as a kind of interrogator. I had a ten-minute scene with Alec Guinness, and it was my first sinister role. Anyway, it was quite successful and we went on tour and everybody was being terribly nice and saying 'Oh, it's wonderful', and all those things that people say, and in Cambridge I came down with measles. So I was taken away to the isolation hospital just before the opening night in London.

RP: Bad luck.

DP: However, I came back to it, and then I did another play with Peter Brook and Alec Guinness at the Arts Theatre. And then everything ran out, and I went back and did about five years in rep.

RP: You did some rather distinguished rep with some rather distinguished companies.

DP: I did two years at the Birmingham Repertory Theatre and a year at the Bristol Old Vic.

RP: What took you back into the West End?

DP: I did two plays at the Arts Theatre during the Festival of Britain year, and then I went to America with Laurence Olivier and Vivien Leigh.

RP: For the two Cleopatra plays?

DP: Yes. Then I came back here and did a play I'd written myself, at the Edinburgh Festival and at the Royal Court Theatre, and I didn't really stop working from then on. I was probably doing a television play every month. I got the Television Actor of the Year award in 1958, I think, so I was doing all right.

RP: You had a tremendous chance in the theatre in a Harold Pinter play.

DP: *The Caretaker*, yes. That was in 1960. I did it at the Arts Theatre, and then at the Duchess.

RP: It really was a magnificent performance in an excellent play.

DP: Thank you. At the same time, I was presenting *Armchair Theatre* on television every Sunday night, and acting in some of them. It really was from then that I became somebody whose name was known, instead of just a face. I remember once being in a café having a cup of tea, and I saw a family sitting in the corner and they were whispering about me, and I heard the little girl say, 'No, Mummy, he isn't – he's the man from the cemetery in Bridlington.'

RP: Let's talk about your films – and their name is legion. How many have you done? Seventy? Eighty?

DP: I really don't know. Some of them I've forgotten – fortunately.

RP: What was the very first one?

DP: *The Beachcomber*, adapted from a Somerset Maugham story. I played a Singhalese servant, and I learned to speak with a Singhalese accent. I dyed my hair blue-black, and I browned up, and I wore contact lenses to change the colour of my eyes. It was a good part – a very funny part. A year went by, and then I was given another part by the same producer – to play an Arab. I think they wanted to use the contact lenses again.

RP: You're very prolific; you've taken most of the films that have been offered.

DP: I haven't been selective enough, but I can't bear not to work all the time.

RP: Which have been the good ones?

DP: The ones I like are the film of *The Caretaker*, Polanski's picture *Cul de Sac* ...

RP: *Cul de Sac* was excellent – an outstanding film.

DP: I think it's the best thing that he's done. I also liked *The Great Escape*, *Will Penny*, *Soldier Blue*, *Outback*, which we made in Australia ... Those are a few of the ones that I like. I don't mean that they're the only good ones – I hope.

RP: Let's talk about the mechanics of film acting, Donald. You are sent a script, you agree to play a part. What comes next? Learning the lines? Thinking of the make-up?

DP: First comes getting on an aeroplane and flying to, say, Los Angeles. Now I used to think that when I got there, somebody would tell me how I was going to play the part; but it isn't true actually. It hardly ever happens. So now, usually, I first of all learn the lines, and decide what I'm going to do – because I'm pretty sure nobody's going to tell me. I don't know why this is. Perhaps it's because they think that I have some expertise which will get them over the problem of having to think themselves about what I'm going to do. So I take the make-up with me, and very often the suit or the costume, and I arrive on the set and present myself to the director and say, 'Well, is this all right?' And they usually say, 'That's great, Don.' And you know ... you go on from there.

Robert Powell

I first saw Robert Powell in person at a large, formal and crowded dinner in a London hotel. It was one of those show-business functions which, although worthy in their charitable intent, are pretty heavy going. The principal speakers were businessmen, and the accent was on commerce. When Mr Powell rose to speak, I sighed, because I thought, Here is the token actor who will do no more than advertise his latest film. But, no! Robert was witty, fluent and outrageous, and he lifted a dull occasion into being a memorable one.

RP: You began your career in radio, didn't you?

POWELL: Yes, I started in *Children's Hour*, doing children's plays when I was at school.

RP: How did you get into that?

POWELL: We had a little theatre and a dramatic society at Manchester Grammar School, and I spent all my time not working but acting. Somebody saw me and dragged me along to the BBC and I did an audition for Trevor Hill and Herbert Smith, and that was it. I think I always wanted to be an actor.

RP: In fact, you started studying law.

POWELL: I had read Classics at school – Latin and Greek and Ancient History, and everybody said I must get a degree, and would be a fool to become an actor, and must get something behind me. I didn't want to continue with the classics, because I didn't enjoy it that much, and the only thing I could read without any previous qualification was Law. We all started from scratch at that, so I dived straight in.

RP: How far did you get?

POWELL: A couple of years, that's all.

RP: Were you doing amateur theatre work?

POWELL: I was running the University Dramatic Society, and writing and directing revues ... that's the reason why I only lasted a couple of years.

RP: So it was an actor's life for you – off you went. Had you any money to fall back on, or were you really taking a chance?

POWELL: Isn't the pride of an adolescent amazing? I refused any help at all from my parents. I insisted that, as I was going against their wishes in becoming an actor, either I did it on my own or not at all.

RP: How long did it take to get your first job?

POWELL: I wrote to three repertory companies, and got a response from the one in Stoke-on-Trent – the Theatre in the Round there. I went there one Saturday for an interview and was given a job for six weeks – three weeks rehearsals, and three weeks as assistant stage manager and carrying a spear in *King Lear*.

RP: There was a snag there: playing in the round, you can't get a prompt.

POWELL: I didn't need one, because I didn't have any lines.

RP: Point taken.

POWELL: No, I did have a line! I played Gloster's Old Man, as he's referred to in the script. I did have a line. I can't remember what it was now. But after we had opened *Lear*, the director asked me to stay on, so at that point everything was forgotten and I became a professional actor.

RP: What happened after Stoke?

POWELL: After fourteen months, I headed for the smoke, in search of fame and fortune.

RP: You were making the onslaught on London a little early in your career. Had you an agent to contact, or anything like that?

POWELL: No, I just wandered off, bright-eyed and bushy-tailed, expecting everybody to say, 'Here is Robert Powell, what an amazing actor!' Unfortunately they didn't; in fact, very few people took any notice at all.

RP: Until?

POWELL: Well, I did this very strange show at the Arts for Brian Epstein, called *Smashing Day*, written by Alan Plater. It was strange only in as much as another actor and I wrote the music for it and played it on harmonica and guitar. We had done it in rep, and Brian Epstein saw it and brought it down to London.

RP: So you compose?

POWELL: After a fashion. I must admit that my associate did about 98% of it, and I sort of hummed a few bars here and there, and said, 'How does this sound?'

RP: And you didn't transfer from the Arts to a bigger theatre?

POWELL: No, but I got a job at the Royal Court, and so far as I was aware, I broke all existing records by understudying fifty-seven parts in one show.

RP: Did you play them all?

POWELL: I played my own six, and then one night somebody was ill, so I played his eight as well. The understudy rehearsals were quite funny, because I was the only understudy and had to play everything. I'd walk in, and the director would say, 'What do you want to be this afternoon, Robert – the whole Polish army?'

RP: What on earth was the play?

POWELL: It was Jari's *Ubu Roi*.

RP: Were you able to stay in London now, or did you go off to the provinces again?

POWELL: It was becoming very difficult, so I wandered off to Scarborough and did a summer season for Alan Ayckbourn, who was a mate, and I went from there to the Octagon at Bolton when that opened, and did six months there. It was that period that almost certainly saw the growth of my confidence as an actor, so that when I came back to London I got a few jobs.

RP: In fact, you landed a leading part in a very successful television series.

POWELL: Yes – in *Doomwatch*.

RP: A splendid series about attempts to stop mankind from committing suicide in various ways ... a different way every week.

POWELL: Of its time it was quite incredible. Sometimes we were ahead of the news and the headlines were following the programme.

RP: You did the series of thirteen, but when the programme came back for another thirteen, you didn't come back with it.

POWELL: Well, I had had enough. I was only twenty-five at the time, and I wasn't married and I had no commitments, and I wanted to do other things.

RP: So your part was killed off in episode thirteen.

POWELL: Literally. Kit Pedlar, one of the writers, came up to in the bar and said, 'How do you want to go?' and I said, 'Irrevocably', and he said, 'What do you mean?' and I said, 'Well, blow me up or something', and he said, 'Wonderful', and then went away in a corner and blew me up.

RP: You began to get some of the classic stage parts under your belt; you did *Hamlet* in Leeds – and then you played Ibsen somewhere.

POWELL: *The Lady from the Sea* at Greenwich.

RP: And some interesting television.

POWELL: Hardy's *Jude the Obscure*, Flaubert's *Sentimental Education*, and various one-off dramas.

RP: You were really having a go at everything, I see a couple of horror movies on the list.

POWELL: We don't talk about those too much.

RP: Christopher Lee parts? Did you have the fangs on?

POWELL: No, I played the hero. It was my ambition to put the fangs on, but nobody actually saw me in that light.

RP: Now let's talk about your career with Ken Russell.

POWELL: Ah yes, how long have we got?

RP: What was the first?

POWELL: *Mahler.*

RP: That was a pretty wearing part, wasn't it? You were on camera practically the whole time.

POWELL: That one was wearing, for a lot of reasons. He's a fairly wearing director to work with.

RP: How did you get on with him? He's reputed to eat actors. Did you establish a relationship pretty quickly?

POWELL: We played cat and mouse for a couple of days. He didn't know who I was and I didn't know who he was. I noticed that Ken's obsession with his work meant that he was giving a hundred per cent the whole time, and it seemed to me only fair if I did the same. Even if you make mistakes, as long as you are trying your hardest he is perfectly happy. He gets very unhappy if somebody slacks: that's where the reputation comes from. We got on very well. I did *Tommy* for him the following year, which was very funny. He rang up and said, 'Would you like to play Tommy's Dad in my next picture?' and I knew the music and said, 'I'd love to.' He said, 'It's just a favour, because it's five minutes screen time and it will take seven days to shoot.' I said, 'Fine, terrific.' He said, 'Seven days spread over eleven weeks.' So I said, 'Ah', and we worked out a deal. Eventually I was on the film for twenty-six weeks.

RP: Still with five minutes screen time?

POWELL: Still with five minutes screen time.

RP: It's just as well you liked the music. What was the next career highlight?

POWELL: My favourite piece of theatre, when I did *Travesties* for the Royal Shakespeare Company.

RP: Oh yes, the Tom Stoppard play. Which really was the beginning of a whacking three years, wasn't it?

POWELL: Indeed it was.

RP: *Travesties* must have been a tremendously difficult play to learn. I mean, it's such a flow.

POWELL: Yes, it is. The comparison is to music; it is very strange. Tom writes so precisely that once you hit the rhythm you can remember the lines, because each word connects later on, four bars later, with another one, which connects four bars later on with another one – and once you catch them and know where they are, then, funnily enough, it all comes.

RP: The rhythm takes you along?

POWELL: Yes. He is one of the greatest wordsmiths. It was while I was doing that, and performing it, that an Italian director came along with a small part in an epic that he was going to make.

RP: A part that one might term the part of all time.

POWELL: A part that no actor in his right mind would ever want to play: the part that no actor can really turn down if he is asked to do it.

RP: Let's stop hedging. This was Jesus Christ. Did you hesitate before accepting it?

POWELL: Oh, very much so, yes.

RP: Have you a strong Christian faith yourself?

POWELL: I believe in Christ and I believe in the Christian ethic and I try to live by the Christian ethic, but I am not – capital R – religious.

RP: How much was shot in the Holy Land?

POWELL: None at all.

RP: None at all?

POWELL: The whole film was shot for four months in Morocco and five months in Tunisia. It is strange that North Africa now is the only place in the world that looks like Palestine did two thousand years ago.

RP: So there was no real sense of being in the footsteps?

POWELL: No, no.

RP: You devised a simple acting trick which was very effective in the role.

POWELL: Yes, when faced with playing Jesus . . . I mean, where do you start? How do you play him? I can't walk six inches off the ground, I am just an ordinary mortal. After a lot of thought, I discovered that I could do something that other actors didn't seem able to do, which was to keep my eyes open for three or four minutes at a time without blinking, even in the strongest light. I thought about it, and I thought about the thread between the eye and the person who is watching. Every time you blink, that thread is broken for a thousandth of a second; so I decided not to break it, throughout the whole film. It was a trick that set this man apart from the other men.

RP: The crucifixion sequence must have been terribly harrowing to do.

POWELL: Indeed it was. In fact, it took about five months to shoot, on and off. I was always threatened by Franco that if I misbehaved I would go back up on the cross.

RP: Franco Zeffirelli?

POWELL: Yes. We were very dependent on the weather to shoot the sequence; he wanted certain heavy clouds. I remember one particular day I was on the cross, and I had been up there many hours, and we'd been shooting in little bits and pieces, and suddenly Franco saw something in the sky behind my head that I didn't know about. He said, 'Robert, we are going to turn the camera now ... please ... you do the whole of the crucifixion scene. It is wonderful behind your head. It is a most beautiful scene behind your head.' So I said, 'What do you mean by the whole thing?' He said, 'All of it. All the pieces, one after another.' I said, 'Including the death?' He said, 'Yes, including the death.' So I did each moment of the crucifixion, one after the other, and finally arrived at the moment when I was about to die. Obviously, to pull myself together and get into it, I paused and there was a voice from behind the camera: 'Go on, Robert, die die die die die die die!' Somewhere in the archives of ITC, that's on film too.

Otto Preminger

Mr Preminger is a large, round man, with a round head which he keeps closely shaved. In his acting days, he had doubtless found the shaven head a useful asset in playing the conventional Hun – although, in fact, he is Viennese. During our preliminary chat, we got along very well together, and I found him cheerful and friendly. However, the fact that the eight records he had chosen were all of music from his own films, showed that he was out for self-advertisement. This began to be even more evident when we started recording, because he began to over-act, larding his talk with heavy-handed mock aggression. He certainly succeeded in getting column-inches in the newspapers, although the comments were not all flattering, and one headline read "Orrible Otto'. It was an abrasive encounter, but I enjoyed it.

RP: Mr Preminger, you're from Vienna and the son of a lawyer. You became stagestruck. Did it happen on any particular occasion?
OP: At the age of seventeen I wanted to become an actor, and at that time a very famous German producer/director, Max Reinhardt, who originally was Austrian, came back to Vienna and started the Theater im der Josefstadt, and he got a very rich Italian to give him all the money in the world, and Reinhardt really knew how to spend it. He sent the pattern of the wallpaper to Belgium and had it remade to the same pattern out of silk, he put in a terrific chandelier which he ordered from Venice, and he opened with Goldoni's *The Servant of Two Masters*, for which he had a neutral set; in other words, there was really no set but a continuation of the auditorium. I had written to Reinhardt, and

151

one of his assistants let me audition, and I became an apprentice actor. My first part, with a few other young actors, was to help take the furniture in and out. My second part for him was at the Salzburg Festival, where I played a nun in *The Miracle*. In that play, there is a long procession of nuns, and in Salzburg all the nuns were portrayed by society women, so he put an assistant, also dressed as a nun, between every fifteen nuns, to tell them what to do. I became an actor first, and then a director.

RP: You became a director at the age of nineteen. Did your ambition lie there rather than with acting?

OP: Yes. I opened my first theatre in Vienna, the Komödie, which still exists, then I opened the Neues Wiener Schauspielhaus, and then, when Reinhardt retired, I took over the theatre where I had started with him, and I ran it until I went to the United States.

RP: Your productions by that time, as a young man in your early twenties, were getting an international reputation.

OP: I wouldn't say international, but they were very successful. Then, in 1935, I had an offer to go to Hollywood, and that saved my life, because if I had been in Vienna when Hitler came to power I would be dead, like many of my friends.

RP: Had you any idea what was going to happen?

OP: Nobody had. The Nazis were already in power in Germany, and my father, who was originally Attorney General of the Austrian Empire and then a very well-known lawyer, laughed and said, 'They'll never come here; it's nonsense.' I'm very happy to tell you that when they did come, in 1938, the President of the Vienna Police, who was his friend, put him and my mother on a plane to Zurich, and they were saved. My brother, with his wife and daughter, walked across the border to Czechoslovakia. We were all lucky to escape.

RP: But you were in New York. How was your English at that time?

OP: I had taken English lessons, but only for six months. In New York, I did a play called *Libel*. Luckily I had done the play before in German, so I knew whether the actors were talking or saying lines from the play; otherwise I wouldn't have known.

RP: Then to Hollywood. You had already directed one film in Austria.

OP: A very small, bad film called *The Great Laugh*.

RP: You could take a fairly independent attitude to Hollywood because you knew you could always set up theatre work in New York.

OP: No, no, I was not independent, I was very anxious to make a success. I watched the production of one picture from the beginning to the end, and then I did two small pictures. Then Mr Darryl Zanuck, who was the head of the studio, gave me an assignment. He had a man, a go-between between the producers and the directors, Gregory Ratoff, who came to me and said, 'You're going to get the biggest assignment in the studio, you're going to do a picture called *Kidnapped*. Zanuck is going to send you the script in a few days.' I got the script, and I couldn't understand it, because it was Scottish and I come from Vienna – I didn't even speak English fluently. So I told Gregory Ratoff, I said, 'Look, I can't do this,' and he said, 'Otto, if you don't do it, you're through; you can just as well resign and go back to Vienna, because Zanuck is producing the picture himself and he'll never forgive you.' I let him persuade me, and I started the picture, and it was terrible what I did. Zanuck and I had a few fights and then he fired me. I tried first to see Mr Joe Schenck, who had been in Vienna and who had brought me to Hollywood, and when I had arrived he had taken me to his house for dinner and showed me the table, and said, 'Whenever you want to come here, you're my guest; you don't even have to telephone.' So when I had this fight with Zanuck, I tried to see Schenck in order to settle my contract. Every day, his secretary used a different excuse, until she laughed herself. I couldn't see him. Eventually, I went back to New York and I did a very successful play, *Outward Bound*, with Laurette Taylor, one of the greatest – perhaps the greatest – actress I ever knew. Then I did a play which I directed, produced, and also acted in, *Margin For Error*, and in the theatre next to us Katherine Hepburn was playing. Often, after the show, we had dinner together at 21 Upstairs. One night, Joseph Schenck came in. He saw me, and came up to me and embraced me. Then he turned to Miss Hepburn, and said, 'I brought this man to the United States, and look what a big success he is.' Then he added, 'Miss Hepburn, how come in all these years in Hollywood, we never met?' and she, in her clipped manner of speaking, said, 'Mr Schenck, I consider that one of the great achievements of my life.'

RP: A nice line.

OP: Then he sat down and had dinner with us.

RP: Of course, you went back to Hollywood, and 20th Century Fox, and Zanuck. You directed *Laura* for him – your great success.

OP: It was my first success.

RP: But you had to do bread-and-butter jobs as well. I'm thinking particularly of *Forever Amber*, which wasn't really your cup of tea.

OP: I was on a contract. I didn't want to do it, and I talked to Zanuck – by that time we were quite friendly – and he said, 'Look, we are paying you. You do it.' I let him persuade me. I think the picture was not very good, although it was a very big success.

RP: Are you nostalgic about your old films? Do you enjoy seeing them again?

OP: I must tell you something about myself. When I'm finished with a film, I deliberately detach myself from it. I see it maybe two or three times with an audience and make some little changes and then I try to forget it. At one time, I was going out with my wife, and she was still dressing, and I turned on the television and they played one of my movies – it was called *Fallen Angel*. We had to leave before the film was over and I still don't know the ending.

RP: You decided to be an independent producer. There were very few of them at that time – twenty-five years ago.

OP: I was one of the first. The major studios financed and released my pictures, but I had complete autonomy.

RP: What was the first film you made as an independent?

OP: I think *The Moon is Blue*.

RP: Which you had previously produced on Broadway. Being independent doesn't mean just choosing the story and the actors: you go right through the whole process – the promotion, publicizing, every part of it?

OP: Certainly.

RP: And you've been something of a gypsy; you've had no real base.

OP: No, I lived for about seventeen years in Los Angeles, Hollywood, and then I moved to New York about twenty-one years ago, and I'm not a gypsy. I've a house in New York. What do you mean, a gypsy?

RP: I mean, you live under cover –

OP: Is this what you do to your guests, insult them and say they're gypsies? I mean, look, I'm not much balder than you.

RP: No, only minimally.

OP: I have as much hair as you, only I shave it, because I think it's awful to have this little hair around and be bald otherwise.

RP: Yes, I know.

OP: If you take my advice, buy yourself an electric shaver and shave yourself.

RP: I'll start tomorrow. But you don't work in a studio any more; you work on location.

OP: For the past fifteen years or so, I've only worked, except for exceptions, in real locales, in real rooms, in real restaurants, and so on. Film is very sensitive now. I could easily shoot you and me in this dark studio, because first of all your head reflects enough light, and my head too. In my latest film, *The Human Factor*, I shot just one scene in a set. There's one scene which takes place in Moscow, and it wasn't worth while going there for one scene, so I had a set built in the studio and you saw through the window, by back projection, Moscow.

RP: You still act occasionally?

OP: Not often.

RP: There are actors who've worked for you who say that you're very tough on the set; in fact that you're something of an ogre.

OP: Who told you that? Which actor told you that? You are incredible ... you read things and you believe everything bad about me.

RP: Do you deny it?

OP: The only things I don't like, that I can't stand, are actors who are late, or who don't learn their lines, otherwise I'm very patient. For instance, in *The Man With a Golden Arm* was Kim Novak, who already was a star, and Sinatra. Sometimes we had to do a scene thirty-five times because of her, and both Sinatra and I were very patient – so don't say I'm tough. Take it back.

RP: Right, I take it back.

OP: Okay. You're lucky that you did.

RP: In your autobiography, I notice that in the list of your films at the back, you credit all the writers, and that isn't usual. It's very much to be commended.

OP: I think the writer contributes a great deal to the picture.

RP: Of course, you contribute a lot to the scripts yourself; you always work with your writers.

OP: I work with the writers very close.

RP: I mentioned your autobiography: two books about you have been published here, but not your own book.

OP: The best thing about my own book is the cover. It is done by my friend Saul Bass, whom I discovered when I did *The Moon is Blue*, and then he did all the titles on all my pictures. I asked him to do the cover for my book, my autobiography, and he called me and said, 'You know, you look much better from the back. May I put the back of your head on the front cover, and your face on the back cover?' And this is what happened.

RP: I hope we're going to see that book, because it has some fascinating stories.

OP: You missed it, it's sold out. I wrote it three years ago ... Don't you ever read anything? An important book like my autobiography comes out and you don't read it. I'll try to find it and have somebody read it to you, because obviously you can't read.

RP: In Vienna, you just failed to give Marlene Dietrich her start, which I found fascinating.

OP: Then you did read my biography.

RP: I have read your biography.

OP: You read my biography, not my autobiography.

RP: I read your book –

OP: Why do you act as if you haven't? Can you never say a true word on this show?

RP: Shall we move on?

OP: We'd better move on, because otherwise we won't finish.

RP: Another thing I found fascinating in your book was the fact that you almost directed Greta Garbo as Katherine II of Russia. That was a new story to me, and it's a great shame that it didn't happen.

OP: I knew Garbo very well, and I think she's a wonderful woman.
RP: Why wouldn't she do that picture?
OP: I don't remember.

Ralph Richardson

This great actor kindly consented to be cast away to mark the 1,500th programme in the series. He claims to be singularly unmusical, although in his touring days he always took a portable gramophone with him. 'Perhaps what I enjoyed most was winding it up,' he said. This was not very surprising, as he had only one record – of 'Tea for Two'. Then, when he was playing Caliban to Gielgud's Prospero at the Old Vic in 1930, Gielgud expressed amazement that Richardson knew nothing about the music of Delius, which was being used in the production. Generously, he sent round a box, containing records by Delius and Bach and other composers. Sir Ralph said, 'I opened my eyes in amazement at the joys of listening to recorded music.'

RP: I believe your father was an artist.
RR: Yes, he was. He was a painter, so was my mother. I was brought up with a very strong smell of turpentine in the house.
RP: As a boy, what was your first ambition?
RR: To be an engine-driver, of course; I was perpetually pretending to be an engine-driver.
RP: What happened to you when you left school?
RR: I went into an insurance office in Brighton.
RP: Were you good at that?
RR: I was terrible. I was absolutely frightful. I used to put the wrong cheques in the wrong envelopes, and I was a terrible scourge to them. But then I had a great piece of luck; my grandmother remembered me in her will and left me £500 for my education, and I thought I was a millionaire. I went to the mana-

ger, Mr Barry, and said, 'Sir, I have some very bad news for you.' 'Oh dear,' he said, 'not bad news again, Richardson.' 'No, no,' I said, 'I have to give you notice – because I've fallen into a great fortune.' 'Oh, Richardson, thank God', said Mr Barry, 'I was afraid I'd have to give you the sack next Saturday.' So I went to a school of art; it seemed natural that I should paint and draw. But then I changed my vocation and went on the stage.

RP: Was there any particular actor or production that inspired you to do so?

RR: Yes, there was. I'd come to a time when I realized that I didn't seem to have any very great talent in the art school, and I didn't know what to do next. Then I went to see Sir Frank Benson play *Hamlet* in the theatre, and when he knelt before the ghost of his father, and the ghost said, 'Remember me', Benson ran his sword along the ground, making a terrible noise. That sound was nothing to do with what Shakespeare wrote; it was something which Benson, as an actor, put in – and it was very effective. What an actor could do just by making a sound excited my imagination. 'I'll try to become an actor,' I said. 'I think that might suit me.'

RP: How did you set about it?

RR: I joined a little repertory theatre at Brighton, and then I got a job in a Shakespeare company.

RP: Did you do well?

RR: Alas, they said, 'This doesn't suit you, this profession. You're never going to be an actor', and that upset me very much, because my £500 had run out and I thought I'd have to go back to the insurance company. But, just by chance, just before they gave me the sack, I learned a little bit of the trick, and there is a trick about acting, in the same way that there's a trick about riding a bicycle, which seems impossible at first, but when you've found the trick of getting the balance, it works. I often wonder if I might have learned the trick of painting if I had stayed at the School of Art at Brighton; and I think that possibly would have suited me better.

RP: In fact, you stayed with that Shakespeare company for quite a long time.

RR: Yes, I did – for three or four years. Touring about.

RP: Of course, you've returned to Shakespeare many times since then. There were those wonderful years when you and Laurence Olivier ran the Old Vic company at the New Theatre. After the drab and grim years of the war, you gave us very exciting productions. We had your Falstaff too.

RR: That was when Laurence Olivier created his superb Richard III, which is one of the unrivalled performances of our time. In fact, people from all over the world came to see his performance. When the curtain went up, he came on as Richard. The setting was very simple; there was a gate, a little wooden gate, and he limped forward and he touched the gate with one finger, and it opened and he passed through. It was nothing very much, it was just to open the play and give him an entrance – but I remember one night there were some Frenchmen sitting in a box, and as Laurence put his finger out to touch the gate – he hadn't yet opened it – one of the Frenchmen cried out, 'Oh, but something of marvellous!'

RP: I seem to remember you took those productions abroad.

RR: Oh yes, we took them to Europe. We took them to Hamburg, where nearly all the city had been destroyed – but the theatre was intact. I remember somebody telling me there about the dreadful fires which had been started – I suppose that their submarine base was a very natural target for our planes – and this person said that one winter, after a big bombing, all the spring flowers came out. They mistook the terrible heat for the spring and showed their beauty. It was very touching, I thought.

RP: An extraordinary story. Looking down the list of your theatre appearances since the war, you seem to have struck a nice balance between the best of the commercial theatre – plays like *Flowering Cherry* and *Lloyd George Knew My Father* – and the classics. Have you tried deliberately to mould your career, rather than take things as they come up?

RR: Yes, I've tried to mould it, I've tried to find changes. If I've been in one kind of a play, I look very anxiously for a different sort of play.

RP: You have been working in that magnificent new building, our National Theatre: how do you take to working in a theatre with such vast resources and with such a vast administration? It's the very opposite of the kind of theatre in which you grew up.

RR: I rather like it. I think I'm more a trooper than a general. I don't mind joining the Army, I don't mind doing things with a lot of other people – and it's very nice to see so many young people improving so much under your very eyes. It's rather like a gardener walking into a greenhouse and seeing people sprouting up. After two or three plays some young actors look quite different. They learn very rapidly there because the two main theatres are very big, and acting has really got to have a size behind it; it's no good mumbling in a cupboard. Acting in a very small theatre can be rather dangerous. You've got to be able to paint big in order to paint small.

RP: You've had a very long and successful career in films; what was the very first one? Do you remember?

RR: Oh yes, I had my best part in my very first one. It was a tremendous part.

RP: What was the film called?

RR: *The Ghoul*. It was a horror film, with that nice English actor who always played in horror films. He was a good cricketer – what was his name?

RP: Boris Karloff?

RR: Yes, Boris Karloff – he was the ghoul. Cedric Hardwick was in it too, but I had the best part – I was a curate. There was Karloff in the make-up room for hours while they put in false teeth and gave him strange eyes, and when I walked in they said, 'Oh, Richardson, we won't bother about you; just put on your dog collar and on you go.' Everyone else in the film was tremendously fraught, but I only came on blandly, and said, 'Oh, your ladyship, how kind of you to ask me to tea. Thank you, I will indeed have a cucumber sandwich. Oh, my lady, how charming,' – and all the time I was putting gunpowder under the house in order to blow it up. I struck a match at the end of the film, which was the most dramatic thing I ever did, and the whole house exploded. I've never had a part like it since.

RP: You worked for a long, long time with Alexander Korda.

RR: I think I worked with him, without a contract, for between eight and ten years. I just stayed with him; he was wonderfully generous and kind to me. He was a very brilliant man; he could light a set, he could design a set, he could photograph a set, he knew everything about the cinema from A not quite to Z – and that was because he didn't know anything about acting. He always thought the actors lived in a magic world of their own, and they must be respected. To actors, he was a very kind, gentle, friendly man; he was not very kind to writers, and to cameramen he was abominable.

RP: He had been a cameraman himself.

RR: He had indeed. He behaved to me like a prince. When the war came I joined up, straight away at the beginning, because I knew I had something to sell and I wanted to sell it while the buying was good. I could just fly an aircraft, and so I joined up. Korda said, 'Ralph, what are you doing in this ridiculous uniform?' I said, 'Well, I've joined up.' He said, 'But you have pictures to make for me, how can you join up?' I said, 'I don't know, it's a tricky time, and I've got to do this just now.' So he said, 'Cunningham,' – he had an accountant there – 'Cunningham, what do we pay Ralph?' So Cunningham told him, and Korda said, 'I will give you half of that until the end of the war.' Which he did. It was years before I worked with him again. He said, 'Now I have some pictures for you. Are you happy now?' I said, 'I am happy, Alex, very happy indeed, and thank you for all you've done for me. But I owe you an awful lot of money, don't I?' He said, 'What do you mean?' I said, 'Well, you've been paying me all the time during the war, and this is a debt I must first of all quickly discharge.' He said, 'Cunningham. Bring me Cunningham.' Cunningham appeared again. Korda said, 'What have we been giving Ralph? Forget it, Cunningham. He does not owe us anything.' Wasn't that generous of him?

A. L. Rowse

As well as being a distinguished academic, Dr Rowse is a poet, historian, biographer and essayist. He was also a self-taught pianist, but he could not reach a standard to satisfy himself, so he gave it up and took to gardening instead. The beautifully kept grounds of his Cornish home testify to his success.

RP: Dr Rowse, you were born just a mile or two from your lovely Regency house overlooking the sea. Did you know the house as a child?

ALR: I knew it as a schoolboy. I used to come down to it, and in those days it was never wholly occupied. I used to sit on the hedge – that's the Cornish word for an earth and stone rampart – and wonder why I wasn't living in it. Well, I have been living in it now, for the last quarter of a century.

RP: You're the son of a china clay worker who earned, I believe, a couple of pounds a week. How do you look back on your childhood? There was obviously deprivation, but was it a happy time?

ALR: I think it was rather a lonely childhood. My people were very hardworking; my father, in about 1922 I think, got the magnificent wage of two guineas a week, but he had set up a little shop which helped out, and I used to help in that. So that, in fact, we were brought up rather better off than the ordinary village people.

RP: You too worked terribly hard; you began winning scholarships. At school, either your elementary school or the secondary school to which you went later, was there any one teacher who inspired you to work, who took you by the scruff of the neck, or was it entirely your idea?

ALR: I've always thought that I owed a great deal to a good elementary schoolteacher, a woman, whom I kept in touch with all the rest of her life. I really think that she was the best of all the teachers that I've encountered in a lifetime devoted to education. Later on, I was encouraged by the headmaster of my grammar school to try for a scholarship to Oxford.

RP: Did you bother with games and other school activities?

ALR: I wasn't any good at games, but I loved being at school. I think that must have been a great help, because I found it so much more interesting than being at home.

RP: You were a choirboy.

ALR: Yes, that was the second string. I owed a great deal to the Church, because it gave me my introduction to music. It helped me to enunciate clearly – which was of use lecturing later on. I adored going to Church, too – the ritual of the Church developed both one's aesthetic sense and one's sense of the past.

RP: And next came a scholarship to Oxford. Now in those days that was a very difficult and an extraordinary thing to achieve. I believe there was only one place for the whole county.

ALR: That was true. Going to Oxford was something of a strain, as you can imagine. On the other hand, rather curiously, even then, young as I was, I realized at once that this was my own true nature and this was where I really ought to be.

RP: At Christ Church you were to read English, were you not?

ALR: I had a scholarship in English literature, but the dons made me do history. I've never regretted that, because history was a better school, provided a better education. But it means that my interests have always been both literary and historical. So one has had the advantage of those two disciplines, which also double the number of brickbats that you're liable to get.

RP: At that time, how did you envisage your future – as a writer, as an academic, as a teacher?

ALR: I think I always thought of myself as a writer.

RP: Were you already writing verse?

ALR: I had started publishing verse when I was a boy at school, in anthologies called *Public School Verse*, although my small Cornish grammar school was not a public school. Later on I came to know quite a number of those who appeared in the early volumes of *Public School Verse*.

RP: Which of your Oxford contemporaries impressed you most?

ALR: I owed most to my friend Lord David Cecil. He was two years older than I, and he was always kind and helpful. With a streak of genius and as an excellent writer, he had a great didactic gift as a teacher. I owed a lot to him, and learned more from him than from any of the dons.

RP: The strain of the amount of work you were putting in meant that you had ill health to contend with.

ALR: That was partly the result of all the strain and anxiety. You see, there wasn't anybody to help or advise me, and it was awfully difficult getting to Oxford in those days from a small county school, with no money. It led to years of illness from duodenal ulcer, which nearly killed me. I'm a reformed character only in old age.

RP: Despite that handicap you took a first, and then you sat for a Fellowship at All Souls – and very successfully. Now there was one frightening ordeal, to have to dine in hall so that one's social graces could be inspected. That must have been rather terrifying.

ALR: You're absolutely right, I could very well have dispensed with that. The examination, well, I was constantly going in for examinations – but I'm not at heart very social and I would have been much more pleased if I had been let off that dinner.

RP: You were a Fellow of All Souls at only twenty-one.

ALR: I was elected before I reached my twenty-first birthday.

RP: There was one pill in the jam; you didn't get the lecturing post you wanted at your old college.

ALR: I never really wanted that. That's why I over-reacted about it, because they asked me to stand for it and then turned me down for someone else from another college – I took it very badly because I had been so proud of being a scholar of Christ Church. Later, when they asked me again, I turned *them* down and cut off relations, behaving badly to them in my turn, as I think now. Over-reacting, just like a proud Celt!

RP: How long have you been in residence in All Souls?

ALR: Nearly fifty years. They kindly enough renewed my Fellowship for three years when I was over-age.

RP: To stay on at one's university so long, isn't it rather like staying in the womb? You're sheltered from the stormy blast to a considerable extent.

ALR: I think you're right about that, but I hope you think I justified the position by working very hard and producing the goods so far as I've been able.

RP: Indeed you have a very impressive list of works to your name, some forty or more. Three volumes of autobiography.

ALR: Those don't count as All Souls research! They were written down here in Cornwall.

RP: *A Cornish Childhood* has already become a classic. Do you still keep a diary?

ALR: I still do when there's anything interesting to write.

RP: Then there's your verse, half a dozen volumes, and a lot of local history, Cornish history.

ALR: I was so interested in everything about Cornwall that my very first All Souls research works were really about Cornish history in the Tudor period: *Sir Richard Grenville of the Revenge*, which has just been republished to celebrate its fortieth birthday, and *Tudor Cornwall*. From there I went on and branched out into the Elizabethan Age as a whole, followed by a good deal of work on its greatest writer, Shakespeare.

RP: What attracted you to the Elizabethan age first?

ALR: I got fixed on the Tudor age from the time I was a small boy of five. We hadn't any books in our house, but an old great-aunt had books, and among them was a history of England, and I got fixed on the Tudors and Elizabeth I. It's odd how one's choices go right back to childhood.

RP: Now, your biographies; you mentioned Sir Richard Grenville, and there's been Ralegh, Swift, Matthew Arnold, Marlowe and half a dozen volumes on Shakespeare. You claim to have unwrapped one of the mysteries of the last four hundred years and discovered the identity of the Dark Lady of the Sonnets.

ALR: It's not very surprising because, after all, I've spent the whole of my life researching into the Elizabethan age, but nothing was known about her until I got down to the manuscripts in the Bodleian Library. That, if anywhere, was the most likely place. She turned out to be the discarded mistress of the Lord Chamberlain, who was the patron of Shakespeare's company. All the circumstances completely cohered, characters and characteristics, people and background, dating, everything. There's not a single respect in which this can be overthrown; it is all unanswerable, for it is the answer.

RP: This is, of course, wonderfully exciting, and it's splendid that in all the drudgery and the dusty work of research at any moment one may come up with what can only be called a jackpot.

ALR: Yes, that's what's so exciting. Obviously, there's a lot of drudgery, but all Cornish people are excessively inquisitive. I've always been inquisitive from the time I was a boy, and I've been able to make several discoveries in the Elizabethan age – not only about Shakespeare but also about Ralegh and Grenville.

RP: The quantity of assorted documentation available to the historian must be enormous.

ALR: Especially in the records of the legal courts; there must be thousands of unpublished documents from all the Elizabethan courts, so that you can't exclude the possibility of finding out more. These subjects are by no means exhausted.

RP: One of your recent published works was *Homosexuals in History*. There was one surprise in it; you gave a certificate of absolute heterosexuality to Shakespeare, which is not the usual verdict.

ALR: But then the people who say that don't qualify to hold an opinion, they don't know about Shakespeare or the age he lived in. There's no sign whatever in his work of any interest in homosexuality. When you come to the Sonnets he specifically tells us that he's not interested in the young man physically at all – it's simply gratitude and affection and a loving response to a most generous nature. All the evidence is that Shakespeare was infatuated with his Dark Lady, and earlier he had got tangled up in matrimony in the usual way, giving the girl a baby when he was only eighteen and a half. So there you are.

Edmund Rubbra

Dr Edmund Rubbra was the first composer I ever met. I was twenty, and my girl-friend was a music student. One Sunday evening, with her and some of her fellow-students, I journeyed to Camden Road, in North London, to sit on the floor of Rubbra's crowded studio, where he officiated at the piano while young musicians demonstrated their prowess. I had never before realized what fun music could be.

RP: The war interrupted life for you, as for everybody else, and there you were – Gunner Rubbra – sitting in an Army hut scoring your Fourth Symphony.

ER: Yes, I was at a remote camp, a cadet training camp on the coast of Wales. They'd given me an office job, because they found out that I could do shorthand and typing. Another composer, Alan Rawsthorne, was there too. He was in charge of equipment, giving it out to new entrants. When a cadet named Hastings turned up, Alan found him a rifle which had the number 1066.

RP: You were eventually put in charge of the Army Classical Music Unit, for which you were made a sergeant. Tell me about that unit.

ER: One day I was summoned to see a Colonel Temple at the War Office, and I was told to form a trio to play nothing – and nothing was underlined – except chamber music of the classical type. So, with William Pleeth, the cellist, and Joshua Glazier, the violinist, we started to get a repertoire together. I hadn't played chamber music, and it took us months to get together a large enough repertoire to go out on tour. We started in Chester, and eventually we expanded into a septet.

RP: Surely, chamber music concerts were a minority interest in the Army.

ER: True enough. For their own sakes, Entertainment Officers tried to get a good crowd to come. On one occasion, we were advertised on big posters as Ed Rubb and his Seven-Piece Band.

RP: Obviously you couldn't use the NAAFI piano; did you take your own with you?

ER: Yes, we had a grand, which we used to take from camp to camp in our lorry. We used to unscrew the legs and pedals and sit on top of it. One day we were told that the next camp had a wonderful piano – a nine-foot grand – and we needn't take ours. When we got there, the piano was up on the stage looking marvellous. We sat down to rehearse, and when I opened the lid I found that at least twenty keys wouldn't play at all. So the sergeant in charge of the piano was sent for, and the officer said, 'Why is the piano in this condition?' The sergeant's classic reply was, 'I can't understand it, sir; this morning there were only six keys that wouldn't play.' It seems that he thought six out of action was all right.

Erich Segal

Mr Segal took piano lessons as a child, but his teacher found that he couldn't read the notes, so the lessons were discontinued. Later, it was discovered that young Segal had been short-sighted. That is a sad story, but then Segal made a fortune out of writing a sad story – a novel called *Love Story*. He likes to run in marathon races, over a distance of over twenty-six miles, which must give him plenty of opportunity for thinking out plots.

RP: Erich, you were born in Brooklyn, and your father was a Rabbi. Was your upbringing very strict and orthodox?

ES: Well, it was strict and unorthodox, because my father wanted me to be a generally cultured person, so he sent me to a yeshiva, a religious school where I learned Hebrew at the same time that I learned English. It was brutal. We started at seven in the morning and finished at six in the evening – and this was five and a half days a week. At the same time, he wanted me to learn all about world culture and to start Latin and Greek, in addition to Hebrew, as soon as I could. 'Be an educated person,' he said. 'Then you can go off and be a Forest Ranger, or fly to the moon – but at least you will do it as an educated person.'

RP: Then to Harvard, where you read classics – and took part in college theatricals, of course.

ES: I was a very bad actor. I had one line in *Hamlet*. I was a courtier, and I said, 'In that and all things will we show our duty.' That was my entire part in *Hamlet*, but it was a good way of getting close to Shakespeare.

RP: After you graduated, did you stay on at Harvard to take your doctorate?

ES: Yes, I was a little too studious. I didn't do the travelling that normally one does between the A.B. and the Ph.D. Usually you take a year abroad, ostensibly to learn and go to museums, but actually to drink and sit in the sun. What was the hurry? I say to myself now. I was thrust into the teaching profession earlier than I cared.

RP: You were also dabbling in the professional theatre.

ES: Yes. Having fulfilled my father's single commandment, I was free to indulge myself in any sort of endeavour I chose ... and I chose not to be an astronaut – there was no such thing in Brooklyn in those days – but to be a playwright. I should stress that I never wanted to be a great playwright, but I did want to be a successful playwright. I scribbled away at plays, and one was produced Off-Broadway and ran a glorious thirty-nine performances.

RP: You became known as a play doctor: at Boston try-outs, you were invited to sit in and say, 'We'll have to fix this ending,' and that sort of thing.

ES: That's a unique profession; I don't think you have play doctors in Britain or, for that matter, in any other country in the world. When a show is in trouble out of town, and by definition all shows that are out of town are in trouble, they never trust the author of the play – even if it's Tennessee Williams, and I'm not kidding you – they call other people in. And they always call in inferior people. And I consider myself one of the inferior ... a graduate student at Harvard, called in to rewrite or fix up or punch up a professional playwright's production. The text of a play in try-out is changed every night, and I'd get to the theatre at one, and write from one to five – because I had my Harvard classes in the morning – and from about four to five the actors would learn the new lines, and I would sit in the back and hear if they lived or died.

RP: Your classics cross-fertilized your theatrical life, because your first book was *The Comedy of Plautus*.

ES: Yes, I'm pleased that it was that book which got me whatever academic attention I've had, because I wrote about this unique classical phenomenon – a truly popular playwright.

RP: And you prepared verse translations of several of his comedies for the theatre.

171

ES: I did that as a sort of follow-up, because translating a play is a great way to get close to the text.

RP: While an undergraduate, you had begun another great interest – long-distance running.

ES: I began to jog, and then I began to realize that I could run a little bit further than the average person. So I ran in the two miles and the cross-country, and then in the Boston Marathon.

RP: Yes, it's the marathon that interests you. What's the distance? – Twenty-six miles or more, isn't is?

ES 26 miles and 385 yards.

RP: How many marathon races have you entered?

ES: I've agonized my way through forty.

RP: What's your best time?

ES: 2 hours and 42 minutes. It doesn't sound very good now, but this was in 1963.

RP: It sounds pretty good to me. Getting back to your show business activities, how did you get mixed up with *The Yellow Submarine* – the Beatles' film?

ES: I really don't know, except that the producer lived in the neighbourhood of Yale, to which university I had moved and where I was teaching. You see, professors in America are much more staid than in England, where eccentricity is not only tolerated but, I think, encouraged and fostered. So the fact that I wrote the odd song and the odd Off-Broadway play – thirty-nine performances or not – was known a few miles up from Yale, which is where Mr Al Brodax lived. So he came up to see me and – to put it bluntly – I worked cheap. I was, I think, the fortieth writer on *The Yellow Submarine*.

RP: And what better man to consult than you if anybody's making a movie about the Olympic Games: you worked on *The Games*, didn't you?

ES: Yes. A Michael Winner production and – if Michael Winner's listening – I still haven't met you, Mr Winner, but I don't like the way you directed *The Games*. With due respect, he said he didn't want to meet writers. I mean, I don't think that's the way to make movies.

RP: There might be writers who don't want to meet directors.

Now, Erich, one day about eleven years ago, you sat down to write a screenplay based, I believe, on an overheard conversation.

ES: It was based on a conversation between two students of mine about a third student who got married. His wife worked to support him through his graduate degree and, just as he got his degree, she contracted a dread disease and died. That's all I used – the bare facts that a student had, at the age of twenty-five, lost his wife. And this little opus – or opusculum, to be more precise – was *Love Story*.

RP: Did you send it on the rounds of the movie producers?

ES: I had no great hopes for it, but my agent did send it around, and it got sent – very quickly – back. I actually lost a job because of *Love Story*. I was supposed to get the job of writing a spy picture which I very much wanted to do – you know, people shooting each other in the streets of Vienna. I lost the job because the producers said I had gone soft. So not only did I not sell *Love Story*, but I didn't get the spy screenplay.

RP: So you rewrote *Love Story* as a novel.

ES: I didn't have much success there either. There was no great rush to publish it; in fact, it was only out of pity that it was published. I owed a book, called *The Death of Comedy*, to the publishers who put out my Latin translations, and they said, 'We've got to keep this man happy. What will it cost to run off a few thousand copies of this novel? We'll publish it, and it'll be forgotten, and he'll get on with his serious stuff.'

RP: How many copies did they, in fact, print?

ES: Two thousand.

RP: And how many copies have now been sold in the United States so far?

ES: At last count – and I've run out of fingers, of course – almost twelve million.

RP: And, of course, there are other languages.

ES: Thirty-three that I know of.

RP: Obviously, you were then commissioned to write a screenplay – all over again.

ES: The stone that the builders rejected – to quote the Bible, if I may – the stone that the builders rejected has become the chief cornerstone. I was feted, wined, and encouraged to write a screenplay, which I did with great relish, since I already had it written.

RP: And a few months earlier, they could have bought it for a couple of thousand dollars.

ES: Right.

RP: It's been a tremendous seller, but few books have had such a pasting from the critics. Did you write it from real emotional feeling?

ES: Well, at the time I was much, much younger than I am now ... and not just the ten years that separates the writing of *Love Story* and the present moment. Naive in spirit. That was the closest I had ever come to death – and death at a young age. Even though it was only the wife of a student of mine, I was genuinely moved. Since I had no reputation as a writer, I had no reason whatsoever to write anything other than what I felt on that piece of blue paper. I'm crazy for coloured paper, so I wrote *Love Story* on blue paper ... if anybody cares.

Peter Sellers

This is the only vintage interview in the book, dating back to 1957.

RP: Peter, what brought you into show business in the first place? Is there a family precedent for it?

PS: Yes. First my grandmother, then my mother and father.

RP: Was it a foregone conclusion that you would be in the theatre?

PS: They always hoped that I would.

RP: How did you start?

PS: I started sweeping my uncle.

RP: Sweeping your uncle? Sounds fascinating.

PS: Well, not exactly my uncle, but the theatre that he was managing – in Ilfracombe. I was sweeping it out for him.

RP: I see – the old adage that you can't walk a stage until you've swept one.

PS: I well and truly swept it – and the hall. I had a good old stiff broom.

RP: In due course, were you promoted?

PS: Yes, I got on eventually to taking the tickets – and then working the limes.

RP: Were you good at that?

PS: I was fair at it. It doesn't take much talent.

RP: Well, you've got to get it in the right place, and it's got to be the right colour.

PS: Yes, it has. I remember one Sunday concert. We had a chap on the bill called Herschel Henlere . . . you've probably heard of him.

RP: Yes, a piano act.

PS: That's right . . . he pulls his gloves off, and they bounce all over the place. Anyway, in the middle of his act, he says 'Strike me pink!' – and the idea was that he should be struck pink by the limes. Well, we had spinners on the limes, and one side was pink and other was green, and I put the green on – and my friend, who was also working the limes, followed me. Mr Henlere was very annoyed about this, and we didn't get a tip at the end of the week.

RP: What were you promoted to next?

PS: I did stage lighting for a while, and then I was assistant stage manager, and then stage manager – but not for very long, because I wasn't good at that. Then I took part in a talent contest. My uncle thought I knew enough about it to do an act.

RP: What sort of act?

PS: Playing the ukelele and telling stories. It didn't lead to anything, but at that time a band came down there – Joe Daniels and the Hotshots – and I was smitten with the drumming bug. Joe's relief drummer taught me, but I wasn't satisfied with that; I wanted to learn classical drumming – tympani and all that – which I did eventually take up. Anyway, I played at one or two little dance halls around Ilfracombe – and then I got a job with a gipsy band, and from the gipsy band I went to Syd Seymour and his Mad Hatters, which I wasn't very pleased about, because it was mostly a matter of hitting things every time Syd fell over. Then I got a job in a dance hall in Brighton, and then I joined the RAF.

RP: Did you do any entertaining in the RAF?

PS: Yes, after a while I was with Ralph Reader's Gang Shows.

RP: Overseas?

PS: India and Burma – and then Germany. I was playing sketches and also drumming. Then, after I got back, I took a job in Jersey at a holiday camp. I was entertainments manager.

RP: Was that fun?

PS: Quite good. Going to bed very late and getting up very early. 'Wakey, wakey, campers' . . . you know. Then I had a crushing defeat in Variety in Aldershot – a terrible thing it was – and then I managed to get a job at the Windmill Theatre.

RP: And it was while you were at the Windmill that you met Spike Milligan and Harry Secombe and Michael Bentine.

PS; Yes, we weren't on the bill together – as a matter of fact, Alfred Marks was on the same bill with me – but I met up with Spike and Harry and Mike at about that time. We all used to meet in a pub in Victoria, and try things out there. Spike was staying with me at the time, and we used to mess around on a tape recorder, and we eventually took one of these tapes up to Pat Dixon at the BBC, and he put on *The Goon Show*.

RP: *The Goon Show* wasn't your first experience of broadcasting, was it?

PS; No, my very first broadcast came about through Dennis Main-Wilson seeing my act at the Windmill, and he suggested I had a BBC audition, which I did. But I had to wait around a long time afterwards – so Dennis thought I might be able to get on a new series which Roy Speer was producing, and which featured new voices. *Show Time*, it was called. Well, I waited around for about three months and heard nothing, so I telephoned Roy Speer and used Kenneth Horne's voice to recommend myself.

RP: You pretended to be Kenneth Horne?

PS: Yes, on the assumption that Roy Speer would know Kenneth Horne and Richard Murdoch, who were very popular then on *Much Binding in the Marsh*. First, I spoke to Roy Speer's secretary, and said that I'd like to speak to Roy, and she passed me over and I said, 'Hello, Roy. Dicky and I have been working with a wonderful act – a really marvellous young impressionist named Peter Sellers,' – and Roy believed it, and I went all through this terrific spiel about myself – and then I told him I was me. Roy said, 'You're a cheeky young so-and-so. Come up and see me.' So I did.

RP: So that's how it all started. Of course, *The Goon Show* has gone on from success to success, and it's led to films, such as *The Lady Killers*, with Alec Guinness, and all the television shows. What do you really hope to concentrate on eventually?

PS: Films. Films, and just an odd television.

RP: Character acting?

PS: Character acting. That's my ambition. Yes.

Stephen Sondheim

This celebrated writer and composer of musicals had exceptional training. It was through friendship with Oscar Hammerstein's young son that he became obsessed by the musical theatre, and he wrote his first show when he was fifteen. Oscar Hammerstein saw his potential, and set him on a course of training: he was to write four musicals, the first to be an adaptation of a well-structured play, the second an adaptation of a not-so-well-structured play, the third an adaptation of a short story or novel, and the fourth an entirely original story. As well as that, he was allowed to be Hammerstein's personal assistant during the production of *Allegro*. He had finished this gruelling course by the time he was out of college, where he majored in music, and he then spent two years studying music privately in New York.

RP: Apart from student productions, what was the first show you wrote?
SS: It was a show called *Saturday Night*, and it was an adaptation of an unproduced play, and it was to be produced by the man who had produced *Kiss Me, Kate*. Unfortunately, he died while we were in the middle of backers' auditions, and the rights of the piece then passed to his widow, who really wasn't interested, so it all disappeared – but it afforded me my first professional experience, in that I had to play auditions for professional backers and professional actors, and I also had to write professional songs. So I had a small catalogue – a portfolio, let's say – to demonstrate to producers around town.
RP: After that big disappointment, what was the next move?

SS: I had to earn a living, so I went out to California and wrote some television scripts for a while; then, luckily, through playing that stuff around, I came to the attention of Arthur Laurents, who was about to write the book of what turned out to be *West Side Story*, and a lyricist was needed, so he brought me to Leonard Bernstein and Jerome Robbins, and we spent two years writing the show.

RP: As we know, the story was roughly based on *Romeo and Juliet*, but instead of the Montagues and the Capulets there was a street gang called the Jets and a group of young Puerto Ricans who called themselves the Sharks. Did you do any research into the way Puerto Ricans live and talk?

SS: No, none at all. As a matter of fact, the only research done on that show was done by Jerome Robbins who went to a gang dance, and he picked up one specific that he thought would be very effective, namely that Puerto Rican boys accepted carnations from the girls, which they put into the cuffs of their pants. Jerry thought this would be wonderfully effective on the stage, which, theoretically, it was until the dress rehearsal, when they all started doing his choreography and the stage was awash with flying carnations – there were trampled flowers all over the stage for people to slip on. That was the one note of authenticity in the piece, and it went out with the dress rehearsal.

RP: In spite of which, it was a verismo musical.

SS: But I think one of the ways to make verismo is to make your own.

RP: *West Side Story* was a big success, and so was your next show, *Gypsy*, in which once again you were the lyricist, to Jule Styne's music. Which was the first show in which you wrote both words and music?

SS: *A Funny Thing Happened on the Way to the Forum*, and that took about four years to write. It wasn't steady writing – it went through a number of drafts. Burt Shevelove and Larry Gelbart wrote the book, and we'd read through a draft and find that the show ran between four and four and a half hours, and every single moment of it was screamingly funny – but obviously we had to do something about it. It wasn't as simple to cut as most shows, because it was intricately plotted, and the only way to cut was not to cut lines but to cut entire sub-plots, but when you cut a sub-plot then you find the entire piece requires restructuring. It must have gone through three restructurings, because I can think of three plots that were cut out.

RP: It was a fairly knockabout sort of show – in fact, there was an aura of burlesque about it – but your music and lyrics were much more sophisticated than the book. Was that deliberate?

SS: No, it wasn't deliberate, and the show is much more sophisticated than it seems. It is a very, very carefully written book; it is in my opinion the best farce ever written, and I include Feydeau's. It is written very elegantly. Its feeling is that it was written over a weekend and just slapped on to a stage, but any actor who's ever worked in it comes away with an enormous admiration for it. Burt Shevelove, whose idea it was, called it a scenario for vaudevillians. He wanted a piece that would hold up under any circumstances but still allow for any group of comedians to invent their own business and lend their individual styles to the piece, so that when it was done here in London by Frankie Howerd, whose style is entirely different from that of Zero Mostel, who played the lead in New York, it was still the same piece. Unfortunately, I was writing more of a salon score, and I think I was influenced by the elegance of the script rather than by its essential low comedy. In fact, I was writing less Plautus, who inspired the piece, than I was Shevelove and Gelbart, and it was probably an error. The result is that the score and the book don't quite match.

RP: Now, skipping a few shows, we come to a romance – a slightly bitter romance, perhaps, but lovely to look at and listen to – *A Little Night Music*. How does that rate in your affections?

SS: Oh, that's my tribute to Ravel, I guess. That's a very French score, although it's not as French as it could have been. We started out by doing an adaptation of an Anouilh play called *Ring Round the Moon*, which was translated by Christopher Fry, but then Anouilh wouldn't give us the rights to do it, so then I remembered the Ingmar Bergman movie, *Smiles of a Summer Night*, which was a darker piece but which gave us the same chance for a romantic musical, which was what we wanted. 'We' being Hal Prince,

Hugh Wheeler and me. I thought I'd better be careful not to make it too French, because it really is Swedish; it has to do with those endless summer days when the night never falls, and the anticipation echoes the anticipation of the characters' sensuality. It's a play about flirtation, so I decided it should be French, but I flavoured it with other things, a little Russian here and there, and even a little Viennese, and made a sort of amalgam, and I think it came out very nicely. It's a piece that I never think I'm as fond of as I really am until I hear it again, and then I say, 'Oh, that's nice.'

RP: I believe you wrote *Send in the Clowns* overnight.

SS: It was the last week of rehearsals, and Glynis Johns needed a number in the second act, where we hadn't thought she needed one, and it had to be ready so that she would have time to learn it, and we would have time to get it orchestrated. When you have to, you have to.

Derek Tangye

Most of us who are in some form of employment say, at least once a day, 'I'd love to get out of the rat-race.' Derek Tangye is a man who has done it. With his lovely and charming wife, Jeannie, he escaped to Cornwall, where they grow flowers and vegetables and write very successful books about the country and about animals and about – well, whatever takes their fancy.

RP: When you were sacked from the *Daily Mirror*, you went on a trip round the world. Had you saved up, or did you work your way round?

DT: I more or less worked my way round. I went by bus across America, I went steerage to various places like Tahiti and Japan, and finished up on the Trans-Siberian Express. But in those days it all cost ridiculously little money; I think the whole year cost only five hundred pounds.

RP: You'd hardly got back from your circumnavigation when the war broke out.

DT: Yes. I joined up in the Duke of Cornwall's Light Infantry and was sent to guard Falmouth docks, armed with a stick.

RP: There's a story that you were appointed the Army's Far Eastern expert.

DT: Having come back by the Trans-Siberian Express, they thought that I had a great knowledge of the Far East – in fact, I'd been in Shanghai for a week – and I was brought out of the ranks and made a captain and put in charge of the Chinese armies. They threw in the Thai armies as well, for good measure. I spent hours and hours sticking little pins in a map, having got most of my information from *The Times*.

182

RP: You were writing a book about your world tour.

DT: Yes, I worked on it late at night. It was called *Time Was Mine*, and it came out in the second year of the war.

RP: Was it that book which led to you meeting your wife, Jean?

DT: Yes, she was press officer at the Savoy Hotel, and I asked her if she could please arrange for my book to be on sale at the hotel book stall, and she did, and I asked her out to dinner. I asked her to tell me her name, her full name, and she said, 'Jean Everald Nicol,' and I said, 'Good God! you're the girl I'm going to marry.' You see, on my world tour I'd had my hand read on a boat, and the palmist had said, 'You're going to marry in 1943 and the girl will be smaller and darker than you, and her initials will be J.E.' So the whole thing was ordained.

RP: You'd switched over to MI5. Although Jeannie didn't know it, you were using your frequent visits to the Savoy Hotel in your work.

DT: Yes indeed, I'd stopped looking after the Chinese armies and I started looking after the West End of London and I began to have a very fascinating time. Of course, the Savoy Hotel, with all its American press correspondents, was a hive of information.

RP: When the war was over, as a civilian, you were still in MI5, I believe.

DT: Yes, I look back on those years with fascination now that all the revelations are being made. I remember I used to walk down the corridors and say to myself, 'Now I wonder which person is the spy.' It was a sort of joke, but I did come across one or two of them. Philby, for instance. I remember going back to Jeannie after having a session with Philby and saying, 'I've just met one of the most hateful men I've ever met in my life.' Now, there was no reason for me to say that because he had been charming to me – but there was something in the air. And then, of course, there was Anthony Blunt. He had access to a lot of information. People read about spies, but they don't quite understand what it means when there is deep betrayal.

RP: Do you think Blunt was a deep spy? Did he do a lot of damage?

DT: I think he did quite a lot of damage but, from my point of view, I thought he was just an overgrown schoolboy.

RP: What about Burgess? Did you know him?

DT: Burgess? Yes, off and on. One forgets in hindsight various factors which influence people. At that time, the Russians were our allies and a lot of us, quite rightly, were very sympathetic to them. We were only anxious to hurt the Germans. So the atmosphere, generally speaking, was not exactly anti-Soviet.

RP: Did you go back to journalism?

DT: Yes, I went to the *Daily Express* to write the William Hickey column. I didn't want to do it, and I knew I wasn't going to do it, and after three days, during which time I was told to change my stories two or three times and attack people I didn't want to attack, I walked into the office and said, 'Take my resignation. I don't want any of your money,' and went out feeling very relieved.

RP: So what did you do instead?

DT: I wrote for the *Continental Daily Mail*, and did a lot of other freelance work, and then I had a brilliant idea to make a fortune. Jeannie and I set up a take-away food shop, and I think we must have been the very first people ever to do it.

RP: Where was it?

DT: In Kingston-upon-Thames.

RP: What sort of food were you offering to be taken away?

DT: Oh, goulash and Cornish pasties and . . .

RP: Proper food! Not like present-day take-away food.

DT: No, it was exquisite food, and the chefs used to look out from their kitchen at the people passing by and shout, 'Fools, fools, why don't you come in?'

RP: So the enterprise wasn't a success.

DT: No, it wasn't. But we had a lot of good food ourselves. Then one day we found what everybody wants to find, the perfect home. It was a cottage called Minack, overlooking Mount's Bay, near Land's End. It was a derelict old cottage, with water coming through the roof and surrounded by derelict land. It was absolutely crazy.

RP: So you decided to abandon the rat race.

DT: And take the escape route.

RP: How were you going to live? Only by your writing?

DT: By growing flowers.

RP: Daffodils?

DT: Daffodils and violets – and potatoes. It was very exciting, except that when we seemed to have a good crop there always seemed to be a glut.

RP: Did either of you know anything about it?

DT: No, it was only a sort of wild, stupid enthusiasm.

RP: At the beginning, did you have any time to write?

DT: Jeannie did. She had a book she wanted to write about the Savoy Hotel during the war.

RP: That was *Meet Me at the Savoy*, was it?

DT: Yes. We had a chicken house where we used to bunch the violets, and I used to lock her in there, because she was very lazy.

RP: And she's written several more books in that chicken house?

DT: Yes, two novels after that.

RP: When did you start?

DT: I started after I felt I'd really got the feel of the land in my bloodstream. I must have been there seven or eight years before I wrote a line.

RP: You wrote what are now known as *The Minack Chronicles*, about that Cornish home and the way you live and survive, and about your animals and whatever.

DT: The first book was *The Gull on the Roof*. We took it to the post office and sent it off, and I shall always remember the result. Both of us were practically in tears, because the agent wrote back saying that it was unpublishable. But from that I learned a tremendous lesson, and it's a lesson for anyone who writes – that you always have to get your book, or whatever it is, to somebody on your wavelength.

RP: You keep going until you find the right people.

DT: And I was lucky enough in due course to find the right people, and then I had another blessed piece of luck: Beverley Nichols was writing a column for one of the weeklies – *Woman's Own*, I think it was – and when he was in the editor's office, he picked up a proof copy of *A Gull on the Roof*. He started reading it, and wow! He wrote a terrific piece about it, and that, of course, excited the publishers and, what with one thing and another, the whole thing took off.

RP: How many volumes of *The Minack Chronicles* have there been so far?

DT: Twelve.

Margaret Thatcher

I was very impressed by Mrs Thatcher. Come to that, I still am. At the time we recorded *Desert Island Discs*, she was about as busy as any woman could be, but she found time to invite me to her home, so that we could get to know each other before we worked together, and she took a tremendous amount of trouble in choosing her records. Our recording came at the end of a long day, and she had a heavy cold, but she could not have been more co-operative or forthcoming.

RP: You were born in Grantham, in Lincolnshire. That's quite a small town, isn't it?

MT: Yes, a small town, and very much a community. I loved living in a town where everyone knew everyone else.

RP: And you lived in a flat above your father's grocer's shop – right on the Great North Road.

MT: Between the Great North Road and the Great North Railway. The lorries used to rumble past at night, and if we went for a weekend in the country with friends, I used to stay awake – it was too quiet.

RP: You weren't an only child, were you?

MT: No, fortunately; I have an elder sister, for which I am eternally grateful. When you've got problems, there's nothing like close relatives.

RP: Your forebears had been craftsmen and tradesmen: one was an organ maker.

MT: Great Uncle John! As a great treat, we used to go and stay with him at weekends sometimes. He had two organs there, and

I was allowed to try to play them but, of course, I was young and it was very difficult. Quite by coincidence, when I went to a local music teacher for my first music lesson – I was five years old – I saw on the piano the words 'Made by John Roberts', and that was my great-uncle.

RP: You've described your upbringing as rather Puritan.

MT: Well, it was very strict. On Sundays, we went to church twice and to Sunday School twice, and the idea that you might have any entertainment on Sundays was just unthinkable.

RP: You won a scholarship to the Grammar school; which subjects interested you most?

MT: That's very difficult to say; I was a fairly good all-rounder, and had difficulty in choosing whether to go on the science side or the arts side. I can tell you what decided me – and I'm sure it's been the same with a lot of young people – we had a marvellous chemistry teacher – a wonderful teacher and a wonderful person – and I'm sure that's why I decided to take science.

RP: Where did you go for holidays?

MT: We went, quite regularly, to Skegness, which was the nearest seaside town. We used to go to a boarding-house, or sometimes we had a self-catering holiday, when we'd buy our own food and cook for ourselves. They were wonderful holidays, and we loved them. Having the shop, my mother and father could never get away together, so my mother took us to Skegness, and then my father went later – in Bowls Week.

RP: During school holidays, did you help in the shop sometimes?

MT: Oh yes, and I loved it. There were always people coming in – and a lot would come in just for a chat. I helped in the shop and I helped behind the Post Office counter, serving out ten-shilling widow's pensions and ten-shilling old age pensions, and learning how to do the accounts. We used to stay open quite late in those days ... until seven o'clock normally, eight o'clock on Fridays and nine o'clock on Saturdays. It was a very full life. You know, it was a much fuller life than sitting in front of television and watching what's going on in the rest of the world.

RP: As a schoolgirl, what were your ambitions?

MT: I had some very strange ambitions. At church we had missionaries coming and talking to us about their experiences, and I remember that I wanted to go into the Indian Civil Service, because there was a tremendous desire to serve – to serve people who were much less well off. And I knew that to do that you had to go to university – and quite apart from that, you know, the opportunity to go to university was to us an almost undreamed-of chance. My father had never done it. In modern times, he would undoubtedly have gone, and almost certainly gone into teaching. He wanted to give us everything that he had never had, and so when we showed any talent or ability he did everything to see that we got the requisite training. I was lucky; I was quite good at school, so it was assumed that I would try to go to university. But it was always with the idea of some kind of service to other people who had even greater problems than we had.

RP: So – a scholarship to Somerville College, Oxford, where you read chemistry. What were your other activities?

MT: Politics, mainly. My father and I had always talked about politics. They were very disturbing but fascinating times, with the rise of Hitler, the problems of the world economy, the great depression. I gravitated towards politics the way other people gravitate towards music or theatre or journalism.

RP: What was your first job when you came down?

MT: It was in the development section of a factory making plastics. We were developing new materials, taking them through the pilot stage and then thinking what they could be used for and where they could be sold. It wasn't pure science, it was applied science, and very interesting. Sometimes I tease some of my Labour MP friends, and say, 'You know, I've had more experience of working in a factory than you have.'

RP: Afterwards, you went to work for Lyons.

MT: Yes, that was on food processing and control – and I also did quite a lot of research work into what's called surface chemistry.

RP: You had a nagging ambition to take a law degree; how does law tie in with chemistry?

MT: People often find that rather mystifying. During my school holidays, when my father used to go to sit on the magistrates' bench I used to go along with him. The law had a very great fascination for me, and I remember, at the age of seventeen, saying to the Chairman of the Bench, who was a lawyer, 'But you see, I'm already on the science side, and I can't change now.' And he said, 'Don't worry, I took a physics degree at Cambridge. The thing to do is finish your Chemistry degree, and then do law. You won't be able to afford to do another degree, but work at it in your spare time, because you'll find there's a whole branch of law for which you need science as well – and that's the branch that deals with patents.'

RP: A lot was to happen before you were called to the Bar, including the contesting, on two occasions, of an absolutely hopeless seat at Dartford.

MT: But, you see, to me it wasn't hopeless. There had been a tremendous political swing in 1945, and we hoped for a tremendous swing back. Looking back, I don't quite think we could have turned a twenty-thousand Labour majority into a Tory gain, but one was young and full of hope. I loved it; we had meetings outside factories, we went round canvassing, and, you know, in tough seats you get the most marvellous band of helpers, who really believe fervently in the cause.

RP: One of those helpers was a Major Denis Thatcher, who was managing director of a paint firm. Do you remember the very first time you met him?

MT: I do. It was the night that I was adopted as candidate, and I thought that I must circulate after the meeting to get to know as many people as possible, and I missed the last train – so he was approached. Would he like to drive me back to London? Mercifully, he did like.

RP: How long afterwards were you married?

MT: Oh . . . that was 1949. Not until 1951.

RP: And two years after that, you took your Bar Intermediate in May, produced twins in August, and took your Bar Finals in December. That was an action-packed eight months.

P. L. Travers

In common with the majority of her millions of readers, I knew nothing about the author of *Mary Poppins* when I interviewed her, because she is a very retiring person who has never sought publicity.

RP: It'll probably be news to many of your readers that you are in fact female and that you shelter behind those two initials.

PLT: Yes, I do, like a bird in a nest. It's a kind of shyness, I suppose, and being anyway a private sort of person – not of the 'Hi Bill, meet Mike' kind – I felt I'd like to be as anonymous as possible. But don't, for goodness' sake, take that as humility. I would really like to have signed myself 'Anon' because, for me, it is Anon who writes the best poetry. So it would really be a gesture of arrogance to have done that.

RP: So at your own wish you're P. L. Travers. And you come from Australia.

PLT: Well, 'My mother bore me in the southern wild', as Blake says in one of the poems I have chosen. But I come, as you put it, from the countries of my Irish father and Scottish mother. I think I was born saying, 'Get me out of here', and most of my life has been lived in England.

RP: But you were brought up in Australia?

PLT: Yes, in the deep country, and looking back now I'm glad of it – the mystery of that hardly inhabited world, its ancientness, its lore, for all its apparent newness.

RP: Were you a bookworm?

PLT: A gourmandizer! There were few books for children.

Nothing was banned, though, so at an early age I read everything I could, from Shakespeare to a Victorian book called *Twelve Deathbed Scenes*, which I loved and longed to emulate.

RP: When you were very young you used to make up stories to tell your younger sisters.

PLT: Well, everybody does that, surely. I don't remember them all.

RP: I believe there's some evidence that one of your make-believe characters as a child was a Miss Poppins.

PLT: A sister says so. I think it's merely hindsight. But one of my childhood books which I still have has the name 'M. Poppins' scrawled on the flyleaf. Not in my writing. I can't think who put it there. Herself, perhaps.

RP: And you liked writing verses.

PLT: Well, I had articulate, poetry-loving parents. And anything either of them liked would find its way quickly to the general breakfast-table. I remember my mother showing a poem of mine to my father and him shrugging it off with, 'Hardly W. B. Yeats!' He measured everything by the best. But then I don't suppose even Yeats would have been W. B. Yeats at the age of six.

RP: So you showed signs of wanting to be a writer very early.

PLT: Oh, but not as a career. I don't have a career. I'm just a woman doing the things all women do and writing into the bargain. I never thought that books were actually written by people. No child does, I think, unless parents and teachers tell them. They are just there, like oranges and sunlight. I remember what a shock I got when Beatrix Potter died in 1943. I never even knew she'd been alive! 'Oh, I could have gone and knelt at her gate!' I said sorrowfully to a friend. 'She'd have swept you away with a broom,' he replied. Which would perhaps have been a proper gesture. Recently a young man, a stranger coming to interview me, ran into my studio, hands out, eyes alight: 'Oh, I'm so glad you're not dead!' he said. Wasn't that an honour? To have been thought not to be alive! To have been 'just there'!

RP: In your teens you began to send pieces and poems to magazines and newspapers, and with a very modest capital you decided to come to Britain.

PLT: Yes, I saved up my fare and arrived with ten pounds, five of which I promptly lost. This, like everything else I planned to do – sweep crossings like Little Joe in *Bleak House* if necessary – was held by my English relatives to be unsuitable and irresponsible.

RP: And of course you had to go to Ireland.

PLT: Of course, to see my father's people. But I had another reason. I had sent a poem with a stamped addressed envelope to A.E., on whose poetry, along with that of Yeats, I'd been brought up, and who was then editing the *Irish Statesman*. And I sent it with no covering letter. I wanted to be, as it were, naked. And, sure enough, the envelope came back, but with a cheque for two guineas and a letter from A.E. saying that nobody but an Irish person could have written such a poem, and if I was ever in Dublin would I come and see him? So of course I went and was soon surrounded by poets, not at all to the approval of my father's people, who did not like the idea of Fleet Street and as for me going round in Dublin with 'men who saw fairies' – well, poetry was all very well in books, but poets, they were another matter! However, I was not to be deterred. And that's why I have chosen poetry for my stay on your desert island. Schubert and Beethoven would make me feel lonely but to hear the words and the voices of my friends, known and unknown, would make it bearable. Such as A.E.'s 'Outcast':

> Sometimes when alone
> At the dark close of day
> Men meet an outlawed Majesty –
> And hurry away.

Maybe there I would meet that Majesty, and not hurry away. Where could I hurry to, anyway?

RP: Was A.E. – George W. Russell – a gregarious man?

PLT: He was certainly no hermit. One of his sayings was, 'You only love what is your own and what is your own you cannot lose.' People thronged to him, I among them, and through him I met Yeats and James Stephens and all that lot – a poet on every corner. Playwrights, too, one of whom I had been warned against. 'There's a terrible great boastful fellow – in Dublin or London, I don't know which,' said my uncle. 'If you meet him, be courteous but do not pursue the acquaintance. His name is George Bernard Shaw.' I never got the chance either to make or pursue that acquaintance. But Shaw was delighted with the story when A.E. eventually told it to him. So, as you see, it was a wonderful world to grow up in and be taken into.

RP: There is a story about your visit to Yeats' Isle of Innisfree – one of the poems you've chosen is about it.

PLT: Ah, one was so romantic then! When I asked the boatman on Lough Gill to take me to Innisfree he replied prosaically, 'It's Rat Island I'll take you to, begob, for that's its proper name.' So off I went to Rat Island, which you could have put into a small-sized room, and cut down branch after branch of rowans to take back to Yeats in Dublin. It was raining when I arrived at his door, looking like Burnham come to Dunsinane, already sick of my adventure and hoping Yeats would not answer the bell. But he did! He looked at me in shocked horror and said, 'Go down to the kitchen and be dried!' Well, I was dried and given cocoa, and I longed to go out at some back entrance and never be seen again. But a maid came and said, 'The master wants you.' Oh God, I thought, what would he say? 'Come and see my canary, she's laid an egg!' he cried. And then, of course, he became the Bard, not acting, just filling out his proper role. And so, with his arm about my shoulders he walked me round his library. 'Do you know how I write my poems?' he asked. If Moses had offered to explain his tablets, I couldn't have been more moved. 'I choose one of my books and then I read it and that inspires me to go on.' He took down a volume and read me the poem to Anne Gregory, glancing sideways at my newly dried head when he came to the lines:

> But only God, my dear,
> Can love you for yourself alone
> And not your yellow hair!

Which was fanciful but good to the ego. He once said to me in a crowded room, a journalist standing by of course, – and well he knew it! – 'Nothing matters to the young but Thermopylae.' Well, Thermopylae didn't matter to me then but later I got a glimpse of his meaning. T.S. Eliot, whose last part of 'Little Gidding' – 'And all shall be well, And all manner of thing shall be well' – I have chosen, never read me his serious poems, though he did quote to me from *Practical Cats*. Nor did Robert Frost ('Choose something like a star'), though it was his dog who ate the beautiful straw hat I had bought to wear when I met President Roosevelt. On the other hand, A.E. would expatiate at length on any poem. He said to me, when he heard of my plucking of the rowans, 'Well, I do hope you won't go cutting down all the willows at Dunfanaghy,' which was *his* favourite part of Ireland.

RP: Did Yeats decorate his library with your branches?

PLT: Not he. But I glimpsed, as I left him, a sprig of rowan in a glass on the table. Ha, I thought, he's teaching me a lesson. And I didn't then want to be taught – you don't when you are young. But later I saw the reason in it. You don't need branches. A little sprig will say it all, as a sonnet will gather into itself a whole epic. That's why I chose Gerald Manley Hopkins' 'The World is Charged with the Grandeur of God'. It would be short enough to say over and over again on the desert island and give me reassurance.

RP: Well, going back to *Mary Poppins*: in 1934, after an illness, you wrote a book, a magical book about a magical person. You've always been interested in fairy tales and folklore, haven't you?

PLT; Well, in myth, really, which comprehends everything – yes, since my earliest childhood.

RP: This book has brought delight to millions of children and grown-ups all over the world. What were you thinking of when you wrote it – were you picking up something from the stories you were told?

PLT: 'No cause, no cause,' as King Lear says in the last act. I just can't say, 'This is how it was.' I'd rather leave it in the Unknown, which is the homeland of all stories. Perhaps it was a message – everything one writes is a message to someone, maybe to myself. It's not primarily a children's book though I am grateful that children read it. And I never thought of it as something to be published, but a friend saw it half-written and took it to a publisher. And soon, so unexpectedly, there were eleven elderly gentlemen applying for the American rights.

RP: How many languages has it appeared in?

PLT: I'm told in *all*, but that's absurd. Lin Yu-Tang translated it into Chinese for his children; all the European languages; in Japan it is read in English classes. When I was in Japan studying Zen Buddhism a Zen master told me that every chapter had elements of Zen. I knew better than to ask which or why. Zen, like Poppins, never explains. It's in Hebrew too, which pleases me, the language of the Bible – and, absurdly, Swahili. Later, the Russians got hold of it and put it about in millions – but what's a million in Russia? A mere nothing. When my agent wrote and asked them, 'What about something for the author?' they replied that if the author would come to Moscow she would be royally treated. But I had already been to Moscow and did not believe that 'Moscow' and 'royal' were words that went well together.

RP: The book is set in Edwardian days, a typically English setting. That's not your own background at all.

PLT: Oh yes it is. In all that southern sunlight we lived, imaginatively, in the North. England was spoken of as 'home'. At that time, Ireland and Scotland and England, I remember, were thought of as one whole. One critic even called *Mary Poppins* 'a cornerstone of the British Empire'.

RP: It's also a very personal book because you have incorporated your own possessions and animals you knew.

PLT: Well, I never had a parrot-headed umbrella. But a maid we had was possessed of one and I was very displeased with my mother when she refused, saying it was unsuitable, to get one for herself. But no, it's not personal, not based on my childhood.

RP: Had you wanted a nanny like this? Was it a kind of dream?

PLT: Not at all. My dreams were of myth and poetry. On your Island I shall look for footprints and come at last on Man Friday and teach him some simple poems. Robert Louis Stevenson's 'Friendly Cow' for one – it's one of my chosen poems. The last verse goes:

And blown by all the winds that pass
And wet with all the showers
She walks amid the meadow grass
And eats the meadow flowers.

If that could be said of me I think I would die happy. Besides, who would ever have thought of sliding up the bannisters?

RP: You, for one. In 1964 *Mary Poppins* became a very successful film in the hands of Walt Disney. How much of a hand did you have in that film?

PLT: Well, I was shown the story-boards, which I did not think were much like my books, so I stayed about ten days in Hollywood talking with the artists and musicians and making an enormous tape of suggestions – in the hope, of course, that I would be allowed to write the definitive script. But Walt had never, he said, worked with an author, but he promised me to be true to the tape. He also said I was very vain to think I knew more about Mary Poppins than he did. 'Well,' I told him, 'vain or not, I do think it.' 'No,' he insisted, 'I'm entitled to my own vision and so is every other reader.' Well, I've always thought that a writer is only half of any book, the reader being the other half, so, thinking it over, I saw the logic of what he said. But I couldn't imagine how anyone could envisage her as a pretty soubrette making cinematographic magic. However, there it was – a very clever, very colourful film, and on its own terms the best Disney ever made, I think.

RP: Did you approve of the cast?

PLT: Well, Julie Andrews is a good trouper and I felt she had the necessary honesty for the part and that she would gladly have put on a black wig and turned up her nose if these things had been asked of her. But they weren't.

RP: It's still being shown all over the world.

PLT: So they tell me. I've seen it once or twice and lots of people enjoy it.

RP: Hollywood wasn't new territory for you, was it? You had lived in the United States for some years.

PLT: Yes, I went there during the war, doing odd things for the Office of War Information. I also spent two summers on an Indian reservation and was given an Indian name. Do not ask me what it is, for I am forbidden to tell it. Everyone there has a secret name which if disclosed to a stranger would bring bad luck both to me and the tribe. Then, after the war I went back and was Writer in Residence at three universities, Radcliffe, Smith College and Clare-mont on the West Coast.

RP: What does a Writer in Residence do?

PLT: You tell me! That's what I asked them. There I was at Radcliffe with a typewriter, reams of paper and not an obstacle in sight. I detest blank sheets of paper. I write everything on the backs of envelopes or bills. I do hope, since the Bible and Shakes-peare are already there that you will let me have for my book a bound collection of old envelopes, and of course a pen or two. I might then be able to write a book while I am on the Island. But at Radcliffe that was impossible. 'But what do I *do*?' I asked the Dean. 'Nothing. We just want to touch the hem of your garment.' 'How frightful,' I thought, 'I can't stay here. Jehovah would blush at that.' But then they asked me to receive students and to lecture, and things started to happen. I talked not to but *with* the students, many of whom are still dear friends.

RP: About Mary Poppins? And was your latest volume, *Mary Poppins in Cherry Tree Lane* then in the making?

PLT: Oh no. There have been two other books, *Friend Monkey* which transports Hanuman, the Monkey Lord in the great Hindu epic of the *Ramayana* to the last years of the nineteenth century; and *Two Pairs of Shoes* which retells two also very old stories – one from a collection that runs parallel with *The Arabian Nights* and the other from *The Mathnawi of Rumi*, the great Sufi poet – and lots of other writing and lectures since then. Yes, we talked about the character, but mostly of poetry and myth. American students make wonderful audiences. They ask questions and argue with you and show whether they like you or not. I am sure if they knew I was going to be wrecked on a desert island they would say, 'Well, be sure to wear something red. Then you can hang it on a coconut palm and a passing plane will notice it and you'll be rescued at last.' But, I ask myself, what if no plane ever passes? I would have to remember *Cymbeline*, and that

Golden lads and girls all must
Like chimney-sweepers come to dust.

And also keep my one luxury near me, the marble, two-foot high Buddha that I found leaning against a lamp-post outside an antique shop in the King's Road. He was going cheap because he had lost his topknot. He would be something comforting, as the last line of Robert Frost's poem has it, 'To stay my mind on and be stayed.' But no! An aeroplane *would* pass. I am on the side of life and would want to be here, whatever happens.

Maria von Trapp

Baroness Maria von Trapp, whose story inspired *The Sound of Music*, made a colourful figure in our studio, because she still likes to wear traditional Austrian costume.

RP: Baroness, I believe you were born in a train.

MVT: Yes. My mother visited relatives, and then she thought it looks as if it were going to be time, and got herself into a train and on the way to Vienna, where her husband expected her. I couldn't wait that long and so I appeared on the train. A conductor had nine children himself and knew all about it, and he played midwife. Then he begged my mother, practically on his knees, to please get off the train. He wanted to get rid of her. 'Go to hospital. You belong to a hospital now.' She said, 'No. My husband expects me with this train and I stay here.'

RP: She was a remarkable woman, your mother. Alas, you never knew her, did you?

MVT: No, she died when I was less than a year old.

RP: So you were brought up by foster parents. Were they kind to you?

MVT: Very.

RP: Did you see your father still?

MVT: Ja. My father had a very hard life. When he was a young engineer, he got married with a beautiful young wife from the Tyrol and, after a year, she presented him with a little boy and he was more happy. And, after another year, she died, and he was really heartsick. He took that baby to a cousin of his, to bring him up, and he disappeared. He sent money, and the money came from

Arabia and from India, from everywhere. After a few years, he appeared again, and he went to the cemetery to visit the grave of his beloved wife, in that mountain village in the Tyrol, and as he came out of the cemetery he had an eerie feeling that he was seeing things. His wife was coming to meet him! It was the little sister, who had been a baby when he had gotten married, and was now sixteen or seventeen. It was so overwhelming that, in no time, they got married, and were very happy. After a year, she presented him with a little girl, who was me. After another year, she died. For my father it was too much. He took that little baby to the same cousin where the boy had been brought up, and disappeared again. When I was six or seven years old, he returned to Vienna and, once a week I was allowed to visit him. I'm sorry that he didn't live longer, so I could have known a little more about him. He had a large apartment, and a whole room was full of twenty or thirty exotic little birds; and another room was practically full of instruments, each one of which he played. He must have been a very interesting person, but I was seven years old when he died, so I was too young really to find out much.

RP: At school, what did you want to be?

MVT: First of all, I wanted to have ten children, because I suffered so much from being an only child, and that should not happen ever again, you see. And I did get ten children. God was good.

RP: You decided to run away from your foster home.

MVT: After my father died I got a guardian, and I say right away to his excuse that he ended up in an insane asylum. He used to beat me mercilessly – for nothing, for every little something. I wasn't spanked, I was beaten. So when I was fourteen years old, I just left.

RP: Where did you go?

MVT: I went to a classmate on the other side of Vienna, in what I call now a tourist section. And I went from hotel to hotel, of which there were plenty, and offered my services as a teacher.

RP: A teacher of what?

MVT: Of anything. I like to teach, and I always wanted to be a teacher.

RP: But in hotels, did they need teachers?

MVT: Some of the kids needed – what do you call them?

RP: Tutors?

MVT: Tutors, *ja*. Well, I wasn't lucky. After I think twenty-eight hotels I still hadn't found something, so I started with the first hotel again and said, 'I offer my services for just anything.' And I was so lucky, because they needed – what is that word now? A tennis match needs somebody who . . .?

RP: An umpire?

MVT: An umpire, *ja*. And I was fresh enough to say yes.

RP: Did you know about tennis?

MVT: Absolutely nothing. But it worked – for ten days.

RP: What happened then?

MVT: Well, I never went back to my foster mother and guardian. I succeeded in the entrance examination to something brand-new in Austria, brand-new in the world – the State Teachers College for Progressive Education. And there I stayed for the next four years. I became a teacher, and I really loved it, and I still do.

RP: Where did you learn your music, because music means a great deal to you. Was it at school or at home?

MVT: In Austria, you don't learn music. You sing, you listen, and if you are good enough, you get lessons. Everybody sings. Everybody listens. It used to be the daily life.

RP: After college where did you go?

MVT: Well, comes a very dramatic moment. It is the custom in Austria that every graduation class makes a graduation trip, and we went to the Tyrol, into the glacier world. I was a good mountain climber, and on the last evening I was the last one. The professional guide was the first one who fastened the rope, and I was the last one who took it off the hook, and I was standing there for a moment, alone, and it was sunset, and this is something I wish everybody to see once, once in a lifetime – sunset in the glaciers. Colours you don't even know existed, you see changing in front of your eyes. It was so terrific, and I thought, 'All this God gave to me; what can I give Him?' And I had a tremendous idea: the best of the best is I give it right back to Him. I shall go to a convent, to a strict one, where I can never go out again. I shall never see this again. I give it back to Him. It doesn't sound logical,

see, but never mind; at that age you don't need to be logical. It
served my purpose. I gave something terrifically big to God. I
went down the mountains and out to Salzburg, asked my way to
the strictest convent in town, which was the Benedictine Abbey,
Nonnberg, and there I appeared. This was really funny. You have
to know the workings of a convent. It was such a strict one that
the parlour had a fence down the middle: on the one side were the
nuns and on the other side was the world – in this case, I. I had to
wait until Reverend Mother Abbess came, and she was very tiny
and very frail and very loving, and she said, 'What can I do for
you, my child?' And I stood there, with the rucksack and the rope
over my shoulder and the ice pick in my right hand, and in this
imposing position I announced, 'I have come to stay here.' This is
not usually the way to enter a convent, I found out later, but she
was so great that she took me – and for two blessed years those
darling nuns tried to turn a boy into a girl, and make a lady out of
that girl, which was awfully hard.

RP: What work did they give you to do? Were you teaching?

MVT: I was teaching. Well, one day, at the end of the two years, I
was called to see Reverend Mother Abbess, and that sounded not
good, so I took a long detour to go to her room, thinking hard,
Just what does she know? And when I came to her room, she said,
'Maria, I want to know how much you have learned in our house.
What is the most important thing in life?' I was so relieved that
this was all she wanted to know, because I really had learned that,
and so I said, with great conviction, 'The most important thing in
life is to find out what is the will of God, and then go and do it.'
'Even if it is hard?' she asked. 'Even if it is hard,' I said. And right
there and then I was told that a certain Navy captain, a Baron
George von Trapp, had been there seeing the nuns that morning,
asking whether they could lend him, *lend* him, a teacher for one
school year, because one of his children had had a bad case of
scarlet fever and had to be tutored at home – and all the nuns
together decided to send me. I was heartbroken. I really wanted
to stay. That was my place. But now I had to eat my words, you
see . . . Even if it is hard.

RP: You intended to take your vows and stay there for ever?

203

MVT: Yes, yes. And I was very close to it, to the finals, you see. So now I had to go, and Reverend Mother repeated several times, 'It's only *lent*.' So, I'm only lent – but I went out and never came back. The children I was to teach were aged from four to fourteen: two boys and five girls, and my special pupil was Maria, and she was twelve. There was a nursemaid for the little ones, and a tutor for the boys, and I was for the middle class. Before long, the other two left, and I had them all, and I loved and I loved them and they loved me. Then, three weeks before my year was over, the three little ones, who were four, six and eight years old, went to their father and said, 'Papa, we've talked it over, and the only way to keep her here for good' – her was me – 'is for you to marry her.' The father said, 'Well, I don't even know whether she likes me.' Now, I was standing in the big living-room on a ladder – what is that kind of ladder called?

RP: Step-ladder?

MVT: Step-ladder. In my left hand I held a bowl of luke-warm water, and in my right hand a little sponge, because the handbook of the German housewife said, 'In spring, a part of the spring cleaning is that you have to wash your chandelier with luke-warm water and a sponge. I was standing up there on the ladder when the kids came running in and said, 'Do you like our father?' I said, 'Of course I do.' They ran back and said to him, 'Of course she does.' That evening, I was back in the big living-room again, arranging flowers, and I had a peony in my right hand and a precious Copenhagen vase in my left hand, and the Captain came in and said, 'This is really very nice of you.' I stopped for a moment putting my peony into the vase, and said, 'What?' and he said, 'Aren't we engaged?' Down went that vase on the floor, and when he saw that I wasn't feeling engaged at all, his very, very beautiful dark eyes clouded over, and he looked sad. I thought, 'Well, how can I help him? I'm going to run and ask Reverend Mother for a message, and if she sends word that it is the will of God that I go back home in three weeks, then it will be easier for him to take.' So I left my peony ... there was no vase any more ... and ran into town, and up 144 steps to my abbey and told Reverend Mother. She disappeared, and I was sitting in the novitiate, and then she came back. She said she had called the whole community together, and they had prayed to the Holy Spirit for enlightenment, and they found out that it was much more important that these children get a new mother than that I go back to my abbey. With that I had to go home, hoping that when I arrived there the house would be dark and I wouldn't have to face anybody. Well, he was standing right there in the middle of the hall, and I ran over and put my head on his shoulder and said, 'They told me I have to marry you.'

RP: And that's how you got seven of the ten children you wanted, ready made. Was there a lot of music in the Captain's house?

MVT: Not when I came. To my great astonishment, these kids didn't sing. I had a guitar, and the very first evening we sat on the floor around the fireplace. We have those very, very beautiful Austrian folk songs – Austrian, not German – from the mountains, and I found to my great joy that all the children are very musical.

RP: Where had you learned to play the guitar? Did your father teach you, or was it at the convent?

MVT: Nowhere. You just take a guitar and play. There was a very big park around the house, with big meadows and gravelled paths, and these seven kids walked on those gravelled paths, which I found absolutely ridiculous. What are meadows for but to run over and play ball on? Nobody had climbed a tree yet, so I showed them how to.

RP: There was a Father Wasner who came on the scene.

MVT: We had a chapel in the house, and a priest coming to say Mass. One day, the bishop sent a new priest, a young one, and he was really music walking on two legs. He introduced us to the wonder-world of the music of Palestrina, Orlando di Lasso, Victoria and all the great masters. And he insisted that we sing by heart, so as not to bury our noses into music but to look at the conductor. In no time at all we sang very well. Eventually, the Saltzburg Festival came round again, and Lotte Lehmann – the great Lotte Lehmann – came to pay us a visit. We happened to be outside in the park, and there was a screen of pine trees, and behind that screen we were singing. She stopped and listened, and she got so excited. She said, 'You have to give a concert at the Festival', and the Baron said, 'My family will never be on the stage.' By saying this he proved that he was no prophet, because this is exactly what we did for the next twenty years. We said goodbye to our former life, to the beautiful estate we had lived in, to the eight servants we had, and we walked to the little railroad station and took a local train to Italy, and we arrived there as refugees.

RP: Leaving everything behind?

MVT: Leaving everything behind.

RP: Did Father Wasner go with you?

MVT: Yes. My husband and I went to the bishop and said, 'Would it be possible?' and the bishop looked out of the window and said, 'I think this is providential. It will prove very important for us here, that Father Wasner goes with you now', and it really did. After the war, when there was great need in Austria, we, with our concerts, were over half the world; all over the United States, Central and South America, Australia, the South Pacific. The American General of the Occupation Army in Salzburg wrote an official letter to the Trapp Family Singers – that's what we were called – asking whether we could do something for Austria, because the people were sick and hungry and desperate. I used to take that letter on the stage during the intermission of our concerts and read it to the people, and we were able to send £275,000 worth of goods.

RP: How many of you spoke English when you first went to America?

MVT: Some of the older children had a little basic school English, which doesn't help, because I remember in one of the schoolbooks it said, 'A grandmother is lying under a sofa.'

RP: Oh, we all know houses like that! Did you revisit Austria quite soon after the war ended?

MVT: I think it was 1949.

RP: What had happened to the house?

MVT: It had been first taken by the Nazis and then by the Russians, and it was badly ruined.

RP: Baroness, you discovered that you had talent as a writer, and you wrote the story of the Trapp Family Singers, which was made into a very successful German film, and since then there's been a musical stage version and an American film version.

MVT: *The Sound of Music.* You know, we never made money because I was too stupid to have a lawyer in time, so we hardly got anything. But many times within our life, where we mingle with the great, I see how difficult it is to be very rich and very good. You are one or the other. And God took over, you see, and avoided the getting-very-rich part. We never made it. We always had to work, and it was good. We enjoyed it, and we didn't fall into the traps which big money provides.

Fred Trueman

I know remarkably little about cricket, because at school I opted for shooting instead. On the rare occasions when I visit Lord's or the Oval, I am intimidated by the expertise which is being aired around me, and on village greens I am nervous that the blacksmith will smite a boundary which lands on me, if I should have become too drowsy in my deckchair to take smart evasive action. But if I have reservations about the game, I have none about the players, and all those whom I have interviewed have been gentle, philosophical and amusing.

RP: Fred, whereabouts in Yorkshire do you come from?

FT: I was born in a little village called Stainton, down near the bottom end of South Yorkshire. It's just the other side of Maltby, towards Bawtry.

RP: Your father was a miner, but you're not really from a mining family, are you?

FT: No, my father comes from a racing background.

RP: Horses?

FT: Yes, he was a buyer and seller; then in the late twenties, when things were bad because of the advent of the motor-car and with horse traffic starting to die, he moved into the Yorkshire coalfields. So that's where I was born.

RP: How many were you in the family?

FT: Seven or eight of us.

RP: So were times a bit tough?

FT: Oh yes, they were tough – but they were very happy times. That's the main thing, you know. Dad was a very conscientious

208

person when it came to the family. They came first – very much so.

RP: Did you help out by doing odd jobs?

FT: Yes, I used to go out picking potatoes in the winter, and topping and tailing turnips; and at harvest time I used to be stooking the sheaves when they came out of the binder: then we'd lift them into the old Dutch barns for stacking and threshing. Of course, seven bob a week was a lot of money.

RP: I've read somewhere that you used to go to church on Sundays three times.

FT: Oh, no arguing, yes. The choir in the morning, and then Sunday School in the afternoon, and then Sunday evening the choir again – and of course choir practice on Tuesdays and Thursdays.

RP: Did your father play cricket?

FT: Oh, yes, he loved it. The whole family did; we were brought up on it. I remember my father talking once about his father in ... it must have been the 1880s or thereabouts ... and he was asked to go to the Yorkshire nets, and when they told him what the pay was as a cricketer – as a fast bowler – he said that he couldn't afford to go and play cricket. Of course, it hasn't altered much nowadays, has it?

RP: So you are the third generation of fast bowlers.

FT: No, my father was a slow left-arm spin bowler, and left-hand bat. That's where I've become ambidextrous from.

RP: How early did he start you?

FT: Oh, I can remember playing a sort of cricket way back at three or four years of age; by five or six, I could bowl at a dustbin lid on two bricks. That's where I learnt to bowl.

RP: Your father was captain of the village team.

FT: Yes.

RP: And you played for your school. Your father wanted you to play for Maltby Cricket Club, but they turned you down.

FT: Well, yes. I went up to the nets to bowl a few people out, and in my pocket I'd got my five bob, which was the customary fee to join, and I was told quite straight that there was plenty of my sort up there already. So I went and joined a little club called Roach Abbey.

RP: Now Roach Abbey played Maltby Cricket Club, who had turned you down.

FT: That's right, yes.

RP: And what did you do to them?

FT: I think I got something like six wickets for eleven runs. I forget the figures now.

RP: You just about devastated Maltby Cricket Club.

FT: Then they tried to get me to play for them, but Dad said, 'He stays where he is. Anyway, you're too late; he's going to Sheffield United.' Which is where I went, under the coaching of one of my dearest and greatest friends, Cyril Turner, the old Yorkshire player, who passed on a few years ago.

RP: How old were you when the County Club began to take an interest?

FT: About sixteen. I was getting a lot of wickets in the local district – figures like six for one, and eight for thirteen, and eight for seven and six for two and . . .

RP: They're rather alarming figures. I believe the County Club sent you out on a Colts tour first.

FT: That was the Yorkshire Boys Under-18 team, and that's where I met Brian Close and Ray Illingworth. We were to become closely associated over a great number of years.

RP: For coaching you had to go to Leeds, which was quite expensive. Did the club help?

FT: Yes, they paid your bus fare and gave you ten bob. That was in the late forties, and what I liked about it was that it was always a new ten-bob note. That was the nice part.

RP: You were working at the pit by now.

FT: My father never wanted me or any of his family to go down a mine, but they wanted me to play for Yorkshire; I was doing one or two great things, and they wanted me to carry on. By then I had reached the age of eighteen, so they wanted me to get a reserved occupation, which I did – down the mines. Then in 1951 Yorkshire made a mistake. On one Monday afternoon they gave me my county cap, but a rule had just been passed giving you five pounds a week if you joined the forces, so on Tuesday afternoon I joined the RAF. I'd finished with the mines for ever. I always reckon if anybody wants a ton of coal they should go down and get their own.

RP: Then one day while you were in the RAF you had a telephone call to say that they'd applied for leave for you to play in your first Test.

FT: Yes, I was stationed at a place called Hemswell, in Lincolnshire, and I received this phone call, and I won't say on the air what I said to this person who rang up.

RP: You thought it was a hoax?

FT: I mean, I never dreamed of playing for England.

RP: Who was this against?

FT: This was 1952 – against India.

RP: And you just about murdered them that summer.

FT: Oh yes, I had a great time. I'll never forget that first Test match. I played in the Yorkshire versus Lancashire match on the Saturday, Monday and Tuesday; then we had the Wednesday off, and I stayed in a hotel in Harrogate – and that's where I first really got to know people like Denis Compton and Godfrey Evans and Trevor Bailey and Alec Bedser. England lost the toss, so we fielded, and the thing that stuck in my mind was, would I be nervous? I went down the steps to bowl my first ball for England, and I was absolutely shattered to find that the atmosphere of the Test Match against India was nothing to what I'd just been through, playing against the old enemy, Lancashire, because the atmosphere of a Yorkshire versus Lancashire match, especially in those days, was electric.

RP: Were you still in uniform when you went off for your first Test tour, against the West Indies?

FT: No, I was demobbed by then. I came out of the RAF in September 1953, and I went off to the West Indies in December.

RP: From what you've said in print, Yorkshire wasn't a very happy club in those days. The old sweats didn't really encourage the youngsters.

FT: I've never said they didn't encourage them, but they probably didn't help them as much as they should have done. I always thought we were in two, or possibly three, camps in one team.

RP: This was still the days of Gentlemen and Players, wasn't it?

FT: Oh yes, very much so. The last Gentlemen and Players match would be in about 1962 or 1963. There were lots of times the Amateurs stayed at a different hotel to you, and in some places they changed in a different dressing-room.

RP: So, in some ways, the early days weren't a very happy time for you.

FT: It was a bit hard, but when you'd had two years in the Forces you could accept discipline ... so long as that discipline was administered correctly.

RP: And when it wasn't? You had a reputation at that time for being a bit of a tearaway.

FT: Yes, I did – but I think that was because I didn't care who people were ... I told them what I thought – spoke straight. Yes, I probably made things a little difficult for myself, but at least I could put my head on the pillow at night and go to sleep with a clear conscience.

RP: You were offered terms by Lincoln City as a soccer player; were you tempted to do the double?

FT: Very tempted. I would have loved to have played soccer as well as cricket, but I was asked by certain people in the hierarchy to think of England and English cricket and my cricketing career, so I thought about it very seriously and I turned soccer down – and then they went off to Australia without me and left me at home for the winter without a job. So I finished up selling furniture.

RP: A long list of successes can get a bit monotonous, so we won't go into all the statistics, but basically you took over three hundred wickets in Test cricket, and that doesn't happen very often.

FT: No, there are only two bowlers that have ever done it, myself and a young man from the West Indies called Lance Gibbs; he's an off-spin bowler and a very fine bowler, and Lance beat me by two wickets. Of course, he played more Test matches than me, being a spin bowler, but he took the record – and I think that anyone that gets over three hundred wickets like Lance did to pass me – deserves it.

RP: How many hat-tricks were there in your career?

FT: I think I got four for Yorkshire: three against Nottingham, one of my favourite counties, and one against the MCC at Lord's. Of course, if you get a hat-trick at Lord's that is a great success, because Lord's is the home of cricket, the headquarters of world cricket, and a most beautiful place.

RP: Looking at the reference book again, your total number of wickets taken in first-class cricket was 2,302. It's said that you used to card index every batsman in your mind: you knew which way he was going to move, didn't you?

FT: Yes, I used to have this photographic memory. I was very lucky, you see; I used to field at leg slip or short leg and I used to watch their first movements. That stood me in great stead, fielding close to the wicket.

Peter Ustinov

I met Peter Ustinov first about thirty-five years ago, at a morning press showing of a film that was so abysmally silly that we formed a bond in suppressed derision. We have met many times since, and our meetings have always been occasions for hilarity. That is not to say that I do not admire the serious side of this gifted man.

RP: You travel a great deal, and I believe your travels started very early.

PU: They started pre-natally, really. I did an awful lot of travelling as extra weight. I think my embryonic state was started in Leningrad, and I was eventually born, after a narrow squeak in Amsterdam, in Swiss Cottage – Adelaide Road, to be precise.

RP: You went to Westminster, one of the most English schools where, in those days, the boys wore top hats and tail coats: were you bright at school?

PU: No, I was a matt finish on the whole. I once said that I thought British education was probably the best in the world if you could survive it; if you couldn't, there was nothing left for you but the Diplomatic Corps. I still feel that quite strongly on occasion.

RP: You were interested in writing and designing and acting and directing; why did you opt for drama?

PU: My mother's family are all painters, and inevitably a family of large size with a tradition of that sort tends to become a mutual admiration society – or a mutual condemnation society, which is just as bad. I was dying to do something slightly different from the rest of them. When I started, I had a letter from my great-uncle, Alexander Benois, saying, 'For centuries, our family has been prowling round the theatre: we have designed them, we have built them, we have painted scenery in them, we have composed and we have conducted – and at last one of us has had the sheer gall to climb upon the boards himself.'

RP: You went to drama school: looking back, do you think that was a good idea, or is a drama school, in the main, a waste of time?

PU: I think it was on the whole a good thing. I disagreed with many things there, and disagreeing in itself was good for me, as it was at Westminster and even at my preparatory school, Mr Gibbs's in Sloane Street.

RP: We know that your first engagement was at the Players Theatre doing a sort of variety turn: what was the first play you were in?

PU: The first play of all was an early version of Chekhov's *Uncle Vanya*, called *The Wood Demon*.

RP: Where did you do that?

PU: At the Barn Theatre at Sheer, in Surrey. I was wearing my grandfather's smoking jacket, which was my only real connection with the past on that occasion. The overture was the Polonaise from Tchaikovsky's *Eugene Onegin*, and I can't listen to it to this day without feeling stagefright. I don't suffer from it any more, but when I hear that music I remember the emotions of being on stage for the first time. I believe I had the first line, which was as difficult to remember as any of Chekhov's lines ... it was something like, 'Will anybody have any more ham?' Those things are very difficult to remember.

RP: You were playing a character part already.

PU: Oh, indeed I was.

RP: What was your first film job?

PU: It was in an absurd film called *Hullo Fame!* I was on a spangled ladder, together with other promising young people, climbing to the ceiling and waving. Jean Kent was on the next ladder, and she got to the top much quicker than I did.

RP: A sort of Busby Berkeley number?

PU: A Busby Berkeley number in a room ten feet by ten feet somewhere in Paddington. My second screen appearance was as Van der Lube in the Reichstag Trial in a film called *Mein Kampf*

– *My Crimes* in which the star, if I remember rightly, was none other than Hitler. I was a syphilitic wretch who was dragged into court and didn't say anything, and perhaps it was just as well.

RP: You had your first play put on when you were – what – nineteen?

PU: No, I wrote it when I was nineteen, and it went on in 1942, when I was twenty-one.

RP: By which time you had joined the Army, having been rejected for the Secret Service.

PU: I had indeed, although I hate to talk about my failures in this way. My father engineered a meeting for me with a gentleman who was supposed to be reading *The News-Chronicle*, which was then a popular Liberal newspaper, in front of Sloane Square Underground Station, which is there to this day, of course. I saw a man standing there who was very obviously not reading his paper but just looking at it, and I was supposed to go up to him and say, 'Excuse me, sir, can you guide me to no. 9, Eaton Square,' and he was supposed to say, 'I'm going in that very direction,' – and then we'd walk off. I did my bit, and the gentleman looked at me, searching my face for evidence of all sorts of things, and as we walked off he said, *'Parlez-vous Français?'* I said, *'Oui, monsieur.'* *'Sprechen-Sie Deutsch?'* he asked. *'Ja, mein Herr.'* 'Good man,' he said. And we walked a few paces, and then he said that I would be informed, and he walked away. I was really wanting to go in the same direction as he was going, but I thought a man in his line of country might hate to be followed, so I went deliberately in the other direction. After all my efforts, I was turned down, which disappointed me as a spy but gave me enormous encouragement as an actor because, he said, unfortunately my face would be very difficult to lose in a crowd.

RP: A very satisfactory reason to be rejected.

PU: Except that a theatrical impresario named Henry Sherek, whom you may remember . . .

RP: Yes, indeed I do.

PU: . . . and who weighed twice as much as me, was accepted, because evidently he would blend into any kind of background.

RP: Well, other talents of yours were pounced on, and you began to work in the Army Cinematographic Unit, with very distinguished people like Colonel David Niven and Captain Carol Reed, and you had a headquarters in the Ritz Hotel. It was said that you were a not-very-dashing private. That must have complicated your existence.

PU: Of course it did, if I had to interview a general. For a private, London was hell, because one had to salute everyone and the pavements are narrow. Bond Street was absolutely impossible. So I looked at myself in the mirror and reached certain conclusions. The greatcoat they had given me fitted me round the shoulders, but it was so long that it reached the ground. I put a safety-pin in the inside of my beret, so that it sucked the regimental badge into a kind of crevice, wore glasses, which I didn't need, all the time, smoked cigarettes in a long holder, and carried an empty attaché case around with me. I saluted nobody, whereas Poles of all ranks saluted me.

RP: For a while you pretended to be David Niven's batman, I believe.

PU: Well, under the establishment of the British Army, which hadn't changed since Waterloo, there was no possible way of a private and a colonel being together unless one was the batman of the other, so that I used to work on the script of the film which we were doing, which was called *The Way Ahead*, in the Ritz Hotel, with David hovering near the door. Occasionally, he'd say, 'Cave,' and I would throw the script aside and pick up his belt and start polishing it, and a general would look in and say, 'Morning', and we'd both say, 'Good morning,' and as soon as the general had gone, I'd throw the belt down on the floor and pick up the script again. It was a series of absurd situations.

RP: Still in your early twenties, you'd had several successful plays on in London and you'd directed a film or two: it was all happening very early. Haven't you since found the Boy Wonder image rather hard to live up to?

PU: Well, thank God the boy has gone out of the door now and forever, and the Wonder with him. Yes, I found it a big nuisance, and I really think it's deceptive. I'm convinced that I haven't changed much since then, and that I say more or less the same things I have always said. The only thing is that now I look different, people listen to me with the respect due to an old mogul, whereas they'd treated me as an upstart because I said the same things far too early. That was something I had to live with.

RP: Are you still ambitious?

PU: I'm ambitious to do things better than I have done. I'm not in a hurry any more; I think life seems much longer as you get older than it did when you were young. Oh, I was in a tremendous hurry.

RP: Which of your plays is your favourite?

PU: I don't know. I think probably *Photo Finish* is, in a way. I think it went further than the others and, of course, was tremendously experimental, in spite of the fact that it was absolutely naturalistic to look at. A play running on four different levels at once is a technical accomplishment of which I'm rather proud, because it actually works when you see it – and I've seen it in the most extraordinary countries. Really, I hate saying which is my favourite play, because there was one more recently, called *Half-way up the Tree*, which I was told by the critics, and even partially by the public, not to be terribly proud of – but it was all right. It was played very skilfully in London by Robert Morley, and ran a long time; it was a disaster in Paris; it went well in Germany but not terribly well in America, and I was told it was a lightweight piece. Then I saw it the other day in Leningrad, played by people who obviously hadn't had the benefit of my advice – because I had no idea they were going to do it, and I can only tell you that I really saw the play as it was written for the first time. At the end, I began to look at it as though it had been written by somebody completely different: they hadn't changed a word, and it was marvellous. They played it terribly seriously, as though it were Chekhov. After a rather solemn first ten minutes, when I thought, my goodness, what are they doing, people began laughing absolutely helplessly at it, and it became the funniest play I've ever written – and yet absolutely of one piece, with no inconsistencies.

RP: Does a bad criticism hurt you?

PU: Certainly it does if it's unjustified. But the first sign of maturity as you're growing up is to learn to live with injustice, because there's no arbiter for these things.

RP: Changing the subject, you've directed a number of operas. Do you find that rewarding and exciting?

PU: Between ourselves, it's a very difficult job to do, simply because you're dealing with singers who, of course, know their parts in a most commendable way. I mean, you very seldom find straight actors who are so up on their parts at the first rehearsal – in fact, you never do. So at the opera, you say, 'This is marvellous.' Then you come to your second day of rehearsal, and it's all exactly the same as the first, because in the meantime they've sung *Carmen* and they've forgotten everything that you've told them. And so it goes on until the end. There are some opera performers who are better singers than actors, and there are others who are good at both; there are a few who are not terribly good at either, and there are others who are so hardened in their profession that they roll with your punch and then, on the first night, when you can't get at them, do exactly what they've always done. So that one starts out, usually, euphorically; by the end, you're thoroughly depressed, and then Mozart, or whoever it is, gallops to the rescue, because you've really rather forgotten the music.

RP: You devote a lot of time to UNICEF.

PU: Yes, I'm a sort of ambassador at large. I even have a little certificate which clips into my passport and which produces different results in different places. In Finland, they put out the red carpet, and I don't even have to go through customs; in San Francisco, they look at it, and they say, 'You'd better open all this baggage.' So it shows that, on occasion, the United Nations themselves are not taken with the seriousness that they deserve.

Natalie Wood

❧❧❧❧❧❧❧
·

This dark-haired film actress with large eyes and a mouth that turned-up delightfully at the corners was, I believe, my most attractive castaway. She was devoid of any sense of self-impor-tance, and had a lovely sense of fun. It is sad that print cannot convey the hilarious impression of a Mexican spitfire with which she embellished the story of the making of *The Burning Hills*. The few hours I spent with her were joyous. Eighteen months later, she drowned in a tragic boating accident off Catalina Island.

RP: You are Russian by parentage?
NW: That's right, though I was born in America. My parents left Russia when they were very young – they were four or five years old. It was during the Revolution, and my mother's family left and went to China, where she lived until she was a teenager, and my father's family went to Vancouver, and eventually they both wound up in San Francisco, and that's where my parents met and got married, and that's where I was born.
RP: Your father was in the film business.
NW: Yes, he was. He used to build miniature sets.
RP: And your mother?
NW: Well, my mother took ballet lessons, but she never was a professional. I think in many ways the fact that I became an actress ... she enjoyed watching it happen, because she had never had a career of her own.
RP: It's hard to believe, but you're a veteran actress. You began at the age of – what was it – four?

NW: Yes, when I was four I did a little bit part, and then I had my first real part when I was five.

RP: Then a whole lot more films followed. Orson Welles, who like all actors doesn't like acting with children, goes on record as saying, 'You were terrifying.'

NW: I hope he was joking.

RP: Obviously you had to be educated. You had lessons on the set, did you?

NW: That's right. By American law a minor, up until the age of eighteen, can only work eight hours a day. Three of those hours have to be devoted to school, then there's an hour for lunch, which leaves four hours of working time.

RP: How many other children were in those lessons?

NW: I was very often alone – so I was often privately tutored.

RP: Pretty miserable?

NW: Well, in between films I would go to a regular school, and I was always quite a bit ahead of the class. I graduated at High School a couple of years early, because of the private tutoring, you see.

RP: Didn't you feel that you were missing a lot of the fun of being a child?

NW: I wasn't aware of it at the time. I mean, I guess I wasn't aware that other kids did other things. I did feel a bit of a misfit at Junior High School, when I was about twelve, because I was so comfortable with adults and rather uncomfortable with kids, having not been around with very many.

RP: How do you feel now when they run one of your early films on television, and you see this little moppet acting away? Can you identify?

NW: Sometimes I do, because on some films, the Orson Welles one for example, I remember very vividly most of the events of the whole thing; I suppose it made a great impression on me. There are certain other films I remember for different reasons. I did a film called *Scudda Hoo, Scudda Hay*, in which I played this tomboy, and I had great fun because we filmed most of it on the Fox ranch, and I was catching turtles and feeding the chickens and swimming in the river and all that, but there are other pictures

221

that I only dimly remember even though I was older when I made them, and I suppose at that time I must have been interested in other things, and so my primary focus wasn't on them.

RP: You must be almost unique, Natalie, in that there was no break in your career; you went right through from child to adolescent to grown-up.

NW: I guess that is quite unusual. I think luck plays a great part in being able to make the transitions. A very good film called *Rebel Without A Cause* came along while I was just a teenager, and the part had such range and depth that it kind of opened the door for me to be thought of as a serious actress, as an adult actress.

RP: How old were you – sixteen?

NW: Fifteen. I was sixteen when it was released.

RP: And you played opposite that cult figure, James Dean. How do you remember him?

NW: I remember him very sweetly, I don't see him as this doomed self-destructive figure that many people see him as. I didn't see that side of him; perhaps I was too young.

RP: He wasn't moody on the set?

NW: He seemed introspective and quiet, but he was always very accessible and friendly, and he was always very considerate of other people. I remember when we were filming at the Planitarium, there were a lot of fans grouped around, and he took great pains when he signed their autographs to try to find out a little bit about them and get to know, and he was never arrogant or big starish. I remember him very fondly.

RP: How many big screen pictures have you made altogether?

NW: Forty-four or forty-five.

RP: In the early days, you'd always worked independently – for any studio that hired you: after *Rebel Without A Cause*, you signed a contract with Warner Brothers, but that didn't altogether work out.

NW: Actually, I was under contract on two occasions before, but as you say I was put under contract to Warner Brothers, and I did a few films and then I sort of went on strike. I presume that's what you're referring to.

RP: The story is that you were on the payroll at about $750, and Warners were loaning you out at several hundred thousand which must have made you hopping mad.

NW: I thought that was fair enough, because they'd given me this chance in *Rebel Without A Cause*, for which I was very grateful, but I felt they were trying to make me do films that I just didn't like. Sometimes we did three or four pictures a year, and I wanted the right to be able to pick one for myself and to keep the money for that one.

RP: Did you win?

NW: I finally won, after about eighteen months on strike, and the only reason I won was because Elia Kazan insisted that he needed me to be in *Splendour in the Grass*.

RP: A nice man, Kazan.

NW: A wonderful man. That was a lovely film, and a wonderful, wonderful experience. To work with Kazan was the epitome, I think it still would be, but it was particularly then, aged twenty, to be able to work with the greatest actors' director in the world – and *Splendour* was different because we didn't shoot any of it in Hollywood. We shot in upstate New York, and we did some in a studio in New York City, and it was all East Coast based. And all the other locations, like the waterfalls, were real; and I've always found that when films are shot that way it's so much better for the actors, because you can concentrate so much more, there are fewer distractions.

RP: You won your upset with Warner Brothers. Jack Warner must have been quite a man to argue with.

NW: The funny thing about it was that we never, ever argued personally. These arguments were all carried on through lawyers, and when we met at parties he was always very polite, and he'd say, 'Hello, Natalie darling, how are you?' And I'd say, 'Hello, Mr Warner, how are you?' On my birthday, he'd send me lovely flowers, and on his birthday I'd send him a bottle of Jack Daniels, and there were little notes back and forth, 'Thank you so much for the lovely flowers', and 'Thank you so much for remembering my birthday', and meanwhile the lawyers were saying that he was saying, through them, 'This child will only work again over my dead body, blah, blah, blah ...' But eventually it got settled and there had never been a cross word between us.

RP: During the Warners era, you did a lot of Westerns. That must have been fun.

NW: Yes, it was great fun. I did one which was quite crazy in a way. It was called *The Burning Hills*, and I was supposed to be a Mexican spitfire, and throughout the filming they could never decide whether I should be doing this with or without an accent, so part of the film was with a Mexican accent and part of the film was without, and finally, at the end, after great deliberation, they decided that I should have the accent after all, so I had to post-record the whole film with this thick Mexican accent.

RP: Which was the first picture you were allowed to choose on your own, without being told what to do?

NW: *West Side Story*.

RP: We will murmur the fact that someone else's singing voice was used.

NW: In *West Side Story*, yes – but in *Gypsy*, which I did afterwards, I did all my own singing.

RP: Well done. Now, you weren't a dancer, so you must have ached all over after that *West Side Story* stuff.

NW: Well, my mother had seen to it that I had a lot of ballet training when I was young, so it wasn't too difficult, but it was quite a rigorous schedule. As a matter of fact, I finished filming *Splendour in the Grass* on a Friday, flew to California on the Saturday, and started dance rehearsals on Sunday for *West Side Story*, which had about an eight-month shooting schedule. The funny thing was, while I was doing *West Side Story* I had no idea that I was going to be offered *Gypsy*, but I just loved that score and all day long in the trailer I would play the songs. It was one of the very nice things that Jack Warner did when he let me play that without any fuss.

RP: You've never done any theatre work.

NW: Unluckily, unhappily I never have. I would very much like to. I couldn't do it now, at least not in New York, because of my life and my husband's work being in California. So I have recently, during the last year or so, been speaking to the people at the Music Centre and hoping to do, preferably, a new play, perhaps at the Mark Taper where they do awfully good work. There've been quite a few revivals that I've been offered at the Armundsen – *Cat on a Hot Tin Roof* and *Streetcar Named Desire* and a few others – but I'd rather like to do a new play if possible.

224

RP: You did *Cat on a Hot Tin Roof* on television, didn't you?

NW: Yes, here in London, with Lord Olivier, and it was a wonderful experience, because it was the closest feeling I've had to doing a play. Although it was for television, we rehearsed it for four weeks and it wasn't on film but on tape, which meant that with four cameras we could do very, very long takes; in fact, we practically did an act at a time.

RP: A lot of your work in recent years has been in television films, although there was a big disaster film I remember. What was the disaster? I didn't see it.

NW: It was a disaster; it was called *Meteor*.

RP: You mean the movie was a disaster?

NW: Yes. I played a Russian translator and, although I spoke Russian as a child, I felt that to play that part I should study up, so I took about three months of lessons, which was the only time I have ever studied it formally. And soon after that I went to Russia for the first time. Peter Ustinov and I did a programme for the BBC about the Hermitage Museum.

RP: Yes, that was marvellous. You conducted us through all those treasures in the old Winter Palace of Catherine the Great. Thirteen miles of galleries, you said.

NW: It was really quite an experience.

RP: Is your Russian as good as Peter's – or better?

NW: Well, I don't know. I would say our Russian is about equal.

Barbara Woodhouse

Very occasionally, someone far removed from show business becomes a star of radio and television. It can be a gardener, a sportsman, a naturalist or, in the case of Mrs Woodhouse, a dog trainer and owner.

But, of course, she is far more than that, as you will learn from her interview.

RP: Do you consider yourself a country girl?

BW: Oh, absolutely. My mother used to call me a horny-handed member of the soil, because that's where she really thought I belonged – and I do. I've been mad on animals and farming all my life, and I farmed for twenty-one years.

RP: As a child, you used to ride a heifer.

BW: Oh, I have even when I've been grown-up; I've ridden my cows when they didn't give milk any more. My daughter's ridden her pony, and I've gone out on a cow. I never see why poor cows should be left to end their days just grazing. Why shouldn't they come out and see the world? When I was a little girl, we didn't have a pony, so I saddled the heifer and she jumped beautifully. My ambition was to go to the White City against Pat Moss.

RP: Surely a heifer isn't very comfortable to ride.

BW: You have a saddle – but their heads are very low; when they jump, they put their heads on the ground when they land. You must be careful and lean back. A heifer can easily jump well over five feet from a standstill; they're better than horses.

RP: You went to an agricultural college; what then?

BW: So many things. I ran a riding school, and later I went to the

226

Argentine, and then I came home and we imported polo ponies, and I played polo at Oxford.

RP: Let's take it step by step. I have a note here that you bought a pony for thirty shillings.

BW: It was sold in the market for thirty shillings because nobody could break it. It chucked me off three times, but the third time I landed with my legs just behind its ears, and that stumped it, because I weighed quite a bit and it couldn't do anything. It was only a tiny pony, and afterwards it became a very nice little animal, and in my riding school it taught all the two-year-olds.

RP: Your riding school got quite big, didn't it?

BW: Oh, it was enormous. I had seventeen horses, and I used to teach all the undergraduates and all sorts of famous people.

RP: Then you began to board dogs.

BW: I had twenty-six dogs, and I used to take them all out in the orchard and train them, so that when their owners came for them they were all beautifully trained. Unfortunately, they got to love me too much, and after they'd gone home they'd all came back. In the end, the owners used to ring up and use bad language and say, 'You can keep the something dog; it doesn't love us any more.' I gave up because of that.

RP: Now – the Argentine.

BW: Where, of course, I had all the horses that I wanted; there were six thousand on the estancia I went to. I was only there as a visitor, but I was given the job of breaking them in for the company. They paid me ten shillings a head to·break my neck or break in the horse.

RP: Was it there that you started this hazardous business, which you've talked about, of making friends with a horse by blowing up its nostrils?

BW: That's not hazardous at all, it's an ordinary greeting in horse language. You blow down your nose, a horse comes up and breathes up yours and thinks you're just another horse and likes to go with you everywhere. They'll never chuck you off. I've never been chucked off by an unbroken horse, but I've been chucked off many times by a broken horse with a lot of vice and wickedness. An unbroken horse has no reason to hate human beings; it's human

227

beings that make horses dislike them, with their cruelty, with their awful bits, their bad hands and their spurs, and making them do endless things that are really not natural to a horse.

RP: The voice plays a great part in training animals, doesn't it?

BW: The voice is nearly everything. Animals understand the tone of voice because that's how they communicate; the birds with their songs and their territory threats, dogs with their whines and their barks.

RP: Your adventures in the Argentine included being at the centre of a whirlwind, getting tangled up in a small-pox epidemic, and catching foot and mouth disease. I didn't know that happened to a human.

BW: It does, but not in quite the same way as it does to cattle; the feet don't get it, but your mouth gets the most enormous blister and your saliva runs exactly like a tap. For ten days, you have to wrap towels round your neck to catch the saliva, and if you ever try to sleep or lie down you'd be choked. It's terribly painful, but after ten days it goes and you'll never catch it again. I caught it by drinking milk from a cow that had the disease, because they don't put them down in the Argentine. In fact, those are the ones that fatten the best.

RP: You were also honorary vet on the ranch, and in fact doctor for the community.

BW: I stitched up a horse once that had torn its skin right down from its eyes to its nose, with an ordinary darning needle. People were always coming to me because they thought the English-woman probably knew. Believe me, the Englishwoman didn't know, but I'd done two years of vet. Once I stitched up a couple of natives who'd knifed each other. I didn't know where all their gut went, because it was all hanging out, but I put it back and sewed them up as I thought it should be, and they were taken sixty miles to hospital on a bullock cart, and when they got there, the medicos had a look inside, said, 'It's okay', stitched them up again and sent them back.

RP: Well done. How long were you there?

BW: Nearly four years. I'd had enough by the time I came back.

RP: What did you do then?

BW: I bought and sold horses.

RP: Successfully?

BW: Very successfully. The funniest thing I ever did was resell a man his own horse. I bought it in the morning as a rogue and sold it back to him in the afternoon as a perfect horse. I clipped it out and titivated it, and he paid me £40 more than I'd paid him in the morning. He had a good laugh in the end.

RP: Then you started the farm.

BW: Yes, I had the top cows in the Bucks and Herts show, the top milk yields for twenty-one years, and they were Guernseys. Again, I bought only cheap ones, because we didn't have much money. Complete strangers used to send me blank cheques and tell me to go and buy their herd for them. I had great fun buying cattle for people.

RP: Which was the first important dog in your life?

BW: A gorgeous, terribly nervous Alsatian which was given to me because it was going to be put down. It had one ear flat and one ear up, and I called it Kazan, after a lovely book about the Wild. If ever I was missing, I was in Kazan's kennel. I just lived with him all the time when I wasn't at school. I hated school, anyway. I was very ill one day and taken to hospital, and Kazan died of a broken heart. He was only two.

RP: You've been especially devoted to Great Danes.

BW: Yes. There again, it was a sad dog that was given to me in the first place because she was going to be put down. Her name was Jean and I took her to the Argentine with me, and she died at thirteen and a half.

RP: Several of your dogs had successful careers in films.

BW: Yes, they were known as 'Take One' Juno and Junia in every big studio in the country. They never had to be spoken to, never given signals: they picked everything up by telepathy. When Juno died, I got cables from all over the world.

RP: Is there any particular canine performance that you remember?

BW: Well, a brave one, when Juno was doing a sketch with Morecambe and Wise. She was waiting to go on and pretend to attack them, when a studio hand passed carrying a 25 lb weight which they use to brace scenery up with. By mistake, he hit her on the jaw. She hesitated for a second, but then went straight on to play her scene. When she came off, she had the most enormous lump on her jaw that you've ever seen – but the show went on.

RP: Of course, you've produced films yourself.

BW: Yes, I met a cameraman at Pinewood who said he was going to be out of work, and I said, 'Well, come on, let's go and make films.' So we set off with my two children, who were then six and seven, and my dog, made up the script as we went along, and the films were on distribution for twenty-one years, ending up on the children's Saturday morning shows.

RP: The dog training you do on television – did that start with road safety lectures?

BW: It started when I went to an agricultural show and saw a dog doing obedience training. I went home and tried it on my Great Dane, and she did it so well that I put her into competitions. She won a lot of major competitions, and then I started a club of my own. It ended up that I trained seven thousand people in seven clubs, one each day of the week.

RP: It's very important that dogs are trained. In this country there are – how many million?

BW: Five and a half million – and getting a very bad name because of people saying horrible things about them which are quite unnecessary. Well-behaved dogs are made by well-behaved own-ers, and, if the owners have the right ideas, then dogs need be offensive to no one.

RP: What about putting on a walloping great licence fee? Would that make the owners appreciate them more and take better care?

BW: No, they just wouldn't have the dogs, or they'd chuck them out and they'd all be strays or something. I think, more wardens – and an on-the-pavement fine like they have in New York. Every dog owner carries a spade to clean up in New York.

RP: Is every dog trainable?

BW: Far from it, I'm sorry to say. There are an awful lot of mental dogs in the country today because they live such awful lives, full of stress. They're left at eight-thirty in the morning when their owners go to work, and they don't see them again until five in the evening, and lots of them are fed all wrongly these days and they're getting schizophrenia.

RP: You claim to train a dog in six minutes.

BW: Yes.

RP: Is that really possible?

BW: Oh yes, I do that in public all the time. In basic obedience, it's very easy. With the right tone of voice and the right signals you can get them to walk to heel, sit, lie down, wait and come, in six minutes, and I've taken the challenge many times.

RP: Barbara, you've written a number of books, none of which is issued by a professional publisher. How do you manage that and how did it start?

BW: I decided to do it myself, hoping that I'd have fun out of it and perhaps produce more sales, because I think very often in publishing they bring a book out and then they forget the old titles, and it's always that they have so many new ones that we get forgotten. So I decided to do it myself. I know nearly all the book-buyers in the country and I used to go trotting round. I'm sure some of them thought, 'Poor old girl, she can't sell her book, we'll take a copy.'

RP: You used to go to all the bookshops, all over the United Kingdom.

BW: Oh yes, I know them all – but I don't have to do that now, because it's them who have to ask me for my books now, instead of me begging them to buy. It's been an experience, and I can recommend it to anyone who wants a challenge.

RP: Fine, cut out the middleman. Barbara, you are one of those people with a degree of extra-sensory perception, aren't you.

BW: Oh yes, I know the future very often, and I can always pick people and dogs and things up by telepathy and the dogs do exactly what I want. In one class I said, 'Now, we won't say sit, come, stay, wait and so on; we'll use vegetable names – asparagus, carrots, onions and cauliflowers, but you'll be thinking what the dog is going to do,' and every dog obeyed. If you said carrots, it sat, if you said asparagus, it lay down – and so it shows it doesn't matter what you say. On television the other day, I spoke in Spanish to a dog: I had never done it before, not in Spanish, and the dog obeyed me perfectly. We decided what we wanted the dog to do, and I gave it the Spanish words and not the English, so it shows that it's what you're thinking that matters. So it's no good calling your dog in a nice voice, as I've told you to do, and then be thinking, 'The beastly brute, I hate it for not coming', because the dog picks up what you're thinking, and won't come. You've got to have nice thoughts, if you want to train a dog.

RP: Do you have the same gift with people?

BW: Oh yes, I'm always picking up people. I save on my telephone bill by doing that. I pick on a friend to telephone me, and within ten minutes she'll do it. My children do exactly the same. My husband is a doctor, and I used to know what was wrong with people when they telephoned. I had the telephone by my bed and always answered the night calls, and I would tell my husband what was wrong with the patients. One day he said to me, 'Well, is it bad? Do you think I ought to go?' and I said, 'Oh no, it isn't' – but he went all the same; he wasn't going to trust my ESP. But it always works. I was once talking at a meeting of a ladies' club, and I said I always knew what was wrong with humans and what was wrong with dogs, and a lady at the back of the hall said, 'What's wrong with my husband?' and I said, 'Madam, your husband has cancer of the jaw', and she said, 'Yes, that's right.' Well, how did I know? It's a horrid gift; I wish I hadn't got it.

RP: You had a premonition of a railway crash once.

BW: Oh yes, my husband always travelled on a certain train, and I told him not to go on it one morning, because it was going to crash. I tried to warn the station master, but they just thought there was another lunatic on the telephone. 'Don't worry, madam, we take great care of our passengers,' but they didn't. The train did crash, and there were a lot of casualties, and it was very sad – but I saved my husband from going on it.

Who Chose What

Catalogue numbers of discs have not been included, because they can so often be misleading. Popular recordings are frequently issued several times and on several different labels, and there is no guarantee that the actual disc used in any programme was the most recently issued. Readers wishing to acquire any listed discs should consult their local dealer, giving the title of the work and the artists concerned: the dealer can then refer to the current catalogues to see if the disc is still available (the performer's name appears in brackets after the title of the piece).

The asterisked record in each case is the one the castaway would have if only one disc could be taken to the island.

Jeffrey Archer   31 January 1981

*Lennon/McCartney *Help* (The Beatles)

Armstrong *Brother Bill* (Bing Crosby and Louis Armstrong)

Beethoven *Symphony No. 9* (Berlin Philharmonic Orchestra and Chorus conducted by Herbert von Karajan)

Coward *A Bar on the Piccola Marina* (Noël Coward)

John/Taupin *Candle in the Wind* (Elton John)

Nino Rota *Incidental Music to 'Much Ado About Nothing'* (National Theatre Ensemble)

It's Hard to be Humble (Mac Davis)

Weelkes *Hosanna to the Son of David* (Choir of St John's College, Cambridge)

The luxury: A plasticine figure of Roy Plomley with a supply of pins

The book: Fred Uhlman *The Reunion*

Lauren Bacall   3 March 1979

Gershwin *Isn't it a Pity?* (Ella Fitzgerald)

Rachmaninov *Piano Concerto No. 2* (Sergei Rachmaninov with the Philadelphia Orchestra conducted by Leopold Stokowski)

*Shakespeare *Sonnet 130* (Sir John Gielgud)

Moszkowski *Etude in A flat* (Vladimir Horowitz)

Brahms *Violin Concerto in D* (Isaac Stern with the Philadelphia Orchestra conducted by Eugene Ormandy)

Coward *Has Anybody Seen Our Ship?* (*Red Peppers*) (Noël Coward and Gertrude Lawrence)

When the World Was Young (Nat King Cole)

Puccini *O Soave Fanciulla (La Bohème)* (Montserrat Caballé and Placido Domingo with the London Philharmonic Orchestra conducted by Sir Georg Solti)
The luxury: Sun-tan lotion
The book: John Cheever *Short Stories*

Lieutenant-Colonel John Blashford-Snell   30 October 1976
Theodorakis *Zorba the Greek* (Orchestra conducted by Mikis Theodorakis)
Jarre *Lawrence of Arabia* (Ron Goodwin and his Orchestra)
Le Clerq *He Played His Ukelele as the Ship Went Down* (Ambrose and his Orchestra)
Hurrah for the C.R.E. (Band of the Corps of Royal Engineers and Chorus)
Diamond *Skybird* (Neil Diamond)
Dvořák *Symphony No. 9* (London Symphony Orchestra conducted by Istvan Kertesz)
Trad. arr. Fairbairn *Amazing Grace* (Pipes and Drums and Military Band of the Royal Scots Dragoon Guards)
★Elgar *Land of Hope and Glory* (BBC Chorus and Choral Society with the BBC Symphony Orchestra conducted by Colin Davis)
The luxury: A case of malt Scotch whisky
The book: Rudyard Kipling *Complete Works*

Mel Brooks   1 July 1978
Porter *Begin the Beguine* (Artie Shaw and his Orchestra)
Beethoven *Symphony No. 5* (NBC Symphony Orchestra conducted by Arturo Toscanini)
★Washington/Young *Can't We Talk it Over?* (Bing Crosby)
Chopin *Prelude No. 4 in E Minor, Opus 28* (Artur Rubinstein)
Mann/Hilliard *In the Wee Small Hours of the Morning* (Frank Sinatra)
Bach *Brandenburg Concerto No. 3* (Bath Festival Chamber Orchestra directed by Yehudi Menuhin (violin))
Kern/Robin *In Love in Vain* (Dick Haymes and Helen Forrest)

Brooks *Springtime for Hitler (from the film The Producers)*
The luxury: A case of Château Lafite-Rothschild 1945
The book: Stendhal *The Charterhouse of Parma*

James Cameron   27 March 1979
Look and Learn Japanese No. 1 from *A Course in Japanese*
Granados arr. Williams *Spanish Dance No. 5* (John Williams)
Bach arr. Segovia *Gavotte from Sonata in E* (Segovia)
Sirba Lui Pompieru Si Am Mindra Mitifica (Gheorghe Zamfir (pan-
    pipes) and his Orchestra)
Straacke *Forty-third Ward* (Win Straacke)
*Dylan Thomas *Under Milk Wood* (Richard Burton)
We Shall Overcome (Pete Seeger)
Sousa *Washington Post March* (United States Navy Band)
The luxury: A case of malt whisky
The book: Lawrence Sterne *Tristram Shandy*

Arthur C. Clarke   23 July 1977
*Elgar *Violin Concerto* (Yehudi Menuhin with the London Sym-
    phony Orchestra conducted by Sir Edward Elgar)
Grieg *Piano Concerto* (Solomon with the Philharmonia Orchestra
    conducted by Herbert Menges)
Vaughan Williams *Symphony No. 7* (London Philharmonic Choir
    and Orchestra conducted by Sir Adrian Boult)
Rachmaninov *Piano Concerto No. 3* (Sergei Rachmaninov with
    the Philadelphia Orchestra conducted by Eugene Ormandy)
R. Strauss *Also Sprach Zarathustra* (Berlin Philharmonic Orchestra
    conducted by Karl Böhm)
Sibelius *Symphony No. 2* (Philharmonia Orchestra conducted by
    Herbert von Karajan)
Beethoven *Symphony No. 9* (Four soloists with the Vienna Sing-
    verein and the Berlin Philharmonic Orchestra conducted by
    Herbert von Karajan)
Bach arr. Stokowski *Toccata and Fugue in D minor (BWV565)*
    (Czech Philharmonic Orchestra conducted by Leopold Sto-
    kowski)

The luxury: Solar-powered short-wave radio
The book: *Palgrave* Golden Treasury

Tom Conti   22 November 1980
Handel *Where'er You Walk* (Kenneth McKellar with the Royal
  Opera House Orchestra conducted by Sir Adrian Boult)
Mozart *Piano Concerto No. 23 (K488)* (Annie Fischer with the
  Philharmonia Orchestra conducted by Sir Adrian Boult)
Seguiriyas y Bulerias (Paco Aguilera and Antonio Gonzalez)
Bacharach *Alfie* (Cilla Black)
Bach *Partita No. 1 in B flat (BWV825)* (Glenn Gould)
★Verdi *Requiem Mass* (Philharmonia Orchestra and Chorus con-
  ducted by Carlo Maria Guilini)
Elgar *Sea Pictures No. 1: Sea Slumber Song* (Janet Baker with the
  London Symphony Orchestra conducted by Sir John Barbi-
  rolli)
Giordani *Caro Mio Ben* (Beniamino Gigli)
The luxury: An upright piano with a stool containing music
The book: A.S. Neal *Summerhill*

Roald Dahl   27 October 1979
Puccini *Che Gelida Manina (La Bohème)* (Enrico Caruso)
Beethoven *Violin Concerto in D* (Yehudi Menuhin with the New
  Philharmonia Orchestra conducted by Otto Klemperer)
Thomas *Fern Hill* (Dylan Thomas)
★Bach *Mass in B minor* (Christa Ludwig with the Vienna Sing-
  verein and the Berlin Philharmonic Orchestra conducted by
  Herbert von Karajan)
Beethoven *Symphony No. 9* (Berlin Philharmonic Orchestra con-
  ducted by Herbert von Karajan)
Fauré *Requiem* (Choir of King's College, Cambridge, and the New
  Philharmonia Orchestra conducted by David Willcocks)
Bach *Orchestral Suite No. 3* (Berlin Philharmonic Orchestra con-
  ducted by Herbert von Karajan)
Mozart *Piano Sonata in A (K331)* (Alfred Brendel)
The luxury: A packet of tobacco seeds and a bunch of grape-
  cuttings from Burgundy

237

The book: *The New Oxford Book of English Verse* compiled by Dame Helen Gardner

Les Dawson 8 April 1978

★Ravel *Pavane pour une Infante Defunte* (Suisse Romande Orchestra conducted by Ernest Ansermet)

Coleman/Burke *Matchstalk Men and Matchstalk Cats and Dogs* (Brian and Michael)

Dumont/Vaucaire *Non, Je ne Regrette Rien* (Edith Piaf)

Mitchell/Applebaum *Passing Strangers* (Sarah Vaughan and Billy Eckstine)

Bell/Creed *You Make Me Feel Brand New* (The Stylistics)

Fields *The Day I Drank a Glass of Water* (W.C. Fields)

Lloyd-Webber/Rice *Don't Cry For Me, Argentina* (Julie Covington)

Chopin *Etude No. 12 in C Minor, Opus 10* (Sviatoslav Richter)

The luxury: A piece of Georgian furniture

The book: Neville Shute *Trustee from the Toolroom*

Lord Denning 17 May 1980

★Vaughan Williams *Fantasia on Greensleeves* (London Symphony Orchestra conducted by Sir Adrian Boult)

Alford *Colonel Bogey* (Band of the Royal Marines, Portsmouth)

He Who Would Valiant Be (Worcester Cathedral Choir)

Rodgers *I Whistle a Happy Tune (The King and I)* (Valerie Hobson)

Haydn Wood *Roses of Picardy* (Webster Booth with Fred Hartley's Quintet)

Battle Hymn of the Republic (Robert Shaw Chorale and the RCA Victor Orchestra)

Gilbert/Sullivan *The Judge's Song (Trial by Jury)* (Leo Sheffield with the D'Oyly Carte Orchestra)

Elgar *Pomp and Circumstance March No. 1* (London Philharmonic Orchestra conducted by Sir Adrian Boult)

The luxury: Tea and a solar method of providing hot water

The book: Palgrave *Golden Treasury*

Mark Elder   8 November 1980

Mozart *Piano Concerto No. 17 (K453)* (Alfred Brendel with the Academy of St Martin-in-the-Fields conducted by Neville Marriner)

Gibbons *Almighty and Everlasting God* (Clerkes of Oxenford)

Verdi *Falstaff, Act 1* (Luigi Alva, Anna Moffo and the Philharmonia Orchestra conducted by Herbert von Karajan)

Dvořák *Overture: In Nature's Realm* (Czech Philharmonic Orchestra conducted by Karel Ancerl)

★Berlin *I Used to be Colour Blind* (Fred Astaire)

R. Strauss *Ein Heldenleben* (Dresden State Orchestra conducted by Rudolf Kempe)

Schubert *String Quintet in C* (Isaac Stern, Alexander Schneider, Milton Katims, Pablo Casals, Paul Tortelier)

Wagner *Die Meistersinger, Act 2* (Gottlob Frick, Elisabeth Grummer and the Berlin Philharmonic Orchestra conducted by Rudolf Kempe)

The luxury: His granny's sherry trifle in a solar-powered freezer

The book: Tolstoy *War and Peace*

John Fowles   10 January 1981

Bulerias (Nino Ricardo and Enrique 'El Culata')

Couperin *Les Barricades Mysterieuses* (Robert Veyron-Lacroix)

Pendem Devla Drabora (Maria Ion)

Vivaldi *Concerto in B, Opus 10, No. 2* (Concentus Musicus of Vienna directed by Nikolaus Harnoncourt)

Berlin *This Year's Kisses* (Billie Holiday with Lester Young (tenor sax) and the Teddy Wilson Orchestra)

As I Roved Out on a May Morning (Sarah Makem)

At the Window (Jimmy Yancey)

Bach *Trio Sonata in G (BWV1039)* (Frans Bruggen and Leopold Stastny (flutes), Herbert Tachezi (harpsichord) with Nikolaus Harnoncourt (cello))

The one record: Bach *Goldberg Variations* (which was not one of the eight because he would not allow the playing of only two minutes of it)

The luxury: A pair of good field-glasses
The book: *The Dictionary of National Biography*

Brian Glover   18 October 1980
Handel *Sarabande* (National Philharmonic Orchestra conducted
   by Leonard Rosenman)
*Dylan *Like a Rolling Stone* (Bob Dylan)
The Lark in the Morning (Maddy Prior with Steeleye Span)
Dumont/Vaucaire *Non, Je ne Regrette Rien* (Edith Piaf)
Prokoviev *Romeo and Juliet* (Cleveland Orchestra conducted by
   Lorin Maazel)
Bach *Brandenburg Concerto No. 3* (London Philharmonic Orchestra
   conducted by Sir Adrian Boult)
Too Young (Nat King Cole)
Lay Me Low (John Tams and the Albion Band)
The luxury: A 1952 MGTD car
The book: John Scarne *Card Games*

Helene Hanff   19 December 1981
Bach orch. Stokowski *Toccata and Fugue in D minor (BWV565)*
   (Philadelphia Orchestra conducted by Leopold Stokowski)
Handel *Comfort Ye My People* (Phillip Langridge with the
   Academy of St Martin-in-the-Fields conducted by Neville
   Marriner)
Barber *Knoxville-Summer of 1915* (Leontyne Price with the New
   Philharmonia Orchestra conducted by Thomas Schippers)
Vaughan Williams *Serenade to Music* (Sixteen Soloists and the
   London Philharmonic Orchestra conducted by Sir Adrian
   Boult)
Bax *Coronation March* (London Symphony Orchestra conducted
   by Sir Malcolm Sargent)
Sondheim *The Miller's Son* (*A Little Night Music*) (D. Jamin-
   Bartlett)
*Bach *In Tears of Grief* (Bach Choir and Orchestra conducted by
   Sir David Willcocks)
Stravinsky *The Firebird Suite* (Chicago Symphony Orchestra con-
   ducted by Carlo Maria Giulini)

The luxury: A Scrabble set

The book: *Memoirs* of Louis de Saint-Simon of the Court of Louis XIV

Russell Harty 21 March 1981

Walton *Overture from Henry V* (Philharmonia Orchestra conducted by Sir William Walton)

When I'm Cleaning Windows (George Formby)

Berlioz *Les Nuits d'Eté: Vilanelle* (Janet Baker with the New Philharmonia Orchestra conducted by Sir John Barbirolli)

In the Bleak Mid Winter (The Choir of King's College, Cambridge)

Prokofiev *Romeo and Juliet: Dance of the Mandolins* (The London Symphony Orchestra conducted by André Previn)

My Way (The Choristers of St Paul's Cathedral)

If You Were the Only Girl in the World (Violet Loraine and George Robey)

Arr. Elgar *The National Anthem* (The Cambridge University Musical Society and the New Philharmonia Orchestra conducted by Philip Ledger)

The luxury: A flag-pole with a Union Jack

The book: Whittaker *A History of Craven*

Earl Hines 24 May 1980

Chant of the Weed (Don Redman and his Orchestra)

Rodgers/Hart *Have You Met Miss Jones?* (Sam Browne with Jack Hylton and his Orchestra)

Sleep (Fred Waring and his Pennsylvanians)

East of the Sun (Tommy Dorsey and his Orchestra)

It Isn't Fair (Bill Farrell)

It Happens to be Me (Ben Webster (tenor sax) and the Ralph Burns Orchestra)

Trust in Me (Dinah Washington and the Quincy Jones Orchestra)

Ellington *Satin Doll* (Duke Ellington and his Orchestra)

The luxury: Physical culture apparatus

The book: Stanley Dance *The World of Duke Ellington*

241

Freddie Jones 7 June 1980

Gershwin *Rhapsody in Blue* (The London Symphony Orchestra conducted by André Previn)

Debussy *Prelude No. 8* (Arturo Benedetti Michelangeli)

Bach *Brandenburg Concerto No. 5* (The Berlin Philharmonic Orchestra conducted by Herbert von Karajan)

A Nightingale Sang in Berkeley Square (Leslie Hutchinson)

Vaughan Williams *Overture: The Wasps* (The London Philharmonic Orchestra conducted by Sir Adrian Boult)

Brahms *Symphony No. 4* (Berlin Philharmonic Orchestra conducted by Herbert von Karajan)

Wagner *Overture from Die Meistersinger* (The Halle Orchestra conducted by Sir John Barbirolli)

Kern/Hammerstein II *Make Believe (Showboat)* (Kathryn Grayson and Howard Keel)

The one record: One of the late quartets of Beethoven 'to explore its implications'

The luxury: A Liebig Condenser for distilling natural products to make a fine tropic gin

The book: Kenneth Grahame *The Wind in the Willows*

Tristan Jones 23 August 1980

Gilbert/Sullivan *A Wandering Minstrel I (The Mikado)* (Richard Lewis with the Pro Arte Orchestra conducted by Sir Malcolm Sargent)

Lennon/McCartney *Hello Goodbye* (The Beatles)

Mussorgsky arr. Stokowski *Night on the Bare Mountain* (London Symphony Orchestra conducted by Leopold Stokowski)

Sedaka *Love Will Keep Us Together* (Dionne Warwick)

★Tchaikovsky *1812 Overture* (The London Symphony Orchestra and the Band of the Grenadier Guards conducted by Kenneth Alwyn)

Warren *Lullaby of Broadway* (Ella Fitzgerald)

Handel *Hallelujah Chorus* (The Royal Philharmonic Chorus and Orchestra conducted by Sir Thomas Beecham)

Boyce *Hearts of Oak* (The Band of the Royal Marines, Portsmouth)

The luxury: A large Union Jack
The book: John Goswell *Modern Wooden Yacht Construction*

Ronald Lockley   4 October 1980
The Twelve Days of Christmas (The Choir of St John's College,
    Cambridge)
Grieg *Solveig's Song (Peer Gynt)* (Ilse Hollweg with the Royal
    Philharmonic Orchestra conducted by Sir Thomas Beecham)
Chopin orch. Douglas *Les Sylphides* (Paris Conservatoire Orches-
    tra conducted by Peter Maag)
★Debussy *Prelude à l'Après-Midi d'un Faune* (Royal Philharmonic
    Orchestra conducted by Sir Thomas Beecham)
J. Strauss *The Blue Danube* (Berlin Philharmonic Orchestra con-
    ducted by Herbert von Karajan)
Fauré *Après un Rêve* (Kiri Te Kanawa and Richard Amner)
David of the White Rock (Harry Secombe with the Welsh Festival
    Orchestra and Chorus)
Trad. arr. Britten *The Foggy Dew* (Peter Pears and Osian Ellis
    (harp))
The luxury: A telescope
The book: Gilbert White *The Natural History of Selborne*

Paul McCartney   30 January 1982
Heartbreak Hotel (Elvis Presley)
Berry *Sweet Little Sixteen* (Chuck Berry)
Britten *Courtly Dances from Gloriana* (Julian Bream Consort)
Be-Bop-A-Lula (Gene Vincent)
★Lennon *Beautiful Boy* (John Lennon)
Leiber/Stoller *Searchin'* (The Coasters)
Tutti Frutti (Little Richard)
James McCartney *Walking in the Park with Eloise* (The Country
    Hams)
The luxury: A guitar
The book: Linda's Pictures

Sir Fitzroy Maclean 11 April 1981

The Barren Rocks of Aden (Regimental Band and Drums of the
Black Watch)

Tchaikovsky *Swan Lake* (Suisse Romande Orchestra conducted
by Ernest Ansermet)

As Time Goes By (Russell Scott (organ))

Lili Marlene (Lale Andersen)

Haydn *Trumpet Concerto in E flat* (Maurice André with the London
Philharmonic Orchestra conducted by Jesus Lopez-Cobos)

Mozart *Voi Che Sapete (Le Nozze di Figaro)* (Fúorenza Cossotto)

★Beethoven *Piano Concerto No. 5* (Vladimir Ashkenazy with the
Chicago Symphony Orchestra conducted by Sir Georg Solti)

The luxury: Pencils, pens and paper

The book: Tolstoy *War and Peace* (in Russian)

V. S. Naipaul 5 July 1980

Poorbi-Dhun (Bismillah Khan (shenai) with tabla and drone)

Tchaikovsky *Serenade for Strings* (Berlin Philharmonic Orchestra
conducted by Herbert von Karajan)

Kern *Smoke Gets in Your Eyes* (Dinah Shore)

Lili Marlene (Lale Andersen)

Bach *Brandenburg Concerto No. 1* (Bach Festival Chamber Orchestra conducted by Yehudi Menuhin)

Mahler *Symphony No. 1* (Vienna Philharmonic Orchestra conducted by Claudio Abbado)

★Beethoven *Piano Sonata No. 32* (Alfred Brendel)

Des Malhar Raga (Ustod Ali Akbar Khan (sarod) and Shankar
Ghosh (tabla))

The luxury: An icon of the Enlightened Buddha

The book: *Teach Yourself Mathematics*

David Niven 30 April 1977

Wonder *You Are the Sunshine of My Life* (Blue Mink)

Trad. arr. Fairbairn *Amazing Grace* (Pipes and Drums and Military
Band of the Royal Scots Dragoon Guards)

Clifton Davis *Never Can Say Goodbye* (Gloria Gaynor)

Verdi *Celeste Aida (Aida)* (Jussi Bjorling)

Casey *Rock Your Baby* (George McCrea)

Delibes *Bell Song (Lakme)* (Maria Callas)

Rodgers/Hammerstein *There's Nothing Like a Dame (South Pacific)* (Chorus and Orchestra conducted by Salvatore dell'Isola)

*Shakespeare *In Peace, there's nothing so becomes a man (Henry V)* (Sir Laurence Olivier)

The luxury: A double bed

The book: *The British Army Survival Manual*

Gregory Peck   2 August 1980

*Beethoven *Symphony No. 7* (Los Angeles Philharmonic Orchestra conducted by Zubin Mehta)

Verdi *Prelude to Act 1 (La Traviata)* (Royal Philharmonic Orchestra conducted by Aldo Ceccato)

Ellington *Satin Doll* (Duke Ellington and his Orchestra)

Mozart *Symphony No. 4* (Vienna Philharmonic Orchestra conducted by Karl Böhm)

Puccini *Che Gelida Manina (La Bohème)* (Luciano Pavarotti)

Beethoven *Violin Concerto in D* (Isaac Stern with the New Philharmonic Orchestra conducted by Leonard Bernstein)

Chopin *Fantaisie Impromptu in C sharp minor* (Arthur Rubinstein)
Theme from *New York, New York* (Frank Sinatra)

The luxury: A case of Château Lafite-Rothschild 1967 and some Brie

The book: Carl Sandberg *Lincoln*

Donald Pleasance   29 March 1980

I Will Survive (Gloria Gaynor)

Bach *Allemande and Courante from French Suite No. 4* (Glenn Gould)

Lennon/McCartney *A Day in the Life* (The Beatles)

Lewis *Blues in A minor* (The Modern Jazz Quartet)

Elgar *Violin Concerto in B minor* (Yehudi Menuhin with the New Philharmonia Orchestra conducted by Sir Adrian Boult)

Rodrigo arr. Evans *Concierto de Aranjuez* (Miles Davis (trumpet) with Orchestra conducted by Gil Evans)

Scouse the Mouse (Ringo Starr)

*Verdi *Requiem Mass* (Vienna State Opera Chorus and the Vienna Philharmonic Orchestra conducted by Sir Georg Solti)
The luxury: Writing materials
The book: Dostoevski *The Brothers Karamazov* and *Crime and Punishment*

Robert Powell 6 January 1979
Janáček *Sinfonietta* (Czech Philharmonic Orchestra conducted by Karel Ancerl)
Gershwin *Summertime (Porgy and Bess)* (Miles Davis with Orchestra conducted by Gil Evans)
Keats *When I Have Fears* (Sir Ralph Richardson)
*Mahler *Symphony No. 5* (Concertgebouw Orchestra of Amsterdam conducted by Bernard Haitink)
Dylan *Don't Think Twice it's Alright* (Bob Dylan)
Stravinsky *The Soldier's Tale* (Israel Baker (violin) with instrumental ensemble conducted by Igor Stravinsky)
Samba de Orfeu from the film *Black Orpheus*
Lloyd-Webber *Variations on Caprice in A minor by Paganini* (Julian Lloyd-Webber (cello) and ensemble)
The luxury: Typewriter, paper and table
The book: H. W. Fowler *A Dictionary of Modern English Usage*

Otto Preminger 2 February 1980
*Raksin/Mercer *Laura* (Frank Sinatra)
E. Bernstein *Frankie Machine* (Orchestra conducted by Elmer Bernstein)
Bizet *Habanera – Dat's Love (Carmen Jones)* (Marilyn Horne)
The Moon is Blue (Sally Sweetland)
Ellington *Almost Cried* (Duke Ellington and his Orchestra)
Fielding *Advise and Consent* (Orchestra conducted by Jerry Fielding)
Gershwin *A Woman is a Sometime Thing* (Porgy and Bess)
Gold *Fight for Survival (Exodus)* (Sinfonia of London conducted by Ernest Gold)
The luxury: A very beautiful watch
The book: His own autobiography

Sir Ralph Richardson   4 August 1979

Youmans *Tea for Two* (Binnie Hale and Seymour Beard)

Beethoven *Piano Sonata No.12* (Artur Schnabel)

Feldman/Fitzgerald *A-Tisket, A-Tasket* (Ella Fitzgerald with the Chick Webb Orchestra)

Gilbert/Sullivan *There Grew a Little Flower (Ruddigore)* (Christine Palmer and Donald Adams)

Chopin *Nocturne in E minor, Opus 72* (Vladimir de Pachmann)

Chopin *Nocturne in B, Opus 62, No.1* (Jan Smeterlin)

The Cruise of the USS Codfish (Bob Newhart)

★Mozart *Clarinet Concerto in A* (Jack Brymer with the Royal Philharmonic Orchestra conducted by Sir Thomas Beecham)

The luxury: Pipes and tobacco

The book: Three novels by Henry James

Dr A.L. Rowse   13 August 1977

Bach *Brandenburg Concerto No. 5* (Stuttgart Chamber Orchestra conducted by Karl Münchinger)

★Byrd *Mass for Five Voices* (Choir of Christ Church Cathedral, Oxford, conducted by Simon Preston)

Duparc *L'Invitation au Voyage* (Dame Maggie Teyte with the London Philharmonic Orchestra conducted by Leslie Howard)

Beethoven *Piano Sonata No. 30* (Artur Schnabel)

Tchaikovsky *Polonaise (Eugene Onegin)* (New York Philharmonic Orchestra conducted by Leonard Bernstein)

Elgar *Cello Concerto in E minor* (Pablo Casals with the BBC Symphony Orchestra conducted by Sir Adrian Boult)

Eliot *The Wasteland* (T.S. Eliot)

Churchill *The Finest Hour* (Sir Winston Churchill)

The luxury: Seurat's painting 'Sunday afternoon on the Island of La Grande Jatte'

The book: Proust *A La Recherche du Temps Perdu*

Dr Edmund Rubbra   23 May 1981

Monteverdi *Lamento della Ninfa* (Nadia Boulanger Ensemble)

Tallis *Spem in Alium* (Cambridge University Musical Society conducted by Sir David Willcocks)

247

Fauré *Requiem* (Choir of King's College, Cambridge with the New Philharmonia Orchestra conducted by Sir David Willcocks)

Stravinsky *Symphony of Psalms* (Choir of Christ Church Cathedral, Oxford and the Philip Jones Ensemble conducted by Simon Preston)

Gregorian Chant *Te Deum* (Benedictine Monks of the Abbey of St Maurice and St Maur, Clervaux)

Byrd *Mass for Five Voices* (Choir of King's College, Cambridge, conducted by Sir David Willcocks)

Tabhair Dom Do Lamh (The Chieftains)

★Schubert *Symphony No. 9* (London Philharmonic Orchestra conducted by Sir Adrian Boult)

The luxury: Manuscript paper and pencils

The book: A.A. Milne *Winnie the Pooh* and *The House at Pooh Corner*

Erich Segal   19 April 1980

★*A Fifth of Beethoven* (The Walter Murphy Band)

Lehrer *Fight Fiercely, Harvard* (Tom Lehrer)

Vivaldi *The Four Seasons* (London· Philharmonic Orchestra directed by Itzhak Perlman (violin))

Milhaud *Le Boeuf sur le Toit* (London Symphony Orchestra conducted by Antal Dorati)

Aznavour/Segal *Our Love, My Love* (Charles Aznavour)

Mozart *Horn Concerto No. 2* (Alan Civil and the Academy of St Martin-in-the-Fields directed by Neville Marriner)

Bruch *Kol Nidrei* (Pablo Casals and the London Symphony Orchestra conducted by Sir Landon Ronald)

Gay *Fill Every Glass* and *Let Us Take the Road (The Beggar's Opera)* (Alexander Young with Chorus and the Pro Arte Orchestra conducted by Sir Malcolm Sargent)

The luxury: A stop-watch

The book: Homer *The Odyssey*

Peter Sellers   4 February 1957

I Want a Big Butter and Egg Man (Bobby Hackett and his Jazz Band)

Rodgers/Hammerstein *I Have Dreamed (The King and I)* (Rita Moreno and Carlos Rivas)

Delius *On Hearing the First Cuckoo in Spring* (The London Symphony Orchestra conducted by Anthony Collins)

Berlin *Cheek to Cheek* (Ella Fitzgerald and Louis Armstrong)

Debussy *Prelude No. 8* (Hans Henkemans)

Victor Young *White (Tone Poems of Colour)* (Orchestra conducted by Frank Sinatra)

Raksin/Mercer *Laura* (Erroll Garner)

Rodgers/Hart *I like to Recognize the Tune* (Mel Torme)

The luxury: A snorkel and face mask

The book: Charles Dickens *The Pickwick Papers*

Stephen Sondheim   16 August 1980

Ravel *Valses Nobles et Sentimentales* (Suisse Romande Orchestra conducted by Ernest Ansermet)

Bartok *Concerto for Orchestra* (Pittsburg Symphony Orchestra conducted by Fritz Reiner)

★Gershwin *Oh Bess, oh Where's my Bess? (Porgy and Bess)* (Lawrence Winters, Inez Matthews, Helen Dowdy, with orchestra conducted by Lehman Engel)

Brahms *Piano Concerto No. 2* (Vladimir Horowitz with the NBC Symphony Orchestra conducted by Arturo Toscanini)

Sondheim *Poems (Pacific Overtures)* (Isao Sato and Sab Shimono)

Ravel *Piano Concerto for the Left Hand* (Robert Casadesus and the Philadelphia Symphony Orchestra conducted by Eugene Ormandy)

Stravinsky *Symphony of Psalms* (Bach Festival Chorus and the London Symphony Orchestra conducted by Leonard Bernstein)

Sondheim *The Ballad of Sweeney Todd (Sweeney Todd)* (Full company conducted by Paul Gemignani)

The luxury: A piano

The book: E.B. White *Collected Works*

Derek Tangye   11 November 1980

Puccini *The Shepherd Boy's Song (Tosca)* (Alvaro Cordova with the Orchestra of La Scala conducted by Victor de Sabata)

Debussy *Reflets dans l'Eau (Images)* (Walter Gieseking)

Bizet *Jeux d'Enfants* (Suisse Romande Orchestra conducted by Ernest Ansermet)

Foster *Jeannie with the Light Brown Hair* (Carroll Gibbons and his String Quintet)

*Rachmaninov *Symphony No. 2* (London Symphony Orchestra conducted by André Previn)

Haydn *String Quartet, Opus 76, No. 5* (Amadeus Quartet)

Grieg *Holberg Suite* (Northern Sinfonia conducted by Paul Tortelier)

Ellis *This is my Lovely Day (Bless the Bride)* (Lizbeth Webb and Georges Guetary)

The luxury: A telescope

The book: Proust *A la Recherche du Temps Perdu*

The Rt Hon. Mrs Margaret Thatcher 18 February 1978

*Beethoven *Piano Concerto No. 5* (Alfred Brendel with the London Philharmonic Orchestra conducted by Bernard Haitink)

Dvořák arr. Boddington *Going Home* (G.U.S. Footwear Band, conducted by S.H. Boddington)

Verdi *Grand March (Aida)* (Rome Opera House Chorus and Orchestra conducted by Zubin Mehta)

Newhart *Introducing Tobacco to Civilization* (Bob Newhart)

Kern *Smoke Gets in Your Eyes* (Irene Dunne)

Mendelssohn *Be Not Afraid (Elijah)* (New Philharmonia Chorus and Orchestra conducted by Fruhbeck de Burgos)

Saint-Preux *Andante for Trumpet* (Pierre Thibaud with orchestra conducted by the composer)

Mascagni *Easter Hymn (Cavalleria Rusticana)* (Chorus and Orchestra of Royal Opera House, Covent Garden conducted by Lamberto Gardelli)

The luxury: Photograph album of her children

The book: Michael Alleby *Survival Handbook*

Baroness Maria von Trapp 1982 to be scheduled

Mozart *Eine Kleine Nachtmusik* (Vienna Philharmonic Orchestra conducted by Karl Böhm)

Schubert *An Die Musik* (Lotte Lehmann with Chamber Orchestra conducted by Manfred Gurlitt)

Mozart *O Isis and Osiris (Die Zauberflöte)* (Richard Mayr)

Mozart *Symphony No. 41* (New Philharmonia Orchestra conducted by Carlo Maria Giulini)

Schubert *Der Neugierige (Die Schöne Müllerin)* (Lotte Lehmann)

Mozart *In Diesen Heiligen Hallen (Die Zauberflöte)* (Richard Mayr)

Schubert *Ungeduld (Die Schöne Müllerin)* (Lotte Lehmann)

*Bach *Brandenburg Concerto No. 1* (Berlin Philharmonic Orchestra conducted by Herbert von Karajan)

The luxury: A statue of the Madonna and Child

The book: *Funny True Stories of Well-Known People*

P.L. Travers   21 May 1977

William Blake *The Little Black Boy (Songs of Innocence)* (Sir Ralph Richardson)

George W. Russell *The Outcast* (John Hewitt)

Yeats *The Lake Isle of Innisfree* (W.B. Yeats)

Gerard Manley Hopkins *God's Grandeur* (Cyril Cusack)

Robert Louis Stevenson *The Cow* (Mary O'Farrell)

Robert Frost *Choose Something Like a Star* (Robert Frost)

T.S. Eliot *Four Quartets – Little Gidding* (Sir Alec Guinness)

*Shakespeare *The Lament for Fidele (Cymbeline)* (John Stride and Alan Bates)

The luxury: Her little marble Buddha

The book: Thick book of blank pages and a pen

Fred Trueman   19 August 1978

Tchaikovsky *1812 Overture* (London Symphony Orchestra and the Band of the Grenadier Guards conducted by Kenneth Alwyn)

Foster *Tables and Chairs* (Yorkshire County Cricket Club)

Robin/Rainger *Blue Hawaii* (The Ray Coniff Singers and Orchestra)

Berlin *White Christmas* (Bing Crosby)

Bizet *Carmen Suite No. 1* (French National Radio Orchestra conducted by Sir Thomas Beecham)

251

McLean *And I Love You So* (Shirley Bassey)
Gordon *Unforgettable* (Nat King Cole)
★Dvořák *Symphony No. 9* (London Symphony Orchestra conducted by Istvan Kertesz)
The luxury: Binoculars
The book: Sir Harold Macmillan *Memoirs*

Peter Ustinov   19 November 1977
Berlioz *Le Spectre de la Rose (Les Nuits d'Eté)* (Janet Baker and the New Philharmonia Orchestra conducted by Sir John Barbirolli)
Prokoviev *Violin Concerto No. 2* (Henryk Szeryng with the London Symphony Orchestra conducted by Gennady Rozhdestvensky)
Mahler *Oft Denk' Ich (Kindertotenlieder)* (Kathleen Ferrier)
Beethoven *Piano Concerto No. 3* (Wilhelm Kempff and the Berlin Philharmonic Orchestra conducted by Ferdinand Leitner)
★Mozart *In Diesen Heiligen Hallen (Die Zauberflöte)* (Martti Talvela with the Vienna Philharmonic Orchestra conducted by Sir Georg Solti)
Speech on the 1909 Budget (The Rt Hon. H.H. Asquith)
Los Dorados do Pancho Vida
Mussorgsky orch. Markevich *Dove Sei Stellina* (Mascia Predit with the Italian Radio Orchestra conducted by Igor Markevich)
The luxury: A bathtub with solar-heated water
The book: An exercise book and pencils

Natalie Wood   10 May 1980
Schubert *Schwanengesang* (Dietrich Fischer-Dieskau with Gerald Moore)
Kalinka (E. Belayaev with the Red Banner Song and Dance Ensemble)
Greensleeves (The Ambrosian Children's Choir and Players)
Beethoven *Piano Sonata No. 14* (Alfred Brendel)
Dylan *Just Like a Woman* (Bob Dylan)
McClean *American Pie* (Don McClean)
Seger *We've Got Tonight* (Bob Seger)

Lennon *Imagine* (John Lennon, the Plastic Ono Band and the Flux
  Fiddlers)
The luxury: A piano
The book: E.E. Cummings *A Book of Poetry*

Barbara Woodhouse   26 June 1980
Ketelbey *In a Monastery Garden* (Albert Ketelbey and his Concert
  Orchestra)
Charmaine (Mantovani and his Orchestra)
Whispering (The Victor Silvester Orchestra)
Romberg/Young *Will you Remember?* (Jeanette Macdonald and
  Nelson Eddy)
Stranger on the Shore (Acker Bilk and the Leon Young Strings)
My Blue Heaven and *Bye Bye Blackbird* (Turner Layton)
Skye Boat Song (Adrian Brett (flute) and Orchestra)
Sweet Talking Rag (theme from her television programme)
The luxury: Her mother's ormolu clock
The book: Her own autobiography